From Newbury with Love

Darling Sarah

Thanks for a delicious lunch
and also for all the other
lunches
teas
suppers
breakfasts
nights
holidays
and love
you've given me since I was 16.

Anna xxx

October 2006

From Newbury with Love

LETTERS OF FRIENDSHIP ACROSS THE IRON CURTAIN

EDITED BY
Marina Aidova and Anna Horsbrugh-Porter

First published in Great Britain in 2006 by
PROFILE BOOKS LTD
3A Exmouth House
Pine Street
London EC1R 0JH
www.profilebooks.com

In association with Amnesty International UK

1 3 5 7 9 10 8 6 4 2

Designed by Nicky Barneby @ Barneby Ltd
Set in 10.25/14pt FF Quadraat
Printed and bound in Great Britain by Clays, Bungay, Suffolk

A CIP catalogue record for this book is available from the British Library.

ISBN-10 1 86197 860 X
ISBN-13 978 1 86197 860 8

For Lera Shestakova and Slava Aidov
And in memory of Harold and Olive

Contents

EUROPE BEFORE 1989

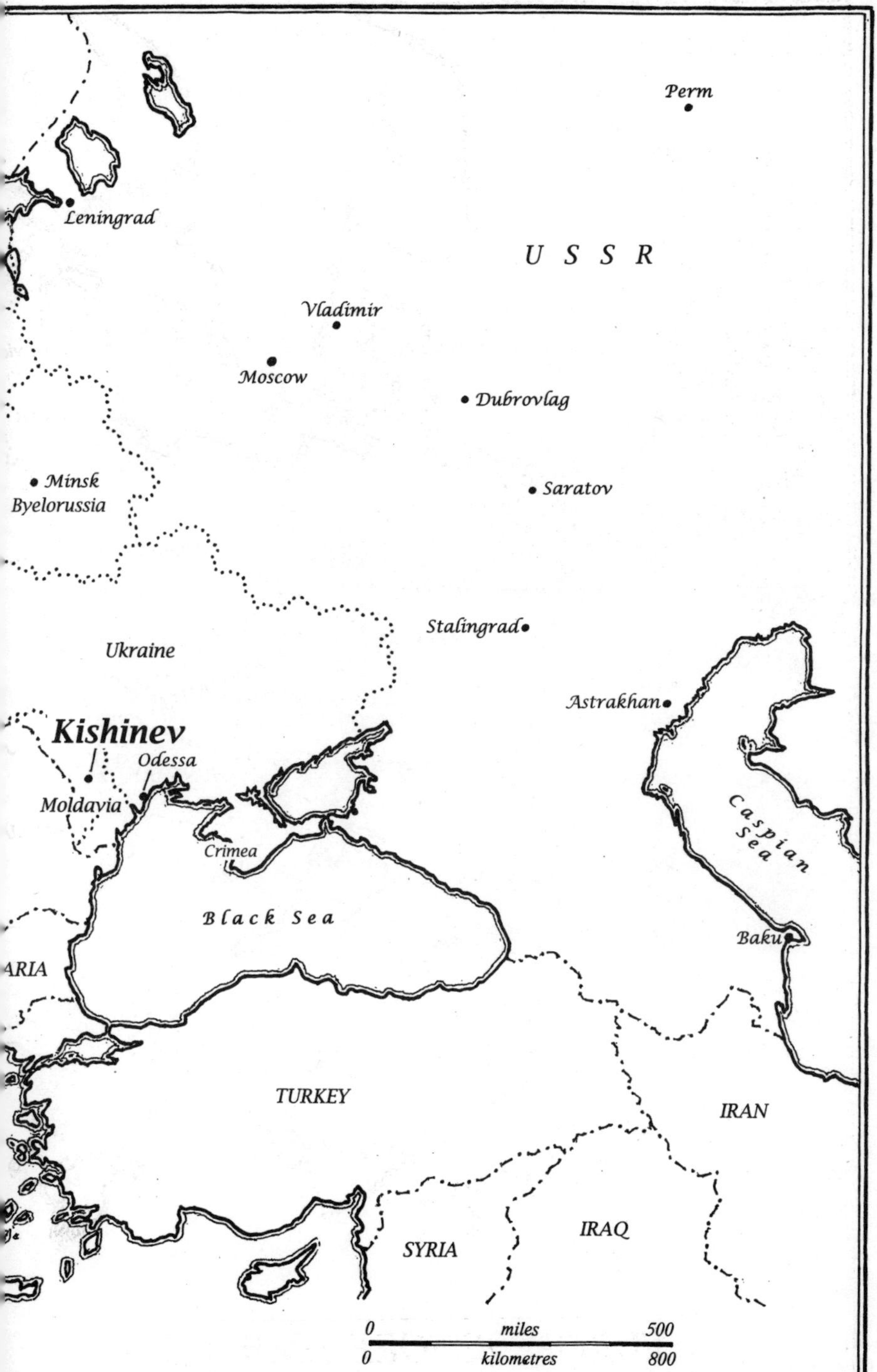
Perm
Leningrad
U S S R
Vladimir
Moscow
Dubrovlag
Minsk
Byelorussia
Saratov
Stalingrad
Ukraine
Astrakhan
Kishinev
Odessa
Moldavia
Caspian Sea
Crimea
Black Sea
Baku
ARIA
TURKEY
IRAN
IRAQ
SYRIA
0 miles 500
0 kilometres 800

Harold, at Sotheby's while President of the Antiquarian Booksellers Association.

Introduction

In 1971 Harold Edwards, an antiquarian bookseller who specialised in buying and selling seventeenth-century books and manuscripts, was living in a cottage outside Newbury with his third wife, Olive. Aged seventy-one, Harold had travelled to the Soviet Union twice, in 1932 and 1964. Those visits, together with his life-long passion for Russian literature and a commitment to human rights, led him to respond to an Amnesty International letter-writing campaign. It was to be the start of a correspondence which would transform the lives of a family living in what was then Moldavia, a small landlocked part of the Soviet Union sandwiched between Ukraine and Romania.

Harold saw a list of children's names and addresses printed in Amnesty International's translation of the *Chronicle of Current Events*, the journal of the civil rights movement in the USSR. They were all the children of political prisoners; the names were in alphabetical order and near the top he saw *Aidova, Marina, 13th June 1963*. Harold decided to write to Marina, then aged seven, because her birthday was one day earlier than his, although sixty-three years separated them. Her father, Slava Aidov, was being held in one of the harshest Soviet prison camps, Dubrovlag, in Mordovia, 600 kilometres east of Moscow. Mordovia had been the dumping ground for political prisoners since 1917 and tens of thousands of prisoners were held in Dubrovlag.

Marina and her mother, Lera, lived an isolated existence in Kishinev, the capital of Moldavia (now called Chisinau in Moldova). In 1971 even so far south of Moscow, in this small corner of the vast Soviet Union, the handful of political dissidents in Kishinev was kept under heavy surveillance. The KGB routinely bugged the Aidovs' telephone conversations, and kept a close watch on the family. At that time very few

Soviet citizens received letters regularly from abroad, so Lera and Marina stood out. Initially, Lera thought that if she wrote on neutral topics like cats, clothes, vegetables and gardens, the KGB would allow the letters to get through. Almost all the letters were addressed to Marina, in the hope that there would be less suspicion of a correspondence between an elderly British couple and a child. Nevertheless, the constraints imposed by the KGB caused great frustration and anxiety and many letters never reached their destination. At one point Lera started to number her letters to make sure the Edwards realised when one had gone astray; parcels from Newbury which never arrived were much lamented. There are also long gaps: some letters got lost, including Harold's first postcard and subsequent letter; holidays, illness, house searches by the KGB and moving apartments in Kishinev also interrupted the correspondence.

All the letters are in English – the Edwards could speak no Russian. Lera wrote her letters using a dictionary, and English-speaking friends would help her translate the replies. She enrolled in English evening classes, and would take along Marina to these three times a week, where the young girl would fall asleep with her head on the desk.

The letters sent between Newbury and Kishinev from 1971 to 1986 form a unique document of a time when the original Bolshevik ideals were changing into something very different. The Soviet machine was developing fault-lines, initially invisible, which would result in the implosion of 1989 and the disintegration of the USSR after seventy-two years of arguably the biggest social experiment on earth.

* * *

Harold was born in 1900 in London; his father left when he was three and the family went to live with his maternal grandfather, a butcher and a self-educated man. Harold grew up surrounded by books in a liberal, non-conformist household; as a teenager his life was changed when he bought *The Conquest of Bread*, by Russian anarchist Peter Kropotkin, for sixpence. Kropotkin's ideas of a social revolution brought about by anarchist communism influenced him profoundly, and during the First World War he said he didn't want to fight

Slava and Lera as a young couple walking together in Kishinev.

his fellow working man and described himself as a conscientious objector. (In fact, he was liable for conscription only towards the end of 1918.)

Harold left school at sixteen and for a short time went to work at Lloyd's as a marine insurance broker. He quickly found office life intolerable and used to say he'd sooner be a tramp than work in an office. In fact he seemed to find the idea of a conventional job for life repellent. He once wrote: 'The thought . . . of a job of any kind is very unpleasant . . . Having to get up in the morning and go to work, to know that was going on for fifty or sixty years and that you got a fortnight's holiday and, if you were lucky, £10 a year rise – it all seemed to be so horrible.' Harold lived in one room in Lambeth, where over his bed he pinned portraits of Marat, Hebert, and Robespierre. He became friendly with a group of Spanish anarchists whom he met in Soho coffee bars, and one of them found him a job as a kitchen porter at the Army and Navy Club in St James's Square. In the evenings, he wrote articles for many of the Socialist papers and magazines such as *Freedom* and *The Freethinker*.

In 1918 Harold became a member of the 'Boss Class', as he called it, having saved enough money to rent the premises of his first second-hand bookshop at 68 Red Lion Street, which he named the Progressive Book Shop, although it sold all kinds of books. Outside there was a large rack, full of all the socialist papers and pamphlets of the day. Three years later, tired of sitting in a shop all day, he sold the business for twenty-five pounds, and started travelling around the country to buy books at auctions and private libraries, selling them on to other booksellers. His interest in the antiquarian book trade, and specifically seventeenth-century books, stems from that time. Harold was to remain a bookseller for over sixty years.

In 1932 Harold travelled to the Soviet Union for the first time, to what was then Leningrad, the Volga and Rostov-on-the-Don amongst other places. Soon after Harold returned from this trip he met Olive, twelve years his junior, the fifth of six daughters of a house painter who had married his childhood sweetheart. Olive had been working as a milliner at the Schiaparelli fashion house, but as soon as they started living together, in the mid 1930s, she began to help Harold in his

Harold standing outside the Progressive Bookshop. Built in the late eighteenth century, the shop's best feature was its window, which could be lifted up so that two shelves of books could be seen and handled. The rent was 10s. a week, rates included.

Olive (left) at the time she met Harold, with her sister Eve.

bookselling business. In 1937 they moved out of London with their small daughter Sally to a cottage in Ashmore Green, just outside Newbury in Berkshire.

At the end of the Second World War Harold opened another bookshop in London, near the British Museum. After buying some significant private libraries in England and Ireland he closed the shop in 1953 and started running his antiquarian book business from the 'bookroom', a clapboard building in the garden of his home back in Newbury. From this building, Harold distributed his distinctive pocket-sized catalogues, and Olive packed all the orders for the business under a naked bulb in the 'packing room', a cubby-hole between their two offices.

By the 1950s Olive was an essential contributor to the business. She suggested an initiative which transformed their pleasant but hand-to-mouth existence into one of relative prosperity: they rented a leviathan Rank Xerox machine, whose output of facsimile bookplates and manuscripts was mailed to librarians and collectors in the USA. This was the first time potential buyers had been able to view the books before buying, and it made a big difference to sales. As they became better off, Harold and Olive could afford good wine, which they loved, to travel more and buy contemporary paintings.

Harold was a prodigious letter-writer all his life, and passionately interested in political freedom. In 1959, after the Chinese invasion of Tibet, and following an earlier Amnesty International letter-writing campaign, he started corresponding and exchanging photographs with a Tibetan Monk in Lhasa. As he started writing to the Aidovs in 1971, he was also in contact with at least two other families of Russian dissidents, but these relationships didn't last, mainly due to the language barrier.

* * *

Born in 1933, Slava Aidov was four years old when he witnessed his grandfather being dragged by soldiers in the middle of the night from his home. All those arrested – the so-called 'kulaks' of the village, men who owned their own farms – were never heard from again. Nobody knows whether they were shot immediately or perished of starvation and cold in Stalin's Gulag. Slava says this experience revealed to him that there were arbitrary and vicious forces at large in the world, capable of destroying people in an instant.

Slava's father was a Red Army officer, and at the end of the war in 1945, he was seconded to Kishinev, where Soviet troops had arrived only five years earlier. As a twelve-year-old boy, Slava could roam free in a place that had been almost completely destroyed by bombing, and whose people had little experience of living under Soviet power.

After finishing school Slava entered the Mining Institute in Tula, a town 200 kilometres away from Moscow. Being an engineer was one of the most prestigious professions in the Soviet Union at this time, so that's what Slava chose to be although it was far removed from his love of languages and literature. When Slava was twenty, in 1953, Joseph Stalin died. Three years later, at the Twentieth Congress of the Communist Party, Nikita Khrushchev denounced the cult of Stalin and those who'd been arrested began to return from the prisons and camps. It was only when hundreds of thousands of these men and women came home to their families that the scale of Stalin's repression was publicly acknowledged. The stories that they told had a profound impact on Slava and his generation.

In this new atmosphere a Professor of History at the Mining Institute organised an unofficial group where students met to talk openly about recent Soviet history, and Slava became one of its most active participants. Now that the threat of sudden and arbitrary arrests had disappeared, people met without fear for the first time. They held parties, danced and listened to music, but most of all they talked. People retyped books at home and in their offices and then passed them around as samizdat (the clandestine copying of literature outlawed by the Soviet government). Towards the end of Khrushchev's rule, the state began to tighten its grip again over the dissemination of ideas and information; official policy allowed criticism of the 'cult of Stalin', but prohibited any criticism of the Communist party or the post-Stalin era.

Meanwhile, Slava graduated and went back to Kishinev. Here he met Lera Shestakova, who had been evacuated to Central Asia at the age of four, during the Nazi siege of Leningrad. Her father had died on the battlefield, and when the Second World War was over she and her mother, a doctor, were left with no place to go, as their house in Leningrad had been destroyed during the bombardments. Lera's mother was offered a job in Kishinev, and they moved to Moldavia. When she finished school, Lera went on to study mathematics at Kishinev University.

Slava and Lera married in 1962, and Marina was born in 1963. They looked forward to their future together. Slava had started his first job, and the couple hoped they would soon be given an apartment of their own, and would live as any other family did: working, bringing up their children and going to the seaside for summer holidays.

In 1964 Khrushchev was overthrown, Brezhnev came to power, and Stalin started to be rehabilitated. Any anti-Stalin criticism was banned once again, and censorship and other controls were tightened. However, the short-lived weakening of pressure under Khrushchev was enough to change the way some people thought. Then aged thirty, Slava read the radical literary magazine *Novy Mir* and listened to the Russian broadcasts of the BBC World Service; he felt he couldn't live within the increasingly repressive system any longer. He went to Moscow, telling Lera he was going to find a job and get a residence permit. There he set up a clandestine group, 'The Union to Fight for Freedom', with some of his friends. The group's main aim was to obtain a printing machine and disseminate leaflets throughout Moscow, calling for people to wake up and start questioning the propaganda that surrounded their lives.

Their plans were doomed, however, as the group were soon betrayed to the KGB by one of their members. In August 1966, before they had even got hold of a printing machine, their room was raided and Slava was arrested. Until this time, Lera knew nothing of Slava's political activities, but in November 1966, six months after he had moved to Moscow, he sent her a letter that read 'I am healthy but I have been put into a military hospital by the KGB'. That day she felt as if her life had ended.

When Slava's trial and imprisonment became public, Lera was shunned by everyone, apart from a very few friends who would visit her

Slava in the apartment before he left Kishinev.

at home. It was dangerous to associate with her; people she knew would cross over to the other side of the street when they saw her and at work they would avoid eye contact in public places like the canteen. To be thrust so suddenly into such an isolated and terrifying situation in the city where she had grown up, surrounded by people she thought were her friends, was hard, and at times the stress felt unbearable.

Like other relatives of prisoners, Lera was allowed four trips a year to the camp; once a year she was allowed to stay for three days, and the other visits lasted only three hours. She would donate blood at the local hospital every two months to pay for her journeys to the camps. This would earn her a good lunch with red wine at the hospital, but also, crucially, some days off work which she could use to visit Slava.

Lera saw Slava in prison for the first time in June 1967 with the four-year-old Marina. It was a two-day train journey with a change in Moscow, where she had to wait for a midnight connection to the camps. She remembers shopping for food and supplies for Slava, feeling exhausted but unable to visit her friends in the city as it would incriminate them, and then having to lay Marina down to sleep on newspapers on the station platform as they waited for the train. They arrived at a small station called Potima at six o'clock in the morning, and from there had to walk to the next station to get a connecting train. The guards taunted Lera as she slipped in the mud, carrying her heavy rucksack.

The visiting families stayed in the nearby town in rented rooms shared with other families. The wives of the political prisoners formed a network, helping and supporting each other. Lera became especially close to Arina Ginzburg, the wife of Alexander Ginzburg. From then on she stayed with Arina whenever she went through Moscow on her way to or from Mordovia; never again did she have to put Marina to sleep on a railway platform. When one of the wives visited the camp they would collect messages about the other husbands in code and pass them on once they got back to Moscow. Marina's name was published in the *Chronicle of Current Events* after Arina was asked to supply lists of the children of Soviet political prisoners. Once, when Slava went on hunger strike in the camp, one of the wives brought out the news and it was passed on through Radio Liberty, which broadcast dissident news from the Soviet Union. Listening to the station at home in Kishinev, Lera heard her husband's name mentioned and despaired

Lera with Marina.

for his life because he had looked so near starvation the last time she had visited him. She decided to go on hunger strike as well, desperate to make some sort of private gesture in support of her husband, however futile. She drank only tea without sugar and ate one piece of bread a day.

When Lera returned home one afternoon in early June 1971, feeling weak from lack of food, she noticed something in her letter box as she was about to open the door. She pulled out a postcard, with a coloured picture of a small town with a tower in the middle of a square, surrounded by houses. It was addressed to Marina Aidova, and she read:

With love from Newbury
Berks
England

Harold and Olive.

Lera stood paralyzed in front of her door; it seemed a miracle that someone living in England could write to her daughter, that this postcard could have penetrated her isolation. It was like seeing an angel.

Note to Readers

All the letters have been faithfully reproduced here as they were originally written, except where we felt linguistic errors or omissions interfered with the readers' ability to understand their meaning, and in those very few cases we have clarified, changed the grammar or corrected the spelling of words.

The Letters

One of the first photographs Lera sent to Harold.

Kishinev
June 6, 1971

Dear Mr Edwards

I am very grateful to you for your kind wishes of a happy birthday for me and I wish you as well, good health and every success in your activities. I am a first class schoolgirl. I learn ballet and study English. And what are you?

Have a good summer.

Thankfully yours,

Marina Aidova

TELEPHONE: THATCHAM 2105 CABLES & TELEGRAMS DRYASDUST NEWBURY

H. W. Edwards *(Booksellers)* Ltd

DIRECTORS: H. W. EDWARDS · O. R. EDWARDS

Members Antiquarian Booksellers Association

ASHMORE GREEN, NEWBURY, BERKSHIRE, ENGLAND

21-6-71

Dear Marina

I am very happy to know that you have received my postcard and to get your reply.

I sent you some sweets a little time ago. Have you received them? I hope so, and that you liked them. When you next write please tell me if there is anything that I can send you from England, and if it is possible I shall do so. Perhaps I can send you some English books for children but I am not sure.

May I say how clever you are to write such good English. I only wish I could write Russian. Alas, I am too lazy like most English people, so am only able to read Russian books that have been translated into English.

You ask me what I am? As you see I am a bookseller, but only very old books. Also I am very old.

We are having a dreadful summer. Rain, rain, rain all the time, and my garden is just covered with water.

Write to me again if you can. Good-bye for now.

Harold Edwards

Kishinev
July 8, 1971

Dear Mr Edwards!*

I have just received your kind letter of June 21, and some days ago your sweets, for which I thank you very much.

I am sending you two photos of mine. Both were made by my mother in our room.

Dear Mr Edwards, I must confess, I do not write my English letters quite alone, it is also my mother, who helps me to write them. However, I understood what you wrote in your letters. I hope, in a short time, to learn English better, so as to be able to write you alone. There are many people here, who speak and write English quite well.

Of course, you can send me English children books, please be quite sure of that. I could also send you books.

Please, tell me. You write you are very old. What do you mean by that? How old are you? I am 8 years old, my mother is 33, her name is Valeria.

We also have rains now, but it is a matter of some days only, usually we have good weather in July.

Soon my grandmother and I go to call on my relatives for two weeks' time.

Yours sincerely,

Marina

* Using exclamation marks in this way is a common rhetorical device in Russian. Exclamation marks are used much more frequently in Russian than in English and don't have the same emphasis as in English.

P.S. I collect postage stamps, and I ask you to go on attaching beautiful stamps to your letters and so shall I (but never enclose them – it is forbidden).*

*Marina remembers: *Some of the parcels never reached us, but others arrived containing only some of their contents. The workers at the post office were watched by their bosses, or by the KGB, so if there were four magazines sent to us, they might manage to steal one. It was a strange time then. When my husband, was thirteen, he went to Cuba one summer for a children's Communist camp, and there were lots of other children of Communists from America, Finland, other European countries, all over the world. My husband made friends there. When he came back, and he started to correspond with those children of Communist parents. This correspondence stopped very quickly because the children didn't receive his letters and he didn't receive theirs. So, even though these were young Communists from Western countries, the authorities in Kishinev did everything possible to preclude contact, because any contact was a potential danger in their eyes.*

TELEPHONE: THATCHAM 2105 CABLES & TELEGRAMS DRYASDUST NEWBURY

H. W. Edwards (*Booksellers*) Ltd

DIRECTORS: H. W. EDWARDS · O. R. EDWARDS

Members Antiquarian Booksellers Association

ASHMORE GREEN, NEWBURY, BERKSHIRE, ENGLAND

16-7-71

Dear Marina

Very many thanks for your nice letter of July 8th, which has only taken a week to get here. I am so glad that you received my letter and also the sweets. I hope you liked them. If not, you must give them away. I always liked sweets very much when I was a small boy, and indeed I am afraid that I still do. Perhaps this is because I do not smoke. I know that sweets and chocolates are bad for you, but I have noticed during a long life that nearly anything that one likes is bad for one.

The English in your letters is wonderful. You and your mother must be very clever. I have tried many times to learn Russian, which I think is a most beautiful language. Alas, I only learn as far as the alphabet and then give up. Perhaps with your help I shall try again.

I am sending you next week my copy of *Alice's Adventures in Wonderland* in two volumes, which I bought once in New York. I first read this when I was about ten years old. It is very famous in England and has of course been translated into Russian. But I feel sure that you will like it. I cannot send it before as I have to go to London for a few days for work.

Later on I will find out what children's books I can get and will send. I expect that some will be too old for you but you have plenty of time.

You ask me what do I mean when I say that I am very old? I mean exactly that. Although I find it hard to believe I am SEVENTY-ONE years old. But do not let that worry you. I sometimes only feel about 15. I have a daughter that is older than your mother. She is 36 and has three children, two boys and a girl who was born only last Christmas and is called Daisy. My wife is not yet 60 but you can see all this for yourself from the photographs that I enclose in return for the two such nice ones of yourself. I am sure you will be a magnificent ballerina.

We live in the country in a cottage that was once our dacha* before the War. We have a large garden almost exactly one desyatin. And we are about 60 versts from London I think. I hope you like my Russian words.

Will you tell your mother that we shall be very happy to send you anything that we can from England either for you or for her. If you would like things to wear you must send the size in inches or centimetres. Newbury has many shops, and things are not very expensive. Be sure to let us know. Perhaps in the winter we can send you a sweater (this is what I am wearing in the photograph, yellow). These are very well made in Scotland.

I do hope you have a nice time with your grandmother. Please give her my best wishes, and of course to you and your mother also.

Harold

*'Dacha' is a summer house. 'Desyatin' and 'Versts' are pre-revolutionary measurements of distance. Harold is using archaic Russian vocabulary.

Kishinev
July 28, 1971

Dear Mr Edwards!

Best thanks for your kind letter of July 16. Both, my mother and I like very much to exchange letters with you, it is interesting to read your letters and to see your photos. On which your wife and the three cats appear so well. We liked you all as we saw you.

As for sweets, I liked them too, but to tell the truth, I do not like sweets so much, I prefer ice-cream. My mother likes smoking, so that she is not so fond of sweets as others are (but nevertheless we are very grateful to you for your attentions).

I have not yet received your book, because it is too early, but I am looking forward towards receiving it.

Two days ago we sent you by registered mail a book on *Fortress Architecture of Early Russia*. Have you received it? Please, acknowledge the receipt. Tell us, please, if you like old Russian art. If you want, we shall send you more books on it.

Now we (the same as many other people here), we watch the English *The Forsyte Saga** in 28 series, a series each day (to-day there is no film). My mother likes very much both – book and film, she says – she would like to watch all the series at once.

As to things to wear, we thank you for your kindness. Sometimes we have bought English things in our shops. For example the shoes my mother wears are English.

I have just returned together with my grandmother from a voyage to the Baltic sea, where I had a really nice time with our relatives.

*Marina remembers: *There was very little foreign television at that time. I was very young of course in 1971, I was only seven or eight, but I remember* The Forsyte Saga *and other films being shown. Primarily they showed Western films which were 'decent', where there was no violence, no sex scenes or anything like that. So in this respect,* The Forsyte Saga *was a perfect example of a very good classical novel, staged well. We had very boring television when we were children, and because we didn't have much to watch, we read a lot.*

What I should appreciate very much is a photo of your daughter and your grandchildren.

Best regards to all your family.

Yours sincerely,

Marina

TELEPHONE: THATCHAM 2105 CABLES & TELEGRAMS DRYASDUST NEWBURY

H. W. Edwards (Booksellers) Ltd

DIRECTORS: H. W. EDWARDS · O. R. EDWARDS

Members Antiquarian Booksellers Association

ASHMORE GREEN, NEWBURY, BERKSHIRE, ENGLAND

5-8-71

Dear Marina

Very many thanks indeed for your letter, the photographs and the fine book, which arrived yesterday. It is very kind of your mother to take so much trouble. I greatly enjoyed looking at it, the more so with the English translations to the photographs. It made me wish very much to see Russia again.

I do hope that by now you have safely received the copy of *Alice in Wonderland* which I sent you. Please write as soon as you get it. I will then send you a copy of *The Forsyte Saga* which you will be able to enjoy when you are older. We too watched the television of this. I think it is one of the best things that the BBC has ever done. I have read that in the version you are watching the words are read by one person only. This is a great pity I think, and it would be so much better if different actors and actresses took the various characters.

Do not, please, write to me as Mr Edwards. Please call me Harold. This is a name that I believe is difficult to pronounce for Russians? It is NOT pronounced as Garold!

I too very much like ice-cream, and we have just bought a small machine that makes really perfect ice-cream. We used it for the first time on Sunday last, and Olive made it with raspberries from the garden. I am sorry that your mother smokes. My wife does also, but no longer cigarettes but small cigars. These are supposed not to be so bad for you. I have tried to smoke many times, but I cannot. It is most unpleasant for me. So I am rather lucky.

Should you ever wish to send me any books I much prefer literature or history. I think some are published in Moscow in English translations. But I have very many in English. All the works of

Dostoevsky, Gogol, Pushkin, Lermontov, Turgenev, Tolstoy and Chekhov and mainly of the more modern writers. I like Chekhov very much. When I was young I read all of Dostoevsky and was greatly influenced by him. I believe he is no longer published in Russia, but all of his works are in print in England.

I am glad that you have had a holiday in the Baltic. Where were you? I hope the weather was nice. We have been having very nice weather here, sun-shine all day, and quite hot for England.

You do not give me any information about your sizes of things to wear. Do please let me know what you would like. My wife will enjoy buying you things in London. And books. Please let me know what you would like and your mother. I shall be only too pleased to send that.

With very best wishes to you all from us here.
I type my letters to you as my handwriting is too bad.
Harold

P.S. Dear Valeria, Forgive me for answering you in this way, but I do not know your patronymic. Please let me know what books interest you. Do you know, I read in *The Times*, that the Trouser Suit for women has arrived in Moscow? My wife has several. It is a very nice fashion if your figure is not too large!

Kishinev
10.8.1971

Dear Harold

I was very-very glad to receive your letter with nice stamps, photographs and the fine books of *Alice in Wonderland*. Your daughter is very pretty and young-looking.

My daughter is now in summer camp for children about 30 km from Kishinev and she hasn't yet seen this letter and books. I write without her. Marina will come in the 20th August and will be also very glad. The book of Alice is very nice but I think it is too old for Marina now. But, as you said, she has plenty of time.

Dear Harold, *The Forsyte Saga* in English we have. Should you ever wish to send us anything I prefer some magazines with pictures of England, London, Englishmen. And as all the women, I am also interested in the latest fashion-papers. And Marina would be interested in the textbook which the children study in the first class, something like ABC-book.

It's very pleasant for me that you know and like Russian literature. I like Chekhov and Dostoevsky too. You're mistaken that Dostoevsky isn't in print in our country. I have the complete collection of Dostoevsky. Have you seen any Russian films from Dostoevsky? Are Chekhov's plays staged in your theatres? Shakespeare and B. Shaw are staged in our theatres as often as Chekhov. I like them very much. Now a Russian film *King Lear* is on. To my mind, it's an excellent dramatization. Not long ago we saw the TV-film *The Picture of Dorian Grey*. I have this book in English and like it very much. I am afraid that I shall not find anything interesting in English translation of literature or history for you here. In English we have only nice books on art. If you want, I can send you the illustrated magazine in English *The Soviet Union*. But I think, it is in England.

Dear Harold, if your wife and you are so kind, as you want to send to Marina things to wear, you can send to her the winter dress for school. The schoolgirls must come to school in brown or blue (better brown) dresses with white collar. The cut may be anyone you like. Her size (in our standard) 34, her height is 133cm now.

As for trousers suit, I am not sure that it suits me, because my figure is not quite large, but I am only of 158 cm height.

I am enclosing photographs of Marina, when she was in the city of Kaliningrad* in Baltic. She had a very good time there.

Dear Harold, from your letter I understand that you had been in Russia, hadn't you?

I am glad that you type your letter, because your handwriting is really too illegible for us. Do you always understand my handwriting and what I want to say?

With very best wishes to you and all your family,

Valeria, or simply Lera

*Kaliningrad was formerly Konigsberg, part of Prussia. After the Second World War, it became part of the Soviet Union, the most westerly city. Lera's grandparents moved there after the war when their house was destroyed during the siege of Leningrad.

TELEPHONE: THATCHAM 2105 CABLES & TELEGRAMS DRYASDUST NEWBURY

H. W. Edwards (*Booksellers*) Ltd

DIRECTORS: H. W. EDWARDS · O. R. EDWARDS

Members Antiquarian Booksellers Association

ASHMORE GREEN, NEWBURY, BERKSHIRE, ENGLAND

23-8-71

Dear Marina & Valeria

I am very pleased to receive your letter this morning and the two photographs of Marina.

Glad also that the *Alice in Wonderland* has arrived safely. I think that if you were to translate it as you read it, Marina would like it. I agree that it is perhaps a little difficult. It is one of the most famous stories written in English for children, and is quite proverbial here. Many books have been written about it. There has even been a Freudian interpretation of it. I can still remember when I first read it before the first war.

As soon as I can I will start to send you *Vogue*, which is a fashion paper here and very popular, and also *House and Garden*. This is a rather silly paper that I take because it has a section on Wine & Food. You may notice that I shall have taken out the last two or three pages. This is because they deal with restaurants in London, and I find it useful to know where to go sometimes. We do not go out very much now. I am very deaf (old age) and this makes for some difficulty.

For this reason I no longer am able to go to the theatre, which was a favourite amusement for us. But I hope this winter to go to the cinema to see foreign films as this will have captions in English and it will not be necessary to understand the speech.

It is odd that you ask me about the plays of Chekhov, for only last night, Sunday, my wife watched the *Three Sisters* which was done in colour. It was very good. I have seen all the plays of Chekhov including the one-act ones. He is continually being played in England. Did you see the very beautiful film of the *Lady with a Dog* that was made some time ago in Russia? It was one of the best films I have seen.

I am glad to learn that Dostoevsky is in print again. You may know that Lenin had a very great dislike of his works, and would not read him. I am trying to remember the Russian plays I have seen in England. Before the war I remember a French company doing a version of *Crime and Punishment*. It was very well done. I have seen Gogol's *Inspector General*, Turgenev's *A Month in the Country*, and Gorki's *Lower Depths* both in English and Russian. I should like to see Bulgakov's *White Guard*. I enjoyed the novel very much.

Yes, I have been in Russia twice. The first time in 1932 when things were rather sad. I had a wonderful journey down the Volga from Nijni Novgorod to Rostov on the Don, and then back to Leningrad via Kiev. Leningrad is one of the most beautiful cities I know. The second time I went with Olive by bus from Ostend in 1964. We did not see nearly as much of Russia as we should have liked, but it was a great experience.

I am writing too much. I will find the books for Marina of course. Do not bother to send me books as I have thousands! Perhaps at Xmas a book on icons?

Wishing you both, my dear Lera, every happiness from my wife and myself.

Love to you all from us,
Harold

The bookroom.

TELEPHONE: THATCHAM 2105 CABLES & TELEGRAMS DRYASDUST NEWBURY

H. W. Edwards (*Booksellers*) Ltd

DIRECTORS: H. W. EDWARDS · O. R. EDWARDS

Members Antiquarian Booksellers Association

ASHMORE GREEN, NEWBURY, BERKSHIRE, ENGLAND

6-9-71

Dear Marina & Valeria

Very many thanks for your letter, which arrived yesterday, and more especially for the book which you have so kindly sent me on Russian Icons. I like this very much, as I have always been attracted by Primitive paintings. I buy what are known as 'modern primitives' and have some rather nice ones. But like everything now in England these are too expensive for us.

In London next week we have an international meeting of antiquarian booksellers for the whole week, ending with a grand dinner at the Savoy hotel. We shall meet many people there, but alas, no one from the USSR.

You mention our garden. You are quite right, it is of great importance to us as we like to grow as much of our own food as is possible, but more especially I like trees and shrubs and flowers very much. All the trees etc. here have been planted by us since we came here nearly 35 years ago. I also like birds very much and we feed them in the winter and always keep water for them. We have a large number here all the year round. I do not know why I should like the country so much. I was born right in the centre of London and have always lived in the centre. My wife, Olive, is also a Londoner and our daughter also was born in the centre. As you probably know, the love of gardens is very usual for English people. There are quite literally millions of gardens in England, each with its own hedge and apart from its neighbours. You may know the proverb or rather saying, 'An Englishman's home is his castle'. I know it is all quite different in Russia where people are so much more friendly to each other.

What are you reading now? I am interested to know. I have just read a wonderful book by Nadezhda Mandelstam called *Hope against Hope*. It must be a great book in Russian, although I am not sure that it has been published in Russia. She lives in Moscow. Do you know the poetry of her husband Osip Mandelstam? Most of my reading is on Russia. I am ashamed that I do not read Russian. When I was a boy at school we were always being told that 'Cato learnt Greek when he was eighty.' So there is still a chance for me.

Glad that Marina has already read *Alice* in Russian.

I see that she is in Form II. I was at her age also in Form II. This was long before the first war.

I must hurry to catch the postman. Write when you have the time.

With love to both of you from us both,
Harold

Kishinev
6.IX.71

Dear Harold!

We were very glad to receive your letter and the three photographs in it. Apparently, you like your garden very much. But we (Marina and I) live in the big five-storeyed house in the 2nd floor and haven't a garden. Our big house has a big yard, there are many flowers, many trees and many grounds for children to play. Children are content.

Marina was content that you praised her dress so highly. Certainly, it has been made by me. I can sew and knit a little.

The weather is fine in our town. We have +25–28 degrees C in daytime, +18–20 degrees C at night. It's the best month in Kishinev. It's warm, dry and there are many excellent fruits, apples, melons, water-melons, peaches.

With best wishes to you from us,

Marina and Lera

TELEPHONE: THATCHAM 2105 CABLES & TELEGRAMS DRYASDUST NEWBURY

H. W. Edwards (Booksellers) Ltd

DIRECTORS: H. W. EDWARDS · O. R. EDWARDS

Members Antiquarian Booksellers Association

ASHMORE GREEN, NEWBURY, BERKSHIRE, ENGLAND

6-10-71

Dear Marina & Lera

We were very happy to get your letter of the 27th September, which arrived safely yesterday.

Glad that at least the books for Marina have arrived. I hope these were the kind you wanted.

Now, last Friday Olive has sent two dresses for Marina. She bought them in Oxford Street, which is London's great shopping street. I suppose it corresponds to the Nevsky Prospekt in Leningrad, although not nearly such a beautiful street. Let me know if these arrive safely (they are for school) and I will then get Olive to buy her a trouser suit. Many children here wear them. This will be much easier to buy than the dresses for some reason.

My daughter runs a Graphic Design Centre together with her husband. This means printing design mainly. When she was at boarding school during the last war she learnt typography, for which she has a natural aptitude. After leaving school she went to the London School of Printing for a year or so. But she decided, rather against my will, to become a fashion model. It was through this that she met her husband. She has, as is very usual in England with those that can afford it, a nurse for the children who lives at the house. Also someone to do the cleaning. She does the cooking usually. All the family are very ardent vegetarians, mainly on humanitarian grounds, not for health reasons. A lot of people here have become vegetarians since the introduction of Factory Farming, which is the intensive rearing of chickens, calves etc. where the birds and animals are never let out of the farm buildings until they are to be slaughtered. It is a form of protest, I suppose, against this cruelty. I may say that when we were in Russia in 1964 we went as vegetarians and we had very little difficulty, except that no one could understand why. So we said that we were Tolstoyans, and after that had no trouble.

I have just ordered a book by Bulgakov on the last year of Tolstoy. This is not the Bulgakov who wrote *The White Guard*, but someone who was Tolstoy's secretary during that time. I regard Tolstoy as the world's greatest novelist, although as a man he left much to be desired.

You ask me what books I should like. The only one that I think it would be possible for you to get, if it is not too expensive, would be a Russian/English, English/Russian dictionary. But when you are next in Moscow, I should like you to look out for any translations into English of Russian writers except the classical ones. For instance, Tvardovsky (who was editor of *Novy Mir* I think) has had some of his poetry translated into English and printed in Moscow. He remarked that to be translated into English and published in Moscow was rather like a girl being taken to a dance by her brother. I am not interested in politics, but any of the minor writers who may have been put into English would be of great interest. But I do not think you would find any in Kishinev?

I was reading a Russian writer yesterday who writes mainly in English, and whom I greatly enjoy, V. Nabokov. He quotes in Russian a saying that impressed me: *vsevo dvoe i est' – smert' da sovest.** He puts this in English, and I think it is very true.

Like you, we are having beautiful autumn weather now. We have been picking the apples and pears. Also nuts in the garden. The last thing will be to pick the quinces. Olive makes a very nice preserve from these. Alas, I have a sweet tooth.

I like the stamp of Dostoevsky you sent. I have just re-read the novel that we call *The Insulted and Injured*. I greatly enjoyed it. Now I am reading *Les Illusions Perdues* by Balzac. Do you know if Marcel

*'There are only two things – death and conscience.'

Proust has been translated into Russian? I hope that I am not giving you too much trouble with my rather garrulous letters. A sure sign of old age.

With love to you both from us both,
Harold

Kishinev
17.10.71

Dear Harold!

Two days ago I arrived from Moscow and found at home pleasing surprise – your parcels with 2 magazines for me and with 2 frocks for Marina. Both of frocks are quite beautiful. She was very happy to receive them and now she puts on now one now another of them, while looking at herself in the mirror. Now Marina has the most beautiful frock in all her class. I shall make a photo of her soon and you will be able to see how well they suit her. Dear Harold, please, receive our best thanks for you and your wife's kindness and the attention you pay to us. But at the same time, I am afraid if it maybe too expensive to you, since it is £8.

Of course, I liked very much the magazines as well, especially *Harpers and Queen*, just because the latter writes more on fashions.

Dear Harold, but we have not yet received your letter. I worry seriously about it. Maybe neither you have received ours of 27.9? As soon as we receive your letter, we shall write you immediately another one.

Please, tell us, if you want souvenirs from Russia? Do you want Russia books? Please, address all the mail to Marina.

With love,

Your Marina and Lera

Kishinev
22.10.71

Dear Harold!

Only some days ago I sent you a letter but today, having received yours, I write again and send you Marina's photograph.

We were very-very glad to get your letter, but it is a pity that there was not a single stamp on the envelope. Somebody took them away. But I hope next time to get the stamps safely.

Dear Harold, you mustn't say that you are giving us too much trouble with your rather garrulous letters. The more you write the better for us. To read your letters, the letters of a man whose life is quite different from ours, is more interesting than the novels. If English were my first language or if I could write to you in Russian I would write much more, of course. Many many thanks for parcels, Marina likes her blue dress so much that she doesn't want to take it off. At end of November I shall be in Moscow and I shall look for books for you. I have sent you a Russian–English dictionary and soon I shall send you the rest.

I have read lately a very interesting book from the Russian history of the XIXth century about 'decabristy'.* I have also read a novel by an American writer A. Hailey *The Airport*. Now I am reading the novel by Remarque, *Shadows in the Paradise*. Do you like the German writer Heinrich Böll? He is one of my favourite modern writers.

You ask about Marcel Proust. Some of his works have been translated into Russian, but it is difficult to find them and I have not read any. I have not heard about Nabokov either. If I find Tvardovsky in English, I send his book to you. Do you have any Russian books in England? If you have, please write about them. I am interested in modern writers mainly. My husband is also a vegetarian. My husband is greatly interested in Yoga system. But nowadays, it is difficult to be a real yogi.

*A group called the Decembrists, members of the aristocracy who tried to overthrow the Tsar in 1825 in order to establish a republic. Five were executed, the others went into exile.

As any woman, I want to be young and slender as long as possible. Your daughter and your wife have excellent figures. How do they manage without gymnastics?

I hope in future I shall be able to work not so much and I'll have more time for reading and sports.*

I haven't quite understood the word 'pattern'. I have no good dressmaker and I sew myself.

Dear Harold, when you receive the dictionaries will it be possible for me to write some places in Russian?

By the way, do you or your wife know German?

Please, excuse me that I ask you too much about stamps. It is not for me, that is why I do it.† Have you received Marina's postcard?

With love to you,

Your Marina and Lera

*A covert reference to the fact that Slava was about to be released in November.

†The friend who helped Lera with writing the letters in English was a stamp collector.

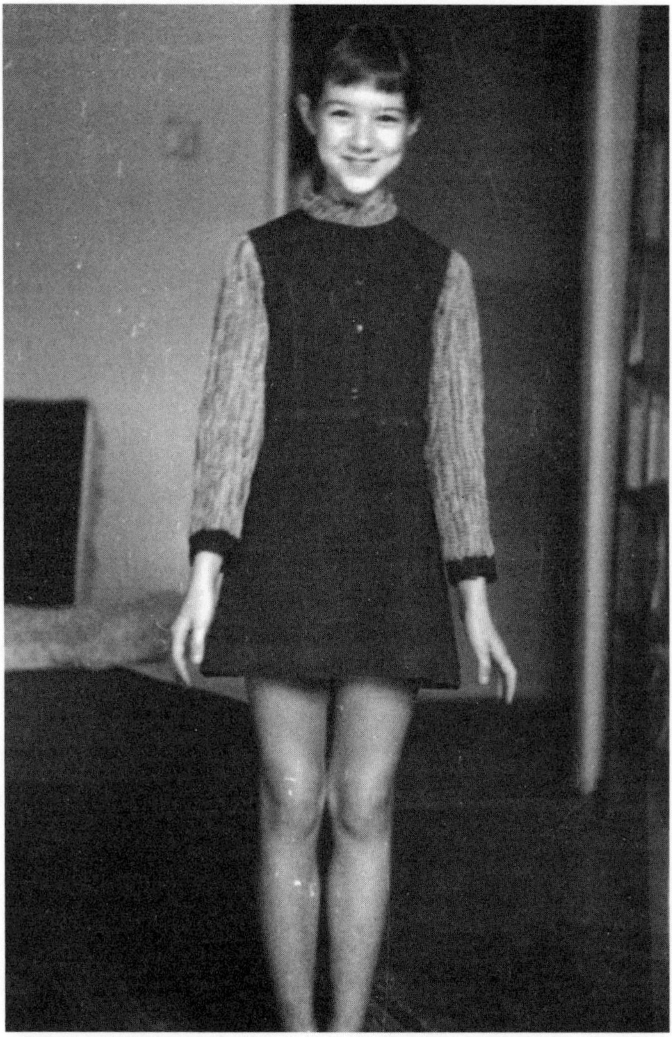

Marina wearing one of the dresses Olive sent.

TELEPHONE: THATCHAM 2105 CABLES & TELEGRAMS DRYASDUST NEWBURY

H. W. Edwards (*Booksellers*) Ltd

DIRECTORS: H. W. EDWARDS · O. R. EDWARDS

Members Antiquarian Booksellers Association

ASHMORE GREEN, NEWBURY, BERKSHIRE, ENGLAND

1-11-71

Dear Marina & Lera

I am indeed in your debt, firstly for the very nice dictionary that you have sent and secondly for no fewer than three letters. So I am answering all these right away, and once more you will owe me a reply. But do not hurry, for I feel that now you are receiving all my letters, even if these take some time to reach you.

Can we send you anything in the way of things to eat for Xmas? All the large shops here make up parcels to be sent abroad, and pack them and send them in accordance with the postal regulations. I do not suppose that many go to the USSR. But this may not appeal to you?

You ask me in your letter of the 17th, do I want souvenirs from Russia? The only things I would like are books in English. But I think that you know that. Did you know that Nadezhda Mandelstam's only book to be published in Russia is in English? It deals with English grammar. Quite unfindable of course. Anything that is not political is of interest to me. I look forward to the book that you are sending. By the way, I still do not know if you have received the *Vogues*? We are sending another two tomorrow. As everything we send to you is registered, it should reach you. And of course, there is no reason why not.

I am so sorry that the stamps were taken off the envelope of my last letter to reach you. It seems rather dreadful, but I suppose it is a temptation. It is such a pity that I cannot send you foreign stamps, as I get very many as most of my business is done with foreign countries and not England. However things may alter.

The photographs of Marina are very very attractive. I really think that I shall have one of them framed to hang in my room.

I am afraid that with old age one does not seem to be able to enjoy the young writers. It is the same in English with the exception of a few. I am now reading one of the novels of Jane Austen called *Persuasion*. It was written in 1815. All her novels are very very fine. Nothing happens, but the characters are beautifully depicted. I think she would be very good in Russian. I have not heard of the two writers you have been reading. Who are they – Hailey and Remarque? When you have more time you must let me send you some English novels, such as D.H. Lawrence, James Joyce etc. These of course were all very modern when I was young. Probably old-fashioned now!

We spent a week in Hastings and then a few days in London recently. It was very nice, but we are always glad to come back here for the fresh air and the quiet. To say nothing of the cat.

We did receive Marina's postcard written by herself. We look forward to the time when she is writing letters. And who knows, perhaps one day we shall see her in England with a Ballet company.

The only book that I have in Russian is the *Poems 1898–1914* of Alexander Blok in 3 vols. printed in Berlin in 1922. It is the first complete edition and the only one with the old spelling and punctuation* by which Blok set such value. His famous poem 'The Twelve' I have read in English.

Vegetarianism. I know how difficult this can make life. We now do eat meat but not very often. This is because I got tired of vegetable dishes. I like cheese very much, but am not very keen on eggs. Olive is far more of a vegetarian than I am. But our daughter, her husband and the three children are absolutely vegetarian. They have been for at least ten years. And very strict. At one time I was interested in Yoga. But I found this much too difficult. It is now very popular in England. There are even classes in Yoga in Newbury.

You ask me about books by Russian authors that I have. There are so many that it would be difficult to answer. I buy almost every book that is translated from the Russian as it comes out. For instance,

*The Bolsheviks reformed the Russian language after 1918, changing the alphabet and instituting new forms of spelling. It was intended by Lenin to encourage mass literacy by making orthography simpler and more accessible.

today I have ordered Kalmykov (A.D.) *Memoirs of a Russian Diplomat, 1893–1917* and a new translation of the poems of Marina Tsvetayeva. Most of the books I have, I am sorry to say, have never appeared in Russia. One book that impressed me very much indeed was by Nina Berberova. She was the wife of the famous poet Vladislav Khodasevich, and it is called *The Italics are Mine*. But I could go on for a long time, and it seems to be rather cruel to mention these books when you cannot read them. The writer I greatly admire in every way, both as a great writer in the old tradition of Russian writing, but also as a very brave man, is A. Solzhenitsyn.* V. Nabokov is a Russian who writes marvellous books in English. He was teaching in America, but now lives in Switzerland. He wrote a fine book called *Speak, Memory* dealing with his early life in Russia. And a very famous novel here, called *Lolita*, which has been made into a film.

I write with shame to say that the only language apart from English that I understand and read very easily is French. At one time I knew a fair amount of German, but it has all gone. Languages are not very easy for English people. We always think every one should understand English, and make little attempt to learn other tongues. The thing is that wherever one goes there is always someone who understands English. Not true of course of Russia, but you must remember that three or four <u>million</u> English people go abroad every year for holidays.

With best love to you all from us both,
Harold and Olive

***It is remarkable that this letter wasn't stopped by the censors, as it mentions both Solzhenitsyn and Nabokov.**

Kishinev
15.11.71

Dear Harold!

We were very-very glad to get your letter and two your post-cards with beautiful stamps. I cannot tell you how pleasant it is to receive your correspondence.

But unfortunately I have not enough time now (before our trip) and cannot write a long letter. Now I shall be your debtor. However as soon as we can, we shall write you a long letter or three.

You write my English is very good. But it is not right. I feel that I am not able to reproduce everything what I think. I think that I look very primitive in your eyes. I can speak English only a little part of what I want. Vyacheslav knows English better than me and it will be easier for me to write the next letter.*

You ask me about the *Vogues*, now I have received them. But I think that these magazines were read by the post women and that's why it took a long time to receive them. Women are women. I liked them, but especially the Pattern book, because fashions in the Pattern book are more acceptable for me.

Dear Harold, excuse me, I do not agree with you about gymnastic. To my mind, to be careful what we eat is not enough to keep a good figure. I think that thinness is yet not grace. And only gymnastic gives grace, plastic movements and beautiful carriage. It is quite possible that we understand this word 'gymnastic' essentially differently. My gymnastic is like ballet, but not like sport on apparatus. And besides that, gymnastics have a beneficial effect on my nervous system.

I can well understand that with old age one does not seem to be able to enjoy the young writers. I can add that it is true for every age: at every age is the best reading – books by writers of the same age. Did I

*Slava is the diminutive form of Vyacheslav. Here Lera is making an oblique reference to Slava's imminent release from prison. Similarly the mention of a journey at the end of the letter is their trip to meet him from prison, and bring him home.

say it right? Did you understand me? You may send me novels by D.H. Lawrence and James Joyce. Also I like Maugham.

The Russian writer which you like, I also like very much.* However, I am not agree with you that he writes in the old tradition of Russian writing. But we thought, English men can not understand him, or rather feel deeply. I do not stop wonder at your knowledge of Russian literature. It is very-very pleasant for me.

I also do not like German, but I had to study it at school and in the University. English I studied only one year at the courses.

Three days ago I sent you our present for Christmas. Did you like our sweets? Which of them do you like more?

Write us as usual. We leave on the 19th November. We shall spend about a week in Moscow, then a week in Saratov† at the 5–10th of December we shall return home. And I hope we shall get your letter.

With best wishes and love for you,

Marina and Lera

*A covert reference to Solzhenitsyn.

†Slava's mother lived in Saratov, in south-eastern Russia, on the Volga.

TELEPHONE: THATCHAM 2105 CABLES & TELEGRAMS DRYASDUST NEWBURY

H. W. Edwards (*Booksellers*) Ltd

DIRECTORS: H. W. EDWARDS · O. R. EDWARDS

Members Antiquarian Booksellers Association

ASHMORE GREEN, NEWBURY, BERKSHIRE, ENGLAND

November 16, 1971

Dear Lera & Marina and Slava*

Yesterday to our great delight your two letters arrived. I think that letters take about 10 days to get here. Our postal service used to be very good indeed, but recently it has deteriorated. We wonder if it is not all due to computers!! We used to get 3 deliveries a day, and now we only have two and one on Saturday. People in a hurry use the telephone all the time.

If possible, will you send me a photograph of you in the dress so that I may have some idea of how you look, and for ideas for future dresses?

There seems an infinity of choice in the shops for young people like you and I would not like to send something that you could not wear or that Slava would not like. My daughter is not a lot of help as she wears very 'trendy' clothes. She was a fashion model before she was married and leads a very social life and is very smart, but I think the clothes she wears perhaps you would not wear? Or would you like something 'trendy'. This means in the trend of fashion, which is ephemeral, and a little exaggerated.

Yes we do decorate Christmas trees here, and most families with children have one. Usually they are real trees, but lately plastic or tinsel trees are becoming fashionable. Perhaps because they can be kept from year to year? I prefer the genuine trees. I should love to see Marina dance. You must be very proud of her, and of her writing.

*It seems that Harold was aware of Slava's imminent release, although Lera herself didn't mention it in her letters – indeed, it might have been dangerous for her to do so. It is probable that Amnesty would have been tipped off about this via a contact in Moscow and passed the information on to Harold.

From her photographs she looks as if she has a sense of humour too.

I too am lately worried about putting on weight. I have given up smoking and have gained 8 lbs already. I am afraid that instead of smoking after dinner, I eat a chocolate, and then another, which is fatal for the figure. I really must learn control!!

A Pattern is made of paper and is used for cutting out from material. All patterns have instructions. I always use them for children's clothes. I do not make clothes for myself as I am not sufficiently expert and it is so much easier to buy them.

Do you think that you could make things from a pattern? Can you get material easily? If so, I will get one of the Simplicity patterns that you liked for you to try.

Thank you for your very charming offer to send me perfume, but please do not. I have lots, as Harold always buys me French perfume for birthday and Christmas presents, and sometimes at any time he is in a loving mood. In fact, there is honestly nothing I want, and as Harold says, I must be a very happy woman. Of course, at your age I was very different.

We look forward to hearing from you soon, and hope you have a very Happy New Year.

Lots of love from us both,
Olive

Olive in her vegetable garden at Ashmore Green.

Moscow
28-11-71

Dear Harold!

I am very thankful for your parcel with books for me, my husband and my daughter, which I get before our leaving from Kishinev 19-11-71. We all like them very much. Now we all three are in Moscow with our friends. Everything is all right. Tomorrow we shall go to Saratov. As soon as we shall be able, we shall write you a long letter and send you several books.

With best love to you both from us all,

Lera

* * *

DAVID BONAVIA WAS THE TIMES CORRESPONDENT IN MOSCOW from 1969 until 1972. In 1973 he published a book called *Fat Sasha and the Urban Guerilla*. The following excerpt describes a party at the home of a Russian dissident in Moscow:

> . . . It was a scene which will live sharply in the memory for a lifetime. One of those present was a quiet-spoken and good-looking young man, a political prisoner who had just emerged from the dreadful conditions of a cell in Vladimir gaol, which he had shared with several others, suffering the perpetual misery of cold, close confinement and semi-starvation. Before being let out, he had been fattened up a bit, and his hair was beginning to grow. His wife, a charming and attractive woman, and their pretty young daughter had come hundreds of miles from the place where they lived, to welcome him and bring him home. When asked what his daughter was going to do when she grew up, he looked at her affectionately, and said with the utmost simplicity: 'She will destroy the K.G.B.' With an impossible combination of tenseness and serenity, he actually seemed to be missing the prison from which he had just emerged, and which, through all the Russias, is still the most feared of punishment centres, though located in a favourite venue for foreign tourists. He said he could never rest in his mind till his friends were released from there, too. All the time in gaol, he had been hungry and able to think of little but food. Now, from nerves and fatigue, he could barely eat . . .

Slava had been taken to the famous Lefortovo prison in Moscow on his thirty-third birthday, 23 November 1966. He was stripped, interrogated and formally arrested on charges of attempting to organise an illegal printing press. It was at that point that he realised how serious his situation was; the Lefortovo is an intimidating building and the prisoners were kept in stone cells with thick walls and tiny barred windows giving hardly any light. There they were kept twenty-four hours a day. On the door of the cell was a list of one hundred rules, a legacy of Stalin's time, such as 'After a prisoner has woken up, he cannot lie on his bed for the rest of the day.' Slava's interrogators offered him a choice: if he gave them names of the others involved he would be released. This wasn't an option for Slava; he couldn't go back to life on the outside on those terms. He was tried in

Slava after his release from prison.

a closed court on 6 March 1967 and given a sentence of five years for the dissemination of anti-Soviet propaganda.

It took several days for Slava to reach the prison camp. He was taken there in a railway gaol carriage filled with prisoners, and it felt like a terrible nightmare. On one side of the corridor, instead of compartments, there were cells behind iron bars that were crammed full of people. Not only was it impossible to lie or to sit; at times it was impossible even to stand properly. They were fed one salted fish in the morning and evening, plus a piece of bread and a glass of water. Within a day the prisoners began to suffer from thirst, which was another refined form of torture intended to break them and humiliate them even more.

Slava had a very vague idea of what was waiting for him in the camp he was going to in Mordovia. There, in the northern part of Russia among vast forests, his train was heading for a complex of prison camps called Dubrovlag. When Slava was in Dubrovlag, there were about 30,000 prisoners held there, of which 2,000 were political prisoners held in three separate camps. The political prisoners were kept apart from the criminals in case they turned them against the Soviet regime. To his great surprise, in the camp Slava found many young people like him who, having experienced relative freedom for a short while during the Khrushchev era, were unable to put up with the Soviet machine any longer, and had begun to resist it. There were poets and painters, priests and soldiers, workers and scientists, and all of them had dared to speak openly about what was going on around them. Other prisoners had been sent there during Stalin's rule, more than thirty years earlier.*

During the day some prisoners worked in factory workshops; others unloaded train carriages or chopped wood in the forests. In the evenings, when they came back to their barracks after a minimal supper, they would talk and tell each other the stories of their lives. They would meet and talk about writers and poets banned by the authorities; they recited poems and shared their knowledge. During such evenings, an abstract painter would talk about the theory of colour in Kandinsky's art, or a priest would explain the ideas of Christianity in the works of Dostoevsky. Slava learned English relatively well in Dubrovlag with the help of a manual he found in the library there. Other prisoners studied Spanish, or Japanese, or some tribal languages of Africa, based on whatever they could find. However, all the books in the library were published in the Soviet Union; not a single book from a foreign publishing-house was allowed in the camp.

Many years later, one of Slava's friends – by now a world-renowned scientist who had been involved in the development of the artificial lung – said he considered it his great good luck to have been in Dubrovlag at that time; to have been so young and to have met so many outstanding people at the same time and in the same place. He said the two years he had spent there changed his life for ever.

Slava's time in the camp was filled with correspondence with Lera;

*Once, staying in the hospital, Slava met a very unusual prisoner. This man spoke with a strong English accent, incredible in the mid sixties in Mordovia. Later on Slava found out that Dale, a young American, had been flying from Thailand to San Francisco, with a connection in Moscow. During a search by customs, a hundred grams of marijuana were found in his luggage. He was taken off the flight, put into a police car and then thrown into a dark prison cell. Dale said everything felt like a dream: the trial, the train, the watch-towers with jailers, the barracks, the frost and the camp surrounded by security guards with police dogs. Fortunately, he didn't have to stay in the camp too long; he was soon exchanged for a Soviet spy.

The prison at Dubrovlag, with the grave of the writer and human rights activist Yuri Galanskov in the foreground. A friend of Slava's in Dubrovlag, Galanskov was imprisoned for founding and editing a samizdat publication called The Phoenix *and also for publishing a report on the trials of dissident writers Yuri Daniel and Andrei Sinyavsky, which was smuggled out to the West. He died in the camp in 1972, at the age of thirty-three.*

he was allowed to write two letters per month. These were censored, and in the event of any minor offence he could be deprived of this right for a month or more. The letters would often arrive with lines crossed over when the censor had found anything inappropriate. Parcels from the family with soap, toothbrushes and note-books were occasionally allowed. For extra food, in spring belly-pinched prisoners planted carrots and onions in far-away corners of the camp, but if the camp administration found those little vegetable plots, they immediately destroyed them. During his period of imprisonment Slava did not eat a single tomato, cucumber or apple; all of these were prohibited. Later he commented that prison life consisted of incremental acts of resistance – you had to resist constantly to retain your human dignity – and that eventually he had felt impregnable in that camp, confident the authorities couldn't touch him.

On one occasion towards the end of his sentence, Slava witnessed a horrifying scene. There was a prisoner in the camp who had been there for twenty years and had lost his mind. He was quiet and harmless, a man whom all the other prisoners loved, felt sorry for and took care of. One evening, coming back from work, this poor man rushed to the barbed-wire fence surrounding the camp and tried to climb it out of despair, unable to withstand the hardships of camp life any longer. A crowd of prisoners shouted to the guards on the watch-tower not to shoot because it wasn't an escape; a doctor should be called and the prisoner be taken to hospital. But they refused to listen and began to fire. The prisoner was not killed immediately but only wounded, and he hung there for a while on the barbed wire, his body convulsing before other camp guards arrived and shot him dead.

This event put the whole camp into a state of shock and for Slava it was impossible to accept what had happened without some form of protest. Along with some other prisoners, he announced a hunger strike until the circumstances of that shooting were investigated and the guilty punished. After three days the gaolers just tied the hunger strikers to their beds, pushed a pipe down their throats and poured in gruel. Slava wasn't allowed to die, but his punishment for the rest of his sentence was to be sent to another prison in the town of Vladimir, about 180 kilometres east of Moscow.

Dating from tsarist times, Vladimir had the reputation of being the harshest prison ever created in Russia. Four people had to share a tiny cell which was piercing cold all the time, even in summer. Originally, the buildings in Vladimir had had large windows which let light in, but Soviet gaolers had considered this too much of a luxury and blocked-up three-quarters of each window with bricks, so there was a constant semi-darkness in the cells. The prisoners were allowed to read and write there, but because of the cold and their permanent debilitating hunger, they couldn't do much except pace up and down.

Wake-up was at six o'clock and during daylight it was forbidden to lie on the beds, look out of the window or speak loudly. Once a day the prisoners were taken for a one-hour walk. In winter, in temperatures of minus thirty degrees, the men were dressed only in light cotton uniforms. Sweaters, scarves and warm socks were taken away, their shoes had very thin soles. Mittens were forbidden. The prisoners had to walk around the prison court for an hour and then, for the rest of the day, try desperately to warm themselves up back in their cells. Slava felt as if he'd been left there to rot.

Marina remembers: As a child, I never knew that my father was in prison; my mother always told me that he was away on a business trip. I thought he had a very important job, maybe working for the military. I remember once when we had just arrived at Potima (the railway station nearest Dubrovlag), we were standing outside the gates waiting be let in, and suddenly my mother saw my father and said, 'Look, here is your Father coming back from work.' A huge column of people all dressed in grey uniforms was approaching the gates of the camp from the forest. 'Why are they guarded by soldiers and police dogs?' I asked my mother. 'They have to be guarded because they have a very important job,' she replied. I started shouting 'Dad! Dad!', and waved my hand, and all of a sudden a hand rose above the crowd and waved back to me, and I heard him shouting, 'Marisha, I am here!' My eyes were so clouded with tears

Slava and Marina after his release.

that I could not make out his face, but I was very happy, I waved even more vigorously and shouted, 'You see, we came to visit you at your work.' Suddenly I heard a woman's scornful voice behind me saying, 'Oh, yes, your father has such a very interesting job here.' I spun round and saw a big woman in a uniform laughing and sneering at me. I began to cry. But that is my only bad memory of Potima.

At the time I was only conscious of meeting my loving father there. Me and my mother would stay inside the camp in an isolated barrack which was called the 'guest house'; there were spy-holes in the doors. When I got bored of staying in our room I would walk out into the dingy corridor and meet other children. (In the early 1990s, when the priest from my church sent me to Switzerland for a seminar about children and Christianity, one of the other delegates, a Russian Orthodox priest roughly the same age as me, seemed very familiar. Finally we realised that we had met each other before; we had played together as children in the corridor of the guest house in the camp where both our fathers happened to be.)

When my mother went to meet my father on his release, I was left for a few days in Moscow, with Arina Ginzburg. There was also a young woman staying there whose name was Vera. One evening she told me she'd been in prison for helping to publish a clandestine journal. I was horrified; up to that moment I had believed only criminals were imprisoned. It was then I suddenly realised that my father was in prison, along with Alexander Ginzburg, not protected by the police dogs, but guarded by them. The shock was terrible. Two hours later my father arrived, I rushed to kiss and hug him and I whispered in his ear, 'I know that you were not on a business trip, you were imprisoned.' After that I think the strain was simply overwhelming, and I collapsed and fell asleep in the middle of the small apartment, oblivious to the noise of twenty people talking until three o'clock in the morning.

After my father's release, we spent several days in Moscow and my parents took me to the Pushkin Fine Arts Museum. We wandered along empty halls of Ancient Greek art, admired the mysterious Fayum portraits, and my parents told me about Leonardo da Vinci. When we entered the hall of Post-Impressionist Art, my father suddenly stopped in front of one particular picture; he seemed rooted to the spot for a long time. He was looking at Van Gogh's *Prisoners Exercising*. I felt then how far away from us he was, and how deeply he felt for the friends he'd left behind, in a similar prison courtyard.

Prisoners Exercising *by Vincent Van Gogh.*

PARK OTELI

AYAZPAŞA

İSTANBUL – BEYOĞLU

Telgr. adresi: **PARK** – İstanbul

İstanbul, 2 Dec 1971

Telefon: 45 07 60

Dear Mr Edwards,

This is to let you know that Vyacheslav Aidov (Marina's father) was released from Vladimir prison last week. He had been sent there after organising a hunger strike at a labour camp where the guards shot one of the prisoners. I met the family briefly in Moscow as they were on their way home to Kishinev. He looked lean but well, but was suffering from some re-adjustment problems and couldn't eat. His will seemed completely unbroken and his thoughts were with his friends in Vladimir jail. (He was in the same cell as Alexander Ginsburg.) His wife asked me to let you know, since I was going to Istanbul on holiday, and also to tell you that all letters are inspected by the censors.

Yours sincerely,
David Bonavia
(*The Times* Moscow correspondent)

TELEPHONE: THATCHAM 2105 CABLES & TELEGRAMS DRYASDUST NEWBURY

H. W. Edwards (Booksellers) Ltd

DIRECTORS: H. W. EDWARDS · O. R. EDWARDS

Members Antiquarian Booksellers Association

ASHMORE GREEN, NEWBURY, BERKSHIRE, ENGLAND

7-12-71

Dear Marina & Lera

At last I am writing to you again. I am really ashamed that it has been so long, but my last letter was such an enormous one that I have run out of thoughts. Also of course, I knew that you were going to visit the town of 'forty times forty churches'.*

First, let me thank you for your gift of the sweets from Kishinev. We have enjoyed these, but there are far too many. Olive is afraid for her figure, and I am afraid for my teeth. So when we next go to London we are taking them for our grandchildren. They are having a big Christmas party for a lot of other children.

I look forward very much to receiving the books. I have been reading a good deal lately of Russian literature. And thank you for the two books that you sent some time ago, and which we have read with great interest. It is very interesting to read contemporary literature, as it gives one an idea of life as it is lived, in the same way that I find the articles from David Bonavia in *The Times* so full of interest.†

I have read a book about which I knew nothing. It is by E.N. Vodovosova and is called *A Russian Childhood*. It is very very good, and gives a picture of life in the 1850s which is almost unbelievable. It is difficult to believe that my grandfather was alive at the same time. She was educated (if you can call it that) at the Smolny

*Moscow became known as the city of forty times forty churches – signifying many, rather than exactly that number of churches, most of which dated from the second half of the seventeenth century, when the city's growing affluence resulted in a wave of new church-building.

†A coded reference to the fact that Harold has received David Bonavia's letter.

Institute.* I had the pleasure of going there on my first journey to the USSR and I remember the place well.

I hope that when you were in Moscow you joined the stampede for the new edition of the works of Dostoevsky in 30 vols? I read about this in *The Times*. I should think it was a very fine edition. I am now re-reading *The Idiot* in a new translation. I think it was the German writer Hermann Hesse who said that no one was ever the same that had read Dostoevsky. I was 16 when I read *The House of the Dead*.

Since I last wrote to you we have been in London to celebrate Olive's sixtieth birthday. I do not really believe that she is that age. We took our daughter and son-in-law out to dinner at a very expensive French restaurant and it was well worth the money. We also did some Christmas shopping, and are going again I hope next week.

There is not much news from here. We have just planted 36 trees and shrubs in the garden, and this week another dozen roses. Every year I like to plant something, but we are gradually getting filled up. London gets more and more unpleasant each year, with so many people and so much traffic on the roads. It was once a very fine city. No longer. What the Germans did not destroy we are busy destroying ourselves. And when I think of India and Pakistan, Ireland and Vietnam I really think that Bernard Shaw was correct when he said the world was the lunatic asylum of the universe.

I must now look at your letters. First again thanks for the photographs of Marina.

Of course, your English is not right. But the whole point is that you are able to write what you mean, and that is quite sufficient. But I think that you will improve now that you will have more time, and I will ensure that many English books are sent. I hope that you do not mind having what we call 'paper-backs'. Otherwise books are very expensive here, as is everything else.

By the way, you are quite right about Gymnastics. This is what we should call (I cannot spell it) Eurhythmics, or the art of graceful and

*The Smolnyi Institute in St Petersburg was a finishing school for aristocratic girls set up in 1764 by Ivan Betskoi, a close associate of Catherine the Great. It became Lenin's headquarters after the Bolshevik takeover until March 1918, when he moved to Moscow.

harmonious movement. Gymnastics is what we had at school, and were quite horrible. Parallel bars, jumping over things etc. I hated the whole lot.

When I wrote about Blok writing in the old tradition, I was of course, referring to the spelling with the hard sign etc. which was changed in 1918. His poetry is entirely in a new tradition.

How was Saratov? I, or rather we, should love to go there. I presume that Jean's Cafe, on the Nyemetzkaya corner of the Nikolskaya, has gone forever? It was there in 1914 together with the hotels Rossiya, Bristol and Tyurin.

I cannot tell you how happy we are that all three are once again at home. A very happy Xmas and New Year from us both.

Harold and Olive

Kishinev
December 18, 1971

Dear Olive!

We returned home some days ago and in the same first day we get your letter of 16th November, and your parcel with trouser suit, sweater and scarf.

And of course our Marina here and then dressed up in her new luxurious suit. I did not resist again such temptations too. Marina showed so as in her name-day* and by no means wanted to part with her new dress, although weather was quite unsuitable for it. Marina in her suit attracted all passer bys' attention.

My husband feels the most friendly senses to you and to your husband and surely he will join us in our correspondence as soon as he will find himself in that world. I hope his depression will not be too long.

With best love to you both from us all,

Lera

*A name-day is the day of the saint whose name one shares. Name-days were and still are religious, but they were tolerated during the Soviet era because it became one of those customs with an almost secular tradition, or at least one which didn't have to be associated directly with the church. It was just like having another birthday.

Marina in the trouser suit that Olive sent her.

Kishinev

31.12.71

Dear Olive, dear Harold!

We were very glad to receive your letter, your photographs and your knitting paper. We like your photographs very much. We can scarcely believe that Olive is 60. To my mind she looks for 40 and no more. As regards to knitting paper, I understand nearly everything without description, because I am a quite good knitter.

And now about books. Dear Harold, I am very sorry, that you sometimes receive not interesting books from us. Unfortunately it does not depend on us, because we are limited in choosing. I hope henceforth you will be more lucky.

You ask me, if I do not mind having 'paper-backs'. Surely I do not mind.

You ask us about Saratov. We do not like Saratov. As compared with Kishinev it is terrible. It is only Volga that can enjoy you there. Our Kishinev is much more European and modern town. In addition we have here an excellent climate and plenty of various fruits and vegetables. Here is so warm, that unfortunately up to now we have not snow. Nevertheless we wear sweaters.

Vyacheslav's spirits are gradually recovered. I hope he will recover definitively soon after he will began to work. Our Marina helps him in that very much. They are in love with each other absolutely hopelessly. Just now they are adorning the New-Year's tree and both are happy.*

Our best wishes to you and your daughter's family from us three.

Love,

Lera

*After the Revolution, the Bolsheviks banned Christmas trees as a sign of bourgeois degeneration. Later, after the Second World War, New Year trees were allowed, but never to be put up for Christmas. In this way, the decorated tree at New Year made it into an important and much celebrated holiday.

Kishinev
January 22nd, 1972

Dear Olive

We were very very glad to receive your warm letter. And I was glad especially. Probably it was because thanks to just namely that letter I felt better – it seems me so – the aroma of your family life, such cosy and such English, that I involuntary recollect your Ch. Dickens. In Winter I especially often admire man's wisdom for their invention of a warm dwelling. And you, Englishmen, happened to be much wiser than all other, because you invented a fire-place.

You asks me about material and its colours: White, red, burgundy, maroon, ecru, all hues of brown, dark green etc. But now here are in *Vogue* dresses of crimpelene crepe and I like them too. You see, Olive, when I asked you about the material and dreamed of sewing the dresses, I was a hopeless fantasist. At that time I did not know yet, what means the 'post-finish' weariness.* Such cases happen not only after marathon race but also after a marathon waiting. Now such 'feats' like sewing are simply beyond me. And that is why I wish, that ready-made dress would fall out of a sky upon me.

Did you see, Olive, the European figure skate competition by TV from Sweden? We all three like that show very much, partly because that kind of sport is very near to art generally and to my art gymnastic in particular.

That show brings to our Marina joy and also grief, because she had very often to go to bed at the most interesting moment (as she presumes).

*When Lera talks about 'post-finish weariness', she's referring to the difficulties and anti-climax the whole family faced once Slava came home: his depression, Lera's exhaustion and growing realisation that she still had to provide for the household because Slava was incapable of working as before. Added to this was the strain of increased surveillance and house raids by the KGB following his release.

Notwithstanding that Slava do not work yet, to my mind, he have already returned upon our sinful earth, although now and than I see he whirls somewhere far away.

We all three send you both our love and the very best wishes.

Love,

Lera

* * *

SLAVA RETURNED FROM THE CAMP SEVERELY DAMAGED psychologically, and it took him a long time to recover and readjust to life. Back in Kishinev, he was under a special curfew for two years, which meant he couldn't leave the apartment at night and had to register regularly at the local police station. His friends had to come to his apartment to meet him, and this meant the KGB often turned up too, to search the house and ask everyone present to show their passports. Some of the other prisoners from Dubrovlag left for Europe and the United States after their release, but Slava always believed he had to stay, to be with his country during this ordeal.

At first Slava found a job as an engineer in a company manufacturing medical devices, but working conscientiously wasn't enough in those days – he also had to take part in mandatory political education lessons, which were held after work. The head of the local Communist Party would turn up and lecture the workforce on the international political situation – topics such as the help the Soviet Union had given to the fraternal people of Angola and Mozambique in their efforts to build socialism in their country. All this was unbearable for Slava; he gave up working as an engineer and became a coal-heaver in a public bathhouse, and in so doing joined the generation of 'janitors and night guardians' – intellectuals who chose to register their opposition to Soviet power in this way.

After his release, Slava didn't actively fight against the authorities, but neither did he play their game. For instance, he always refused to vote. To him, the electoral system was a cynical exercise in obedience intended only to discover who actually turned up to vote for the only candidate on offer and who abstained. Slava was always one of those 0.01 per cent of people who would not vote. Naturally, the KGB kept a strict record of those who didn't attend elections, and Slava was always on the list of those silently disagreeing, a troublesome splinter for the authorities.

Slava was fascinated by books on philosophy, theosophy and religion, but as such books were largely samizdat distributions it was a crime to possess any, and the KGB would seize them on their raids. His small flat in Kishinev became a mecca for all would-be dissidents and thinkers, including young poets, artists and philosophers; it was one

Slava with a friend in Kishinev.

of the few places in Kishinev where they could openly discuss philosophy, and subjects such as Buddhism, Sufism and Christianity. Among them was a group of young people who had started a local rock group. In the USSR rock music was treated as a debauched product of the West, and much frowned upon: Slava would never have called himself a rock-music fan, but members of the band came to him to listen to his ideas.

As the band became more and more popular, they began to hold unofficial concerts, until finally an article was published in a Kishinev newspaper denouncing them. They were described as 'advocates of a destructive foreign culture', as 'puppets who were guided by the insidious influence of the enemies of Soviet Power'. Slava, the musicians and their friends were all taken in by the KGB and interrogated for days on end. Members of the band had to give detailed explanations of the meaning of their lyrics, which KGB officials scrutinised very closely, attempting to decode words with the potential for corrupting Soviet youth. Luckily however, by this time perestroika was approaching, and the matter was never pursued as far as it would undoubtedly have been in previous years.

TELEPHONE: THATCHAM 2105 CABLES & TELEGRAMS DRYASDUST NEWBURY

H. W. Edwards *(Booksellers)* Ltd

DIRECTORS: H. W. EDWARDS · O. R. EDWARDS

Members Antiquarian Booksellers Association

ASHMORE GREEN, NEWBURY, BERKSHIRE, ENGLAND

February 4, 1972

Dear Lera, Marina and Veaceslav

Thank you Lera for your lovely letter of January 22nd. I do understand that the effort of dressmaking just now would be just too much for you and you are sensible to accept that fact. We were rather touched about your reference to a fireplace. I agree it is very pleasant and we have one, and it is lovely with logs burning, but it is rather primitive and I am often thinking of replacing it with an electric heater, but then postpone it until another year. We heat the rest of the house with electricity and just have a coal fire in the sitting room.

Yes I did see the skating competition on TV and thought of you. The Russian skaters were quite superb, and we see it in colour which makes it even more attractive. I think it can hardly be called a sport, but is much nearer to ballet. Do you skate? I tried when I was young but was hopeless at it, and Harold was never any good at any kind of game or sport, except he used to ride a bicycle. Books have always been his main interest, so it is fortunate that he was able to earn his living with the only thing that interested him. (When younger he was also keen on girls!!)

The Sholokov and the other novel have just arrived. Thank you very much for these, which we look forward to reading. Fortunately it will not be necessary for you to send any more books, as Harold has found that he can buy all the books he needs from the Russian shop near the British Museum, which sells most publications.

About my grandchildren. Dylan is 7½ and very blond and attractive, but perhaps a little spoiled. He is keen on cars and most mechanical things and is happiest in the country where he can ride his bicycle furiously. He is not very advanced at reading and writing.

Barnaby is nearly 3. Not so beautiful as Dylan but has a very charming character and will play by himself for a long time happily. Daisy is one year old. She is extremely pretty and we all think will be the most intelligent. We bought her a Russian doll of the kind that fits one into the other in a set of six, and she very soon learned how to do it.

We hope to be in London in two weeks from now, and I intend to ask my daughter to help me to choose a dress for you. Her eye will be better than mine for such a pleasant task.

Love to you all from us both,
Olive

Daisy, Dylan and Barnaby as children in the garden of their house in Yorkshire.

Kishinev
February 24, 1972

Dear Olive and Harold!

We were very glad to receive your letter of February 4th and your wonderful parcel. We all three are very glad that Harold have got better.* And since he is planting now we hope everything will be all right – garden is a such good doctor! The best doctor! And judging by the photographs, your garden is just such one.

Parcel. Both sweaters are beyond any praises and compliments. Especially charming is a light-coloured one. My husband is such beautiful in it, that I am afraid to let him come out of house.

Now about books. Of course, I suspect that in such town as your London must be and such 'curious shop' as the Russian shop near the British Museum, where you could buy even such thing as our Russian books. But in my soul, I hope you never find it. For me it was very pleasant work to find and to send you some books. And now I hope your new book-shop will be only my competitor and not more.

Just like you, our Marina takes care of wild birds. And in general she so likes all animals and birds, as if they all are her the best friends. Last summer we were in zoological gardens in Moscow. I hoped it would give her pleasure. But it happened so that we had to leave the zoo very soon because of Marina's tears. She bitterly cried before every cage with wild beasts. And on the next day she declared that she decided to become a manager of the zoo and to set free all these poor beasts and birds. By the same reason she does not like the circus, although she likes clowns and conjurers.

*Harold probably had flu or a winter cold – nothing serious.

Dear Olive, it was very interesting for us to read about your grandchildren. Write us and in the future about all your family. Our Marina calls her favourite doll Olive. I hope that you do not take offence at her.

Love and the best wishes to you both from us all three.

Yours, Lera

P.S. Dear Olive, when are your and Harold's birthdays?

TELEPHONE: THATCHAM 2105 CABLES & TELEGRAMS DRYASDUST NEWBURY

H. W. Edwards (*Booksellers*) Ltd

DIRECTORS: H. W. EDWARDS · O. R. EDWARDS

Members Antiquarian Booksellers Association

ASHMORE GREEN, NEWBURY, BERKSHIRE, ENGLAND

March 2, 1972

Dear Lera and Marina

Thank you for your letter of February 24th which arrived today. I bought the black sweater just in case you might like it. That style is fashionable here with the young men. They don't need to wear a tie, but anyway in London some of the young men dress in very fancy clothes and in all sorts of colours, and there is no longer any conformity of clothes except by the middle-aged. Also with the girls in trouser suits and the boys with long hair it is sometimes difficult to tell which is the boy and which the girl!! I must admit I rather like it, when they are well groomed.

I am touched that Marina has called her doll Olive. Are there any books that Slava would like us to send? Or perhaps journals?

With lots of love from us both,
Olive

Kishinev
March, 18, 1972

Dear Olive and Harold!

Just now we have received your last letter and as usually we very very enjoyed this. All your letters are joyful events in our family. We wait for them just as for letters from our best friends.

We all like the drawing by Dylan and hope he will be a famous painter in the future. Our Marina cannot draw so good, but although she can improvise dancings for herself and dances them almost also inspiredly and feelingly as Isadora Duncan danced. The other day we were at my mother's birthday (she is 61) and enjoyed Marina's dances there. Especially good she dances Russian and Gipsy dances and improvisations on Chopin's waltzes (she has a wide range in 'programme').

I am very glad that you have received all our books. At 10 March I sent you a book on Russian town Murom. There are icons in it. I hope that the Russian shop in London cannot compete with me here.

Dear Olive, your parcel with fashion papers I did not receive unfortunately yet, but I do not give up hope to get them. By the way all our acquaintances were in perfect raptures over your *House and Garden*. One of them lost his rest and probably will find it again only after arrangement the English fire-place in his House.

And certainly, all your magazines give me a lot of pleasure. Besides I use them. For example, I was ill during four weeks and did not work and for this time I knitted a black sweater for myself, such as in your knitting paper. And now I wear it with your black belt and I am very glad. All our friends like this my attire.

Two days ago I have sent you one book *Painting of Ancient Pskov*. I hope you may receive it just to Easter, of course if it will be more lucky than your magazines.

You ask me about Easter. Of course, it is not official holiday in our country, but we celebrate Easter in our family and like it very much. You know, that our Orthodox holidays (and Easter too) are later than your holidays by two weeks? I think we celebrate Easter somewhat differently than you. Tell us, please, about your Easter.

Dear Olive, excuse me, please, my tactless curiosity, but I should like to know very much, what is your vegetarian menu. By the way, for Slava it is of definite practical value.

About books. Slava would like to get some books on Yoga. Next time I shall write you exact titles of book. I think Slava will be writing you soon himself.

Dear Olive, we all send you our love and wait for your letters.

Yours true,

Lera

TELEPHONE: THATCHAM 2105   CABLES & TELEGRAMS DRYASDUST NEWBURY

H. W. Edwards (*Booksellers*) Ltd

DIRECTORS: H. W. EDWARDS · O. R. EDWARDS

Members Antiquarian Booksellers Association

ASHMORE GREEN, NEWBURY, BERKSHIRE, ENGLAND

22-3-72

Dear Marina, Lera & Slava

We were delighted to receive your telegram. It was very good of you to let us know that the things had arrived safely. We are now awaiting a letter from you.

I should have written before but once again I have been in trouble. When last in London I managed to fall flat on my face in the very road where I was born 73 long years ago. I took myself off to the hospital which very fortunately was quite near and found that I had a broken wrist and had also to have three stitches in my face. The stitches were removed last week in Newbury and I hope that the plaster on my wrist will be taken off in a month's time. I could not type this letter but my machine is electric and the slightest touch is sufficient. The very nice old nurse in the Newbury hospital asked me how I had done this. When I told her, she said, 'I suppose you wanted to kiss the pavement.' I rather liked this. No need to remind you of the old Russian proverb, 'Sorrow is here. Open wide your gates'.

Like you, we also say 'Touch wood'. Do you know the African proverb, 'No man can lick his own back'? I do not really know what it means but I like it.

I wonder if Marina is not a little too young yet for Dickens? *The Old Curiosity Shop* is very good of course. Do you know I went to school about three minutes away from the original Curiosity Shop which still stands in the centre of London.

It is very strange that you are asking me about Gurdieff & Ouspensky. How alike we are in many ways, as I too at your age had a great interest in these writers. I have a little book by Ouspensky written in English and published in Moscow in 1914! I have read all of

Ouspensky. He is very interesting and I feel sure that he had something. For me, however, I have not the will power that I know you have and my mind is always going after too many things. But I have never been able to read Gurdieff. I have not the key that will enable me to understand him. I think there is a great deal of truth in their work, although in the end it seems to me that all the religions and philosophies come down to 'self control' or awareness. Would you tell me what you would like me to try and send to you? It seems quite a matter of chance which books get to you. As you know, long ago we sent a vegetarian cookery book and some children's books, none of which arrived. I cannot understand why. I still have some children's books which I should like to send, if not for Marina then for her school.

As usual I have been reading too much and doing too little, but now I have an excuse not to work. Poor Olive is busy at this very moment cutting the grass. She said to me, 'It is just like the Firth of Forth bridge'. This is a very long bridge in Scotland which as soon as it has been painted, the workers start again at the beginning. I have read some stories by Tendryakov just translated from *Novy Mir*. I enjoyed them. Also a very large selection from *Novy Mir* has been translated, of great interest to me. Also the reminiscences of Galina von Meek who was the niece of the woman who supported Tchaikovsky for many years. I liked this as it gave an account of life in Moscow rather than in Leningrad.

I find I always prefer to read about things rather than doing them. Not a good characteristic I fear.

As usual I write too much. One of these days we must meet and in true Russian style will sit up all night talking.

Olive is marching up and down with our electric grass mower and my conscience tells me that I should go and pretend to be doing something.

Much love to you all from us both,
Harold

TELEPHONE: THATCHAM 2105 CABLES & TELEGRAMS DRYASDUST NEWBURY

H. W. Edwards (*Booksellers*) Ltd

DIRECTORS: H. W. EDWARDS · O. R. EDWARDS

Members Antiquarian Booksellers Association

ASHMORE GREEN, NEWBURY, BERKSHIRE, ENGLAND

March 26, 1972

Dear Lera and Marina

Thank you for the lovely book on Murom which arrived yesterday. It would be lovely to visit such a town. Have you been there? The beautiful photographs of the paintings, architecture and icons are a real pleasure to see. Also thank you for the book on Russian cuisine. We will have a Russian dinner from the book soon. I will buy a bottle of vodka, we will drink a toast to you there.

All is well here. We did a lot of gardening and as a result the garden looks magnificent. I cut the lawn, which took me nearly a day using our electric mower, while Harold sat admiring me!

We do hope that all is well with you? We do love to hear from you and such books as the one on Murom are just to our taste. We only do not want you to spend such a lot of your money on us. We have some paperbacks here which I will pack and send to you this week.

Is Marina learning English? We could find some simple children's books for her if she would like that. I remember that she rather liked the ones we sent some time ago.

Harold sends his love and many thanks for your kindness to us and we hope you all have a happy springtime.

Love,
Olive

Kishinev
April 6, 1972

Dear Olive and Harold!

We were very glad to receive your letter of March, 26 and Harold's post-card with a view of your Newbury. And now we could understand your love to your 'provinces'. In my childhood all fairy-tales histories happened just in such town, as your one. We all are interested in other places very much.

Dear Olive, you quite wrong fully reproach me with my extravagances. Everything it is explained by our very cheap post services. There judge yourself. By my pay in 120 rubles in month I am able smooth to afford to send you only registered letters, because it cost me 28 copecks, and to send a book in England cost 30–40 copecks (1 ruble = 100 copecks). So you see, Olive, I am not such great squanderer.

Two days ago I received your parcel with a dress for me. This dress is quite charming! I am delighted with the skill of your tailors. This dress sits on me so perfect, as if it had been sewn especially for me. I shall put it on at Easter, it will be at 9 April. I am sure in Easter's Sunday will be very warm. As usually.

But with *Vogue* and *Style* I am not such lucky. To my great grief I did not receive it yet. And now I despaired to get it. I suppose somebody from post women did not resist the temptation to see it, and then she forgot the whole world and certainly her official duty. What a pity!

Dear Olive, could you help us in our new misfortune? Plenty of time I read in different magazines about some fluoride-pills to cure a child's caries. This curse of our time did not go past of our own house. It seems me such pills are produced in England and France. And I am afraid, if we do not step in it just now, our Marina will be forced to meet the dentist in the nearest future. Marina do not realise such not very jolly perspective yet and that is why she is very gay now as usual. And even more than usually because at last has come long-expected spring. Marina is delighted in the life as a newborn child.

Do you know, Olive, Russian perfume 'Krasnaja (red) Moskva'? If see, foreigners like it and buy it in Russia. I can send you a bottle of this perfume if you like it. In general, I should like to do any pleasant thing for you, but I do not know what. Oh, my English – my misfortune!

We all three are glad that you both are well. Our April is quite warm, almost as in summer.

Slava and Marina send you their love. Soon I shall write you more.

Love, Lera

P.S. I think it is not necessary to register your letter to us, but magazines I am not sure.

TELEPHONE: THATCHAM 2105 CABLES & TELEGRAMS DRYASDUST NEWBURY

H. W. Edwards (Booksellers) Ltd

DIRECTORS: H. W. EDWARDS · O. R. EDWARDS

Members Antiquarian Booksellers Association

ASHMORE GREEN, NEWBURY, BERKSHIRE, ENGLAND

17-4-72

Dear Lera and Marina

We are very glad to receive your letter this morning.

It is quite cold here, and has been so for some weeks, after having two weeks of quite beautiful weather when we were last in London. We were out and about without top coats which is very unusual in March.

This is a very busy time for us in the garden. Everything seems to happen at once. We have already planted potatoes and shallots, and the first peas have begun to appear above ground. We have had our best year for daffodils and narcissus. Also snow-drops. These very early bulbs are always very welcome after our very dismal winters. The grass has all been cut for the second time, and looks very green and attractive. Soon roses will be here. Our ground is very heavy clay, and things like roses do very well.

You sent me a book by Vladimir Soloukhin which I enjoyed. Another by him has just appeared in England. It is called *Searching for Icons in Russia*. We both enjoyed this very much. One can learn a very great deal about Russia from this book, quite apart from Icons. The title in Russia is *Black Boards* and was published in Moscow in 1969 under the general title of *A Winter's Day*. Do try to buy this and read it. But perhaps you have?

I am now re-reading the whole of Dostoevsky slowly. I am in the middle of *The Idiot*. Was Russia ever like this I wonder?

Now for poor Marina. I have never heard of fluoride pills. Fluoride is added to the water supply in some parts of England. There is a good deal of controversy about this. It is regarded as an infringement of the liberty of the individual, as there is no way of avoiding it if it is added to the water. I do not think it would worry me very much. But I doubt if it is really all that good. As you know, sugar is the great enemy. I am afraid that going to the dentist is the best remedy. But I do know this is very easily said. I always put off going until the very last moment. Both Olive and Sally are very good indeed and go regularly.

Give Princess Marinka our very best love, and tell her to eat apples after meals!

Forgive a very dull letter. And write again soon. Your English is very good. It is always quite understandable. What about the Yoga books?

Love to you all from us both,
Harold

Harold and Olive at home in Ashmore Green.

Kishinev
April 26, 1972

Dear Olive

We have received your warm letter of March, 26 and as always were very glad. I should like to write you a long-long letter. But my English unfortunately do not permit me to do it. Now I began to study English unassisted with the help of manual *Essential English for Foreign Students* by Eckersley, printed in London. I hope it will help me in the future to become more liberated in letters to you. Probably because of my superficial knowledge of English some passage in my letters seem rude or primitive to you. But I do not feel it and think that all is well.

Dear Olive, it seems me that you are offended with Slava for his such long silence. You see, it is not easy to explain in letters his present emotional state. He is very glad to receive your letter as I am and he loves you as dearly as Marina and I. Don't be offended with him, please. (He do not know that I write you about it.)

Of course, Marina is learning English. But she is not able yet to write letters.

We have almost summer here. Lilac and chestnut-trees are blossoming. As to weather, I think we live in paradisiacal cosy nook of Earth.

You write you buy Russian wodka. But we drink only dry wine. We have here not expensive wine and we are able to afford to buy it rather often.

What are you and Harold reading now?

We do hope you are well.

With lots of love from us all,

Your Lera

P.S. I hope you may excuse me my grammar mistakes.

TELEPHONE: THATCHAM 2105 CABLES & TELEGRAMS DRYASDUST NEWBURY

H. W. Edwards (*Booksellers*) Ltd

DIRECTORS: H. W. EDWARDS · O. R. EDWARDS

Members Antiquarian Booksellers Association

ASHMORE GREEN, NEWBURY, BERKSHIRE, ENGLAND

May 22, 1972

Dear Lera

Very many thanks for your letter of April 26th and forgive me for not answering before.

You must not apologise for your English. We find that you are very fluent and certainly never 'rude or primitive'.

We hope that Slava is getting better and working happily now? We like to have news of him, but it is not necessary that he write to us. We perfectly understand.

Harold is reading a life of Hogarth but he is reading so much all the time that it would take pages to tell all. He reads a lot of history, I am more frivolous.

We still have not had any good weather yet, except for an occasional day or two. We are going to London this week, for the annual dinner of the Antiquarian Booksellers Association which we usually enjoy. One wears evening dress for this, and there are speeches and a dance afterwards. It's a nice opportunity to meet our colleagues.

Much love to Marina and Slava, and I will try to find her a pretty dress for her birthday.

Love from us both,
Olive

TELEPHONE: THATCHAM 2105 CABLES & TELEGRAMS DRYASDUST NEWBURY

H. W. Edwards (*Booksellers*) Ltd

DIRECTORS: H. W. EDWARDS · O. R. EDWARDS

Members Antiquarian Booksellers Association

ASHMORE GREEN, NEWBURY, BERKSHIRE, ENGLAND

June 6, 1972

Dear Lera and Marina

Thank you for your letter of May 23rd, which arrived on the 30th which is very quick. What lovely photographs of you all and what a very handsome family you are. I do like Slava in his glasses, they suit him very well, and I see that Marina has inherited your generous mouth. Thank you very much for these.

We did receive the book *The Painting of Ancient Pskov* and I thought that I had written to thank you for it. If not I do so now. It is a lovely book.

All is well here. Harold caught a dreadful cold when we were in London and was in bed for a week, but is better now. The weather is still quite cold which is unusual for June and although we are used to the English climate we are still always expecting it to be better than it usually is. The only good thing about our climate is that it is hardly ever extreme, i.e. never extremely cold or extremely hot. It is said that it is the reason for the English temperament!! It certainly makes us philosophical.

Did you ever receive the novels and vegetarian cookery book? They were sent by registered post.

We are doing very little these days. My sister's 70th birthday here was a great success and she enjoyed it. Our booksellers banquet went off quite well. The food and speeches were good and it was pleasant seeing so many old colleagues, but alas many absent faces. The band afterwards for dancing was noisy and bad we thought but all the younger booksellers seemed to be having a lovely time. The clothes are much more informal than they used to be, although all the men were in dinner jackets. Some of velvet, and some with red velvet bow ties, very dashing. We are going to London next week. Harold's birthday is on the 14th June and we will celebrate it in London. He sends his love to you all and many thanks again for the photographs and the book.

Love to you all,
Olive

Marina and Slava walking together in Kishinev soon after his release.

Kishinev
June 25th, 1972

Dear Olive and Harold!

I am very glad that you did receive the book on Pskov, and what is a pity, that I did not know, when is Harold's birthday. I have one more book for you, which I shall get you this week.

June 13. We celebrated Marina's birthday. There were many guests – adults and children. It was very gaity and Marisha (it is her home name) was very satisfied. And in that day a pigeon, which built a nest in our balkony, hatched 2 nestlings. We all three were happy and interpreted it as a good omen for our family. Now Marina has new cares – of pigeon's family.

Now of 'female problems'.

You ask me, Olive, what kind of clothes I like. However 'to like' and 'to wear' not always coincide. Of course I cannot permit myself to wear 'trendy' clothes, as Sally does. But that is not why I'd not like it. Simply my way of life does not permit me to wear too extravagant clothes. And besides it demands good dress-maker. Therefore I wear mainly such clothes which I can sew or knit myself. But generally speaking I like 'bold' clothes and welcome other women who do not fear bright clothes.* You write me, that my dress is simple, ordinary, but here everybody ask me, where I bought such original dress. So that, Olive, you see it is simply impossible that we should not like your things. Probably you think Slava do not like his black sweater. But it is not so at all. He likes it and weared the whole Winter and Spring. Now we have an awful heat here, 34 to 36 C. Slava and Marisha like summer heat, but I dream of the cool and rain. Every Sunday we go to the lake, we swim and tan. We all three like swimming very much.

*The conformity of dress in the Soviet era, and the lack of choice, meant everyone wore rather dark clothes and very few colours.

We did not receive your parcel with novels and vegetarian cookery book. If it is not difficult for you, send me please some carbon-paper and tape (or band?) for typewriter.

We hope you both are well.

With the best hot feeling and love to you both,

Lera

Odessa
July 29, 1972

Dear Olive and Harold!

It is already more than a fortnight as we have been resting in Odessa,* on the Black Sea coast. We live in a splendid district near the sea in the apartment of some friends of ours. They are out now since they prefer cooler places for their rest. And so they are now in Leningrad. As you know, we dreamed of a warm sea for a very long time. Now we have it. And how warm water there is here! Temperature of sea water, 24–25 degree C!

Our Marina spends so much time in the water, that we are beginning to be afraid that she will become like a mermaid before we end our leave. Slava and I are swimming and reading all the time. Do you know our modern writers Trifonov and Aitmatov? I like them very much.

Dear Olive and Harold, we have not received any letter from you for a very long time. And now we console ourselves with the sweet hope, that your letter is waiting for us at home. We shall be there on the 1st of August.

We hope you both are well.

Have you received our parcel with Russian souvenirs – wooden spoons and salt-cellar? With love from us three to you both,

Yours truly,

Lera

*Odessa is a famous port on the Black Sea, in Ukraine. Cultured and lively, during the Soviet era it had a different atmosphere from other cities due to the large numbers of Russian sailors coming in and out of the port. Western goods and clothes were freely available on the black market. They were traded by sailors and this barter economy was tolerated by the authorities.

Kishinev
15.8.72

Dear Olive and Harold!

Here we are at home and received your last letter. As always we were very glad of it.

We all three were very glad to return home. Odessa is a big beautiful city, but we were very tired of its too mercenary spirit. And in general wherever we are always like to return home, in our 'lair' as we call our flat.

You are very envious of our heat, but we – your coolness. Our weather now is absolutely insufferable, especially at the work. In Odessa also was such hot, that did not save even sea.

Dear Olive, unfortunately you did not write in your letter if you received Slava's letter of 3.6.

I am very pained we did not receive your parcel with *Vogue*, carbon paper and typewriter ribbon again. I am sure if you would take an interest in a fate of this parcel there in your Newbury we shall receive it here in Kishinev obligatory. I hope it is not too difficult to you.

You say, Olive, that you like Slava's spectacles. That is only why you have seen him in his spectacles only in photo. Really it is not good, as it is too small for his face and plastic of rim is inferior quality.

My birthday was at 30 of June. I do not like it and do not celebrate it. I am 34 now. Sometimes I think it is very much, sometimes I feel very young. And I never sorry for my 18 year. Now I perceive life better, than at 18 years. And now I am more optimistic than before. Now I understand that happiness of man is only in his perception of life. One man has everything and feels misfortune, but another will be happy in any conditions. To like life – happy God's gift, is not it? (Oh, my pure English! Do you understand what I wanted to say?)

We all three send our love to you. Both and Sally with family.

We should very like to receive your and Sally's photographs.

I send you 2 of our photos.

Lots of love to you all,

Your Lera

Leningrad
[undated; possibly October 1972]

Dear Olive and Harold!

I love you very much and I am very anxious why we do not receive your letters. We know nothing about you for three months and it is awfully for me. Unfortunately I do not know your daughter's address and cannot ask her about you. Are you well? Maybe you are angry for me because I was too boring with Slava's spectacles? Now I bought it him. Maybe you are ill.

I am in Leningrad now in business trip. Slava was here too, but only 3 days. We lived by our friends. It was simply wonderful! We walked all the time and admired of the beauty of Leningrad. Now Slava went home and I live in the hotel 'Baltiyskaya' in the central part of the city. From the window I am see the Nevsky Prospect.

Unfortunately here there are no books interesting for you. But I hope I shall find them in Moscow. I have not Russian–English dictionary here and I am not able to write a good letter without it. I dream to return home and to get your letter and to know that you both are well.

Your Lera

TELEPHONE: THATCHAM 2105   CABLES & TELEGRAMS DRYASDUST NEWBURY

H. W. Edwards *(Booksellers)* Ltd

DIRECTORS: H. W. EDWARDS · O. R. EDWARDS

Members Antiquarian Booksellers Association

ASHMORE GREEN, NEWBURY, BERKSHIRE, ENGLAND

December 7, 1972

Dear Marina and Lera

I was so delighted to receive your telegram for my birthday. Did you get the telegram that I sent on December 1st, thanking you for yours? Sally and Nick came down from London with Daisy (the baby who is two years old this month) and stayed overnight for my birthday and Sally cooked the birthday lunch and I had a very lazy day. They went back to London in the evening.

The last letter I had from you was that of 14.11.72 with the photographs of you, Slava and Marina with the dog, which are all charming, and the postcards of Leningrad. Last week we received two parcels of books: Zadornov, *Amur Saga*; Gouchar, *The Cyclone*; Bondarev, *Hot Snow*; Granin, *Those who Seek* and Paustovsky, *Selected Stories*. The last one I am reading now. We have his autobiography in 5 volumes, which Harold has read, but I have not. Thank you very much for these which I know we will enjoy.

I am very sorry that you have not been getting our letters and I do not understand it. We have been having a rather difficult time as Harold has had an operation on his eye for a detached retina. This is now over, but he has to go into the hospital on Monday next for a little adjustment. The surgeon says he need only be in for two nights. We think it will be all right. He has some sight in the eye, and we are hoping that after this treatment it will heal and he will be quite better. I will let you know how it goes.

I do hope that you are all all right? And that you had a pleasant holiday? We have been doing very little because of Harold's eye trouble, but we did go for a week to the seaside.

Much love to you all from us both, Olive

In Harold's handwriting on the back: 'Dryasdust digging his own grave, also titled Still Life with Birdhouse*'.*

Kishinev
2/1/73

Dear Olive and Harold

Just as you did it last year so and I write my first letter to you in this one. We received your letter of 7/12 and your telegram for Christmas with Russian words which touched and pleasured us very much.

There is a beautiful genuine fluffy Christmas-tree in our room and smells needles.

Marina stays home from school because of the vacation but still she has ballet activities every day. During their vacation they appear on the stage and children have the delight of seeing them. They even go to other cities to act there. When at home, Marina reads all the time. Now she is mastering Julius Verne and is beside herself when reading his *Captain of Fifteen*. Slava and I read many beautiful books, some of them were mentioned by Harold in his letters last years.* It is a pity but we are poor speakers of English and cannot write of our impressions.

Lately our Marina invents fairy tales and write them down. We must say she succeeds in it. She has a large word stock and she operates it successfully. Now she is dreaming of becoming a writer. But her dreams of future are changed every year. So it is dark now what really will become of her.

With love, your Lera

P.S. Now I intend to number letters for you to know whether all my letters are being received.†

*Code for Lera and Slava having read Solzhenitsyn in samizdat form.

†In fact, numbered letters appear only erratically in the subsequent correspondence, and then peter out altogether. The numbering hasn't been reproduced here.

Kishinev
22.1.73

Dear Olive and Harold!

There is no slightest exaggeration to say that the day we receive your letters is a kind of holiday for us. We got your letter of 30.12.72 on the 21st of January. It was Sunday, we all were at home and when a postman carried an envelope everybody wanted to read it the first. But it was I who first got possession of it and began reading and translating the letter loudly.

We are very glad that Harold is better now. We hope he will be quite well on receiving our answer.

The 1972 was difficult for us too. My grandfather whose photograph with Marina you saw, died. I was sick first one illness then another throughout the year which brought no pleasure to my family.

And certainly, we also were glad to see the end of 1972 and to welcome the New Year, like you we hope that it will be better.

It is rather cold here now, but with no snow in the streets. Marina has skis and for several years she dreams of genuine snow to fall down. But still it is not snowing.

Can one ski in Newbury in Winter? Marina and I made a feeder-box for pigeons at our balcony. Now all wild pigeons from our yard feed at us and are in the habit of taking food right off our hands and recognize us in any clothes.

When Marina or I come home they fly to the balcony and wait for the time we shall feed them.

What is a pity you did not receive Slava's letter! He will write you in the nearest future. We hope this letter will bring more welcome news than antecedent one.

Dear Olive, you write 'forgive me awful typing, but it is very cold and foggy today here and I can't seem to get warm'. I did not understand why it is so cold in your flat in Winter. We have a central heating at our home and it is always warm even when it is cold outside the doors.

Hope to receive a letter from you soon.

Love, Lera

Kishinev
6.2.1973

Dear Olive and Harold!

We were beside ourselves when receiving your letter of 12.1.73. I say 'beside ourselves' because your letter says all your severe troubles are now behind you and you feel yourselves much better this New Year.

You say: 'people are in a hurry use the telephone all the time'. At our flat we also have a telephone which I detest and considered to be my bitter enemy. Man comes home tired very much and does not know what it is to be done first and what after, and telephone rings hourly and involuntarily he begins to envy the ancients – they did not hurry and had time enough to do everything. Sometimes I think that people of the 20th century have no time to realize the problems they meet with deeply. They always have to do something. The best heart dream of mine is to crop all business activities and only read and read. But, alas, it is far from being fulfilled.

Of course, we are very proud of Marina. This is the best happiness of ours in the world. We consider her to be the best girl to be found elsewhere. But still, I assume our opinion to be very much preconceived. Probably, all parents have the same.

As for her sense of humour you realized it to be quite right. She feels no troubles with sense of humour. Even now she likes to read humoristic magazines and knows numberless jokes (certainly, of child's character). It is thousand pities you did not see her dancing.

Generally I praise her to the skies but I am in hope you will conceive and excuse me.

With love to you both from us three,

Your Lera

TELEPHONE: THATCHAM 2105 CABLES & TELEGRAMS DRYASDUST NEWBURY

H. W. Edwards (*Booksellers*) Ltd

DIRECTORS: H. W. EDWARDS · O. R. EDWARDS

Members Antiquarian Booksellers Association

ASHMORE GREEN, NEWBURY, BERKSHIRE, ENGLAND

February 14, 1973
St. Valentine's Day

Dear Lera, Marina and Slava

This is the day when tokens of affection are sent to loved ones, usually cards with entwined hearts, cupids with bows, and flowers etc. It's rather commercial, but the thought is pleasant. Do you have such a day? It used to be a 19th century custom, when the cards were very pretty and decorated with real lace, silk and so on, and the modern ones are sometimes very vulgar but often pleasant and sometimes funny.

We have had a very mild winter here so far, but today it is cold and has snowed a very little in the night. We do not care for snow. No Marina, one cannot ski in this part of the world. There are no mountains and the Berkshire Downs have very gentle slopes and it is mostly cultivated land in any case. The only skiing in this country is in Scotland and even there they have artificial slopes made of plastic snow when there is not enough snow. People who want to ski go mostly to Switzerland.

Your query about my feeling cold is because I always write in the bookroom, which is a building in the garden, and which houses our stock of books and typewriters etc. and is not centrally heated, but is heated by electric fires and when it is very cold, it takes some time for the bookroom to get warm.

We are very sorry that you too had a sad 1972. Let us hope that this year will be better for us all. Harold is very much better now and is beginning to take an interest in work. We are looking forward to the spring. Just now we have some promise of it in the garden. We planted some Siberian primroses last autumn and they are now in bloom. Lovely colours, blue, red, pink, yellow and they are said to be very hardy.

We also have some Siberian pinks, which are like carnations, but smaller, and have a lovely smell. They bloom in the summer.

I have not been reading very much as I have been knitting for Daisy and making pyjamas for the 2 boys. Also the television is rather a menace to reading, although Harold does not watch it, except for the news, and he does read a lot.

Much love from us both to you all,
Olive

TELEPHONE: THATCHAM 2105 CABLES & TELEGRAMS DRYASDUST NEWBURY

H. W. Edwards (Booksellers) Ltd

DIRECTORS: H. W. EDWARDS · O. R. EDWARDS

Members Antiquarian Booksellers Association

ASHMORE GREEN, NEWBURY, BERKSHIRE, ENGLAND

27-2-73

Dearest Marina & Lera

I think it is about time that I wrote to you and not Olive for a change, although my letters never seem to reach you.

I do sympathize very much with your desire for peace and quiet. It was for that reason we took this place so many years ago. The telephone can be a great enemy I know. I sometimes wonder if I have gone deaf in order not to hear it? There is a pupil of Sigmund Freud by name Georg Groddeck who has a theory that one only falls ill because one wants to. There may be some truth in it.

We too have been busy feeding the birds in the garden. In fact we do this every day as we save all the pieces that are not eaten for them. We also have what we call monkey nuts hanging up on trees in the garden for the very tiny birds that we call Tits. They fly around and eat all day long. In fact we feed all the birds we can with the great exception of pigeons. We have millions of them and it is the only bird I would not feed as they eat so much of the green crops here. Also it is forbidden by law to feed them in London from one's windows as they make so much dirt. We have had much trouble with them in our flat in London. The drain pipes have to be cleaned out every year or so.

I am now reading the *Collected Short Stories* of Henry James in 12 large volumes. I have got to Vol. 6. He is a great American writer who died in 1915, and is much admired here. Nothing happens very much in the stories, but they are of great psychological interest. I wonder if he has ever been translated into Russian? I rather should think not.

Do you know of the work of a Leningrad poet, Viktor Sosnora? He has been reviewed here with much praise.

I really must stop. I suppose it is the fault of old age that one goes on and on.

With our very best love and wishes to you all,
Harold

Harold, drawn by Nick.

Kishinev
10.III.73

Dear Olive and Harold

Soon it will be two years since the time I first knew that somewhere on the edge of the world lived the Edwards who knew our Marina and write her letters. It was a welcome news for me, almost a present of the kind that makes our life look like a holiday. Your first congratulations card sent to Marina reached me as well (not in original of course). That time I accepted it as perhaps single evidence of the fact the earth being a big beautiful ball. Those days my sensation of the world suffered with primitively geometrical concepts as for the world's arrangement. Many thanks for your marvelous present!

This is not the first time that I try to give you my hearty thanks for your sympathy and kindness, I hope this attempt of mine will be more lucky.

For Marina your letters made the world to be such reality for her. Whenever she travels by a big map, she of course, reaches to point out the Edwards. And what an incentive she has to learn English now! She studies with the same delight as in her ballet. Olive formerly in one of your letters you asked me about my work. Perhaps you think my literary interests somehow connected with my work. Occasional interests, I confess, live in the exercise of the mind. And I in every way, shield my literary interests from acquaintances.

Still I am very interested of Zen-Buddhism and Sufi.

Please, do not think I am possessed by occult magic. True, it is not so. But if I were born in another time I, no doubt, should have gone in that world. Today this is only my hobby just as your flowers for you. And had I such beautiful garden as yours I would rather prefer English flowers to the Orient's magic.

A lot of love from us all,

Your Slava

Lera, Marina and Slava together in their apartment.

Moscow
21.3.73

Dear Olive and Harold!

I am in Moscow now living here for a full week. My chances proved to be fair enough these days; here I am on a business trip to the city.* Marisha and Slava stay at home together. I am lodging at our good friends here. My business activities take a half of my day time, the rest I spend on theatre going or museums, or else I am just walking the town which enjoys me greatly.

Life runs a bit different pace here in Moscow as compared with that of Kishinev, it is great fun to me to watch people in streets here. Everyone here is rushing along at far greater tempo than in Kishinev. The peculiarity is that everyone is reading here when in metro (i.e. underground) in a trolley-bus etc., even kids go in for that. As to me, I have nowhere to hurry to, so every possibility is provided to calmly enjoy watching all that fuss.

I gave a ring to Kishinev and Slava told me they had received Harold's letter, which they both, he and Marisha, enjoyed much. I do regret I have not read it. We all are really pleased with the fact that you, Harold, now are back to your routine work and activities.

It was at my first day in Moscow when I came to Kuznetski street where I used to buy books for you. But unfortunately to my great regret I could not find anything new or interesting as compared with my former visit there in November. I do hope to come to Moscow soon and by that time, I think, we (i.e. me and the 'Progress' publishing house)† shall have something to please you with.

With love ,

Your Lera

*At the time Lera was still working as a translator for an engineering firm.

†The Progress publishing house in Moscow published English translations of Russian authors – including modern authors.

Kishinev
30.3.1973

Dear Olive and Harold!

At last I am at home. I hope you received my letter from Moscow which told you that I was on business trip there.

Dear Harold, your card tells we are 'too generous and extravagant'. Generally speaking, these properties are peculiar to the Russian people and accordingly to our family. But in this case these properties are not applicable to us, because we love you sincerely which feeling automatically excludes all talk of generosity etc.

I am very glad to know the book pleased you. We live in a multystoried house right over the bookshop, where books on art are being sold. I go there every day after my office-hours. It is a pity but Russian books on art in English are published very seldom. Practically I sent you all such books. Sometimes they sell beautiful books on icons but only in Russian. I do not know whether you are interested in them or not.

I send you the list of books which I can buy for you now. If some of these items of this list will present some interest for you, please, write me of that.

Our Marisha begs us to send her to Moscow next year to learn ballet. In Moscow there is the object of her dreams, the best ballet school of the USSR, the Bolshoi.

Sure, we stood against it at first, but now we are changing our minds. The ballet school provides the background as any of conventional high schools do enabling one to enter any institute,* so she is not obligatory to go in for professional ballet dancing (Slava and me are unanimous on that). Still another point is that humanitarian subjects children learn at high school are better taught there which suits us well. The greatest objection we still hold is that the girl would be bound to lead the major part of her life apart from the family, visiting

*I.e. any university.

us on her vacations only. We detest the possibility to lose our control of the kid at such an early age. Will you write, what you think about all that? The fact is that family environs and good education make opposite sides here. Oh, there is one more thing to keep in mind, i.e. the admittance is far from easy there, the contest is horrible, though Marisha is excellent on ballet dancing, her chances to stand the competition are high enough. Frankly I would be just glad if she fails her entrance exams there for that would settle problem which appeared to be unsolved for a complete year at our family.

I am afraid, Harold, you could reprimand me hard on the point. Sure you would oppose my views on the situation. And how about you, Olive?

It is real Spring now. Tomorrow we go to the lake to lie in the sun. You are, probably, enjoying good Spring time there, the thing you have been awaiting so hard!

We all three send our love and best wishes to you both and to Sally's family.

Your Lera

1. M. Sholokhov. *Virgin Soil Upturned.*
2. Soloukhin. *White Grass.*
3. Sobolev. *The Green Light.*
4. L. Tolstoy. *Resurrection.*
5. J. Herman. *Eternal Battle.*
6. V. Kalverin. *Two Captains.*
7. Dostoevsky. *The Idiot.*
8. Zadornov. *Amur Saga.*
9. Alexin. *My Brother Plays Clarinet.*
10. Bondarev. *The Hot Snow.*
11. Gorky. *Mother.*
12. Fedoseev. *Mountain Trails.*
13. Kuprin. *The Garnet Bracelet.*
14. L. Kassil. *The Queen of Snow.*

Kishinev

31.3.1973

Dear Olive and Harold!

We were too glad to receive your letter of February 14, 1973 and to know of St. Valentine's day. The 14th of February is my mother's birthday and her name is not Valentina, but Anna (she is 62). I shall tell her that on her birthday they celebrate St. V's day in England.

It is a pity, but we have no possibility of reading much. We get home from work at 6pm. Then we have a supper and rest. Sometimes we watch a TV. Generally, my daily home routine are: cooking, and sometimes sewing, knitting and reading. Sometimes we read aloud for something especially interesting to be read simultaneously. Usually it is Slava who reads, while I am busy round the house. Our friends visit us very often and sometimes we ourselves pay a visit to somebody. At 12 we have to go to bed for me get up early in the morning. That is the reason why we always have a lack of time. They say the Englishmen are not in the habit of visiting one another without an invitation card and what is more, they do not visit on week-days. Do they meet one another in café with cups of tea or glasses of wine in their hands?

When I get tired because of our friends' frequent visits, I begin to envy these habits of yours.

From one hand it is very pleasantly to see people whom you are interested to speak with but from another hand it is very tiresome to see them daily.

Do you see figure skating? Do you like our Pachomova and Gorshkov?

A lot of love from us all to you both,

Your Lera

Kishinev
2-4-73

Dear Olive and Harold!

We have been very-very pleased to receive your letter of 7.3.73. Those time gaps separating the letters have so much increased these days that at times we apprehend our correspondence might be imperiled.

This spring has come all of a sudden here, quite abrupt and with no warnings. Though, we understand it must be cold in the pre-Easter week (we call it Strastnaja week, i.e. the Week of Passion). At least this is what the experience tells us it has always been so, in our days and in the days of our grandparents. Of those days we have dyed eggs and the sweet bread (koulitchi) only. And it is a very small fraction that we have now of the festive mood which had always been inherent to Russians at Easter days, for just a few families celebrate the Easter feast nowadays.

Just a few days ago an exhibition from the USA on tourism and recreation facilities was being stationed in Kishinev.* Sure we did not fail to visit there. I should not say we have been greatly impressed by the exhibits, but what attracted us most was a good chance to have a talk with living Americans. The attraction was added by the fact that they nearly all spoke good Russian. The impression is that some of the Americans were showing an open and frank interest not only towards the literature of Russia but generally towards Russia itself. The Americans specifically were pleased with the easiness about the Russians contacting them for talks or acquaintances.

Love to you all,

Lera

*This was a very unusual event during the Cold War, and one which the Aidovs never experienced again.

Lera walking down the street in Kishinev in the dress that Olive sent her.

TELEPHONE: THATCHAM 2105 CABLES & TELEGRAMS DRYASDUST NEWBURY

H. W. Edwards (*Booksellers*) Ltd

DIRECTORS: H. W. EDWARDS · O. R. EDWARDS

Members Antiquarian Booksellers Association

ASHMORE GREEN, NEWBURY, BERKSHIRE, ENGLAND

9-4-73

Dear Marina, Lera & Slava

I think it is my turn to write to you. It was nice to hear from Moscow. I liked it very much when I first saw it in 1932 and before most of it had been pulled down. When you next go please take a walk along the Petrovka.* I have a sentimental attachment to it from a novel I once read and greatly enjoyed. Needless to say about a girl.

We were so happy to have the long letter from Slava, the first we have ever received. It was such a nice letter to receive.

I read that the weather in Russia is quite warm and that the spring sowings have begun. Here we are still having very cold weather. Quite bright sunshine but very sharp frosts. This makes gardening rather difficult, but we have put in onions (something I am very very fond of) radishes, lettuces and beetroot. In the greenhouse tomatoes, capsicums and leeks. We shall soon put in potatoes and all the green vegetables. I hope this does not seem too greedy? But for many years I have thought it a good thing to grow one's own food. At least one knows what one is eating.

Now for books. I will send you what I can find on Buddhism. I went through exactly the same interest from the age of 34–45. I no longer have this, as I find it quite impossible to believe in re-birth. But as a religion I find it most sympathetic, especially the doctrine of 'ahimsa'.† Many years ago I had two or three books written by a Russian scholar in English and published in Leningrad in the 1920s. The name was Tcherbatsky. Very scholarly works on Buddhist

*Petrovka is the famous shopping street in Moscow.

†Ahimsa is the Buddhist doctrine of non-violence.

philosophy. I once had a very large Buddhist library but I have very few books now on the subject. Yoga I have always felt was for the East and not the West. 'Non-attachment' has always appealed to me but alas I have never been able to practise it!

Like you I read more old writers than new. We have one writer here that I am sure is unknown in Russia – Anthony Trollope. He wrote almost the exact period as Dostoevsky but very differently. Rather like Charles Dickens but not quite as good. But very readable. I should think that Dickens would be very good in Russian and soon Marina will be reading him I hope. The books that you have sent me I have not found very readable with the exception of Paustovsky (whose autobiography I have in English and much enjoyed), V. Soloukhin and especially Leonid Zhukhovitsky. Most of the others seem to me to be rather mediocre.

But I could go on for a long time – too long – on Russian literature which, as you know, is a passion of mine. I would like to send you English books but unfortunately you do not appear to receive them. But do let us know what you would like from us here. It will be a pleasure to send. But books do appear to be the most unlikely for you to get.

Much love to you all from us both,
Harold

Kishinev
13.4.1973

Dear Olive and Harold!

Two days ago we received your letter and a very nice letter of your Dylan. We were greatly impressed by his boyish spontaneity. We all liked him and not we only. His letter impressed our friends as well. Marina was affected and looked as if it were her birthday.

I assure you that day when we got Dylan's letter, England became nearer to us.

We got your photos as well and once more looked into a pleasant spot of your nice Ashmore Green.

Dear Olive, you apprehend just in vain that your reverend husband Mr. H.W. Edwards, might have been taken for a peasant. No! Should he array himself in garb of a Russian peasant of past, all the same we should recognize in him a member of the Antiquarian Booksellers Association. Though, I must confess appearance of the past peasant evokes a warm and sad feeling in me. And if you understand this feeling you may envy us because a real peasant is not a relic to us, but just the same real thing as your post-man and your neighbours for you.

I am very grateful to you for your razor. Every morning I take it in my hands and, naturally, I remember your refined English technology. There is a Russian proverb which says that you should do the first step successfully and the whole day will be successful. Your razor, Harold, helps me to follow this proverb.

We have a warm and tender spring. It makes us hopeful for good future. This warm, kind cyclone seemed to touch your Albion as well and I hope you together with us enjoying the spring.

Much love from us all,

Slava

TELEPHONE: THATCHAM 2105 CABLES & TELEGRAMS DRYASDUST NEWBURY

H. W. Edwards (*Booksellers*) Ltd

DIRECTORS: H. W. EDWARDS · O. R. EDWARDS

Members Antiquarian Booksellers Association

ASHMORE GREEN, NEWBURY, BERKSHIRE, ENGLAND

26.4.73

Dear Marina

I intended to answer your letters this morning, but the weather has been so beautiful I went out into the garden instead. So I am starting at 4:30 and will not finish it I am sure.

First we must thank you very much for the sweets that you sent and the books and cards. All arrived quite safely. We sent the sweets to the grandchildren in Yorkshire, and have since heard that you had already sent some to London. I know that nothing will stop you from sending, and I only wish we could send you all we would like, but alas, books seem to be the one thing that get lost.

What a very nice book the one in French on Architecture. And very easy to read. It is the nicest production that I have seen from the USSR. Seeing the illustrations I can only wish to see them in reality.

From your list of books that you offer me I should like one, Alexin *My Brother Plays Clarinet*, because I like the title. Three on the list you have sent me. I have the Tolstoy, the Kuprin and the Dostoevsky & Gorki. I cannot get on with Sholokhov. I find most of the books that have been translated into English and published in Russia are too unsophisticated for my taste. I suppose it is because I have been brought up on the classical writers. These fortunately I find I can read many times. How nice it would be if we could meet and talk about books.

I think your Easter is later than ours? I do hope that you will be having 'Siernaia Paskha'* and the 'koulitchi'. Think of us when you are eating them.

Where were you born in Leningrad? I have a very good map of St. Petersburg in a Baedeker Guide to Russia. Printed 1914. Fateful year. I should like to find it on the map. But perhaps it was one of the new suburbs? I remember Leningrad so well as I was there for nearly 2 weeks with nothing to do, and no money. I was put in a seamen's home on the Vassilievsky island. A beautiful large house. The town was very empty. The fact that I had no money was no trouble as there was nothing to buy whatsoever. This was in 1932 when things were bad. I was also in Saratov but remember absolutely nothing of it! I liked Rostov where the girls were so attractive. Kishinev I think I should like.

All English people complain about the weather, but one of our kings, Charles II, said, quite rightly, that it was the only country where one could go for a walk every day of the year. Also all English people discuss the weather at great length especially with strangers. I find I never telephone Sally without asking what the weather is like.

Nobody in England ever makes unexpected visits. Perhaps to one's parents or children but that very seldom. We have lived in this village for 37 years and have only been in two houses in that time. We have a very high opinion of the value of privacy. There is a saying 'An Englishman's home is his castle'. It is a very small island and very overcrowded, so that it is essential to be polite and careful of other people.

D.S. Mirsky's *History of Russian Literature* in two volumes was written by him in English when he lived in London. It is quite the best history we have. He was a prince and also wrote a life of Lenin. He went back to Russia about 1935 and then disappeared. I should have liked to have known him.

I think that if Marina wants to go to school in Moscow for the Ballet it would be a good thing. Sad for you both of course. But we

*'Siernaia Paskha' is a dish for Easter made out of soft cottage cheese. 'Koulitchi' is a special Easter cake.

had the same problem with Sally here. There was no school that we, or she, liked in the neighbourhood. At nine she went to our best modern school, Dartington Hall in Devonshire, where she was for 8 years. It was the best thing we could have possibly done. It has made her for life. We think here that it is a sign of a good home if a child is happy to leave it. It shows that the child is independent and I believe that is good. It is very sad when the children go back to school, but the holidays are very pleasant. I am not sure that being a ballerina is what you want for her. Sally trained as a typographer but left to become a fashion model. It was the best thing that could have happened as she got married very quickly and happily.

Olive agrees with me on this highly important subject. By the way she is the same age as your mother, or will be in December. Please give her our best wishes.

With lots of love from us both,
Harold

Kishinev
26.4.1973

Dear Olive and Harold!

Two days ago we received your big and interesting letter. In fact, despite that we experienced constant fears about the lot of every letter, we seem to be rather lucky correspondents (knock thrice at the wood according to the Russian sign).

Now our Marina as well as you is being busy with gardening. That time she and her female friends made new flowers bed, after which she came home excited and said: 'How pleasant it is to do useful things.' That brought back to me the Chinese proverb, saying that during his life, one must grow a tree and bear a child. I told Marina that according to this oriental wisdom the half of her life programme may be considered fulfilled and her answer was that she did not think of the Chinese to be very clever – she dreams to have three kids at least.

Marina has not read Dickens yet for Dickens is next year's programme. Perhaps, it will be *The Old Curiosity Shop* that she will read first. Even now we foresee in advance how much tears would be shed over poor Nell's destiny.

We have not read Sosnora yet and do not know anything of him but still we hope his poetry will reach us too.

Recently I got acquainted with Uspensky's book on Gurdjiev. Uspensky and Gurdjiev and Tcherbatsky are contemporaries. As for me, I am very interested in Gurdjiev and his ideas. Gurdjiev was a man of unusual destiny and worked as a Sufi missionary in Russian and Europe. At the time he has been referred to and spoken about throughout. Judging by that you must have heard of him. For you are interested in Russia and Orient it is almost inevitable for you to hear of him. With fresh impressions of Gurdjiev I made an attempt to deepen my new knowledge of Sufi, but the only result was that my interest in this surprising philosophy was incensed more. Now I have to repeat to you a phrase formerly said by me: 'You are the only person who can help me to slate this thirst of mine.'

True, Sufi does not present hot problem for me, but still their philosophy is interesting (to be more precisely, rather curious).

As for my interest in Yoga and Zen, I will never compare it with curiosity. In fact there is something in practise of Yoga that deeply impresses and often hypnotizes young souls with promise of quick and big victories. I passed this phase long ago. Now in Yoga as well as Zen I am interested in their ethics and in his ways of spiritual elevations.

We all are quite well.

A lot of love to you both from us all,

Slava

Kishinev
5.6.1973

Dear Olive and Harold

I intended to write this letter with Slava – he concerning one subject and I – another, but still I feel my letter would be so long that Slava will have to write his one separately. It is only to be said that Slava was very glad to receive your books, because they were just what he wanted.

Now we have a lot of vegetables here. This time it is very easy to be a vegetarian but sometimes I cannot contrive something new from vegetables. Now they sell green onion, radish, dill, parsley, celery, lettuce, cucumbers, strawberry, cherry, sweet cherries.

And maybe it will represent some interest for you, we have mastered new dish for our family – oaten milk porridge. We are very much delighted with it and are ready to eat it every day. You, the Englishmen, have the best mastered technology of cooking oatmeal dishes and as for me I have to make many experiments to obtain best results. Surely your cooking book could rather help me.

Dear Harold, whenever I receive your message I am very glad for your knowledge of our literature and wonder how well you know the subject. The fact you can read in English even something from our *Novy Mir* especially gladdens my heart. In case you meet the stories by Yuri Trifonov read them obligatory. How I wish you could read *The White Ship* by Tchingiz Aitmatov, which was printed in *Novy Mir* a couple of years ago. This novel touched me to tears. It would be wonderful in fact to meet and speak not in the letters but at the table with cups of tea in our hands. But alas, we live too far from one another! And what is more, our poor English would never cover conversation. When we write letters vocabularies and different books are handy for us and as for speaking it is an apple off another tree.

Dear Harold, I have a request to you from the sphere of books. I am very much interested in the medicinal starvation. Do you have some literature in England on this point? A month ago I underwent a course of medicinal starving, not to lose flesh of course, for I have no such a problem, but to receive treatment for allergy. I started in very unskilled way, but still the results obtained were excellent and I reached my purpose without any medicine.

During last time we saw some foreign films: Italian *Robbery in Italian Manner*; French *Spinster* and *House under Trees*; Spanish *Spanish Women in Paris*; English *Cromwell*. They were all were interesting, every in its own manner. *House under Trees* is the film with detective plot. As for us it is not that we were much interested in the plot itself, it is that we were simply interested in the life of people in the family, in the relationships between people, in their countenances. Every good film as well as every good book is always a small holiday for us.

Now a few words of your gift for me once again. No it is not very hot here and I can wear my new dress every day. I like it all over – fashion, fabric, colour and how it fits me. It cools me when it is hot and warms when it is cold. There is no familiar woman in the city who would not have asked me where I had got this dress from. Generally speaking, Olive, you must know that thanks to you I feel myself a little bit happier every day.

Much love from us all,

Your Lera

TELEPHONE: THATCHAM 2105 CABLES & TELEGRAMS DRYASDUST NEWBURY

H. W. Edwards (*Booksellers*) Ltd

DIRECTORS: H. W. EDWARDS · O. R. EDWARDS

Members Antiquarian Booksellers Association

ASHMORE GREEN, NEWBURY, BERKSHIRE, ENGLAND

June 8, 1973

Dear Marina, Lera and Slava

Thank you for your lovely long letter. Harold misled you about our not having people in our house. It is simply that we do not have close friends that live in the village. Most of our friends live far from here and we have many visitors, especially in the summer. They are mainly other booksellers, University librarians and so on. However, very few people call without telephoning first as this is 'not done' in this country.

Kishinev sounds delightful. In fact, Sally and Nick talk about going there one year. What would you think of that? I fear that in the state of Harold's health we ourselves would not be able to go. He has not recovered perfect sight since his eye operation and is a little nervous of being out alone, since falling over.

We hope to go to London next week as we want to take Sally and Nick out to dinner on Harold's birthday. He will be 73. No we do not need another Russian–English dictionary thank you, but feel very guilty at not being able to send you any word in Russian. We are both mentally lazy I fear.

I am just going down the road to collect eggs from the farm. We look forward so much to hearing from you soon.

Lots of love from us both,
Olive

Kishinev
June 30, 1973

Dear Olive and Harold

A few days ago we received Olive's letter of June, 8. And serious deal of time has elapsed since Harold's letter in which he wrote about his London's misadventure. So now we all hope Harold threw of the after effects of his London's fall. In that letter Harold himself says about this event with negligence and humour of professional soldier which almost convinced us of that this case will have a happy end.

We received a telegram exactly on 13th June. Your telegram was composed of the Russian expressions which were in existence in the last century. They are still met nowadays but only as adornments.

Cannot be that Sally and Nicolas are going to visit Russia? This news impressed us very deeply. Do Sally and Nicolas have more concrete intentions and plans on that point? Should it be so we should like very much this to be in the warm months. Summer is to be considered as the best Kishinev's merit, although Lera and I prefer Autumn.

Harold, I am very thankful to you for your parcel with books. You presented me with the entire world which I am delighted with and which carries me away. But still I feel that it would be impossible for me to live long in that beautiful idyll. I consider myself to be an enemy of our present pragmatism but still our epoch contaminated me with the taste to concrete things. Probably on that very reason I have preferred Yoga long ago and I am preferring it still now.

As before, Harold, you remain my sole good intermediary between me and missionaries of Yoga and Sufi. I wonder if there are somewhere in the West the schools of Gurdjiev's followers? As for me, it would be senseless if there were not now Gurdjiev. We are all safe and sound. Within the next few days we are going to come on the Black Sea coast to have our holidays there.

With love,

Your Slava

TELEPHONE: THATCHAM 2105 CABLES & TELEGRAMS DRYASDUST NEWBURY

H. W. Edwards (Booksellers) Ltd

DIRECTORS: H. W. EDWARDS · O. R. EDWARDS

Members Antiquarian Booksellers Association

ASHMORE GREEN, NEWBURY, BERKSHIRE, ENGLAND

12-7-73

Dear Marina

So far we have had a wonderful summer except not enough rain. I suppose next year it will be far too much rain. It is very difficult to satisfy gardeners. Next week I will send you two vegetarian cookery books and will hope that you receive them safely. I agree with you that it is rather difficult to contrive nice meals from vegetables only. We use a good deal of cheese which is produced here all over England. I do not remember any Russian cheeses? Oatmeal we do not much care for. It is the national dish in Scotland. Too stodgy and too fattening I think. We always have tea and toast with butter and marmalade for breakfast and sometimes a boiled egg. For lunch we have nearly always cheese and a form of Swedish bread called Rye-King which is very hard indeed and rather like a biscuit. With this we have some kind of raw vegetable especially onions which I can eat almost at any time. In the evening we have our main meal. For this we have avocado pear or tomatoes, etc. to begin, followed by a large green salad. Cheese or an egg dish, potatoes and then home made ice cream or fruit. And always red wine with this. In the winter we do have some kind of meat and very seldom fish. And always vegetable soup to begin and a cooked pudding to end. I forgot to mention that we always have a drink before dinner. I always have sherry and Olive sometimes has whisky which she likes very much like so many English people. I don't like it at all. I write all this to you because it is always so difficult to find out how other people live.

Do write and tell me what you have. Do you drink vodka? I liked Narzan water* very much and the red Caucasian wines. Russian brandy not at all.

How grown-up Marina looks in the photograph of her at the lake. Is she learning English? She will need it when she comes to England one day I am sure. Our large new room is nearly finished complete with bath, so we now have two bathrooms. When are you coming to see us? I cannot see why not as it will cost you nothing apart from your fares. But perhaps this is a dream. Dear Lera, I can find nothing on medicinal starvation in English. Plenty I think for the reduction of weight. It is now a crime to look fat.

I am now awaiting the arrival from Holland of a book that deals with Kozma Prutkov. Does this name mean anything to you? It is the pseudonym of Count Aleksei Tolstoy and the brothers Zhemchuzhinikov. I have read a little in English. It is very very funny indeed. The date is the middle of the 19th century.

As always I write too much.
Much love from us all,
Olive and Harold

*Narzan water is a famous Caucasian mineral water – still produced and drunk. Harold visited Narzan in 1932.

Yalta
17.7.73

Dear Olive and Harold

We have been swimming for a three weeks already in a warm Black Sea. Now we are in Crimea, near Yalta. You must know this town. In three days we will be in our native house. The best part of any like journey is home-coming. And now we feel it very well. We shall write a long letter to you from Kishinev.

Your Lera

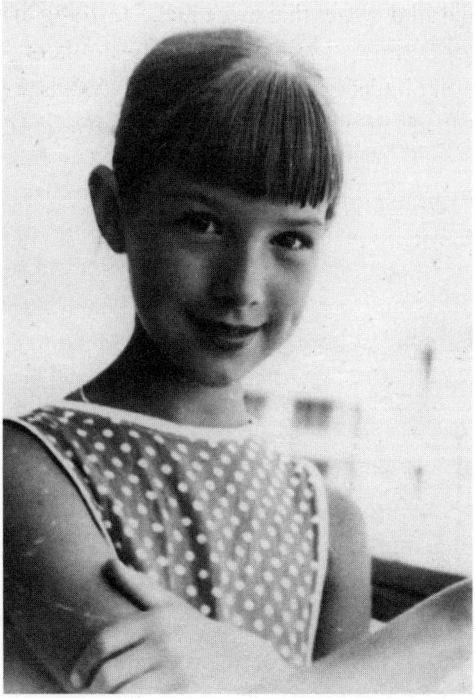

Marina on holiday in the Crimea in 1973.

Kishinev
14.8.1973

Dear Olive and Harold,

We are very glad to receive Harold's letter and to know that you are well.

And we have received the sandals too. But alas. We thought sandals meant kind of footwear to be used in the hottest weather, something like buskins, of course not so laced – two or three strip of leather over foot. And something like that we did get in Yalta.

We are not again at home. Marisha is out in a children's recreation camp being located next to Kishinev but still in the woods and detached enough from the civilized world. We have been on a visit there today and found out she looked much freshened up and healthy there. There is a charming wood and Marisha likes it much better there to play with her children companions, than to linger about alone at home. Not the last thing about is that we are having intolerably hot weather now and the camp's forest and swimming pool are just the things to smooth it down. In general we are truly pleased to see our 'town-born' child living out in nature.

It was very interesting for us to know at last what is your vegetarian board. And it is still half-truth only about your board, the rest part of the truth we hope to find at your table. Of course, it is only my dream. To-day dream, and who knows what will be to-morrow.

I see, Harold, you do care to know what our meals are and when we are having them. I shall not fail to write on it sometimes. Now, in summer we are having mostly raw vegetables, fruits and curds. Of drinking liquids we consume mineral water and stewed fruits (compote) only; it is too hot to drink our beloved dry wines even, not to say of vodka. Generally speaking they mostly neglect vodka, cognac and strong wines here, in Moldavia, nearly all take dry wines, red and white brands. I personally like the white brands. The rest of our meals I would leave for my next letter and for Slava.

Of course we know Kozma Prutkov. And that was just another astonishment to us to find out you are aware of him. Are there any more Englishmen possessing the same profound knowledge on Russian literature and deep love of it?

We hope you are all well and we shall hear from you soon.

With love from us three to you both,

Your Lera

TELEPHONE: THATCHAM 2105 CABLES & TELEGRAMS DRYASDUST NEWBURY

H. W. Edwards *(Booksellers)* Ltd

DIRECTORS: H. W. EDWARDS · O. R. EDWARDS

Members Antiquarian Booksellers Association

ASHMORE GREEN, NEWBURY, BERKSHIRE, ENGLAND

21-8-73

Dear All Three

We were so happy to get your two letters which arrived together. I had just said to Olive that I was afraid you were not well as it was such a long time since we had heard, apart from your post cards from the Crimea. But all is well thank goodness.

I am delighted to read that my 'Russian' is so old-fashioned. That is just how I should like it to be, old orthography, hard and soft signs and everything else. I expect it is because I read mainly 19th century writers where sometimes the Russian phrase is left in. One phrase comes from Tolstoy I think, and the other from the Russian Orthodox liturgy. 'Every hour brings sorrow, and the last hour brings death' is a phrase sometimes engraved on 17th century clocks. It is not, I hasten to say, exactly what I think!

Can we send anything in the food way, such as tea, biscuits etc. And may I make a request for myself please? If you can find *Russkii Yazyk dlya Vsekh** I think it might help me. I think there are six books. Not the records which go with it as I have no gramophone.

I seem to have recovered from my fall in London, but my wrist will never be quite the same again. Do you know the saying of Nietzsche 'What does not kill me, will strengthen me?'

We are glad that you drink wine. We have it every day, and in fact wine is said to be 'the old man's milk'. We always drink red, because Olive has some kind of allergy to white. Vodka I am afraid to drink. It is too strong for us.

Do you know our English writer, Arnold Bennett? I should think he

*The literal translation is 'Russian Language for All' – a Russian-language teaching manual.

has been translated into Russian. He is very good and I am sure you would like him.

As always I am writing too much. We are having beautiful weather, and the farmers are very happy as they are getting in the harvest. I hope that this is the case with you. I think Moldavia sounds a very nice place. I can understand how much you miss Leningrad however.

Give Marina our special love, and tell her I will try to make my Russian more up-to-date next time. Write soon.

Much love from us both,
Harold and Olive

Kishinev
15.9.73

Dear Olive and Harold!

Probably you are in waiting for the manual on the Russian language. It is a pity but they have no such a manual on sales. As soon as this manual appears in the book shops I shall send it to you without fail. I wonder could you keep your linguistic enthusiasm by that time.

As for English writers I read recently *The Day of the Sardine* by Sid Chaplin and *Love . . . Love?* by Stan Barstow. As for Arnold Bennett I read none of his books. Surely judging by your books your way of life differs much from our one, but there is something in common with us. But when I read the Japanese writers I have such a feeling as if their books being written by the other planet inhabitants. Do you like them? I find them to be very interest. But it may really be accounted to my limited chances rather than to uncertainty of my views. All works of foreign writers are available here (translated versions, sure) only through our magazine called *Inostrannaja Literatura*.* So our choice of works to be read is limited to the magazine's offer. And as to the individual translated works they enjoy so great popularity here that the bookshop sell them off in a jiffy. So they are really rare things to get.

By the way we like your old fashioned Russian and it is not imperatively to impart him contemporary features.

We laughed very much at our old English with 'Buskins' placed not to the point.

Now Marina has new hobby – a hedgehog which lives at our kitchen.

Best wishes to you both and Sally's family from us three.

With love,

Your Lera

*Foreign literature.

Kishinev
28.12.73

Dear Olive and Harold,

I do not think you have received my previous letter, that is why I am writing all over again.

First of all, one time more of parcels. Both dresses for Marina are wonderful and suit her very much. The brown dress with red collar especially makes her like a Little Red Riding Hood from Fairytale. The blue dress turns her again from fairytale girl into modern civilized schoolgirl.

Probably, you do not know that I spent the whole November lying in hospital because of not very painful but rather unpleasant illness. My diagnosis is heightened function of Thyroid gland. Mainly it results in quickened tachycardia as well as in the nervous system heightened sensibility. But alongside with negative there are positive sides for woman in my illness too, because it raises my metabolism which means I can eat any amount of what I like without both keeping to a diet and without fear to gain weight. That is why I to some extent, cherished my illness before, and did not undergo a course of patient lingering treatment till recent times. Only now I decided to pay serious attention to my health and fully recover from illness.

Recently I have read a novel *Star in Life* by Alan Sillitoe, the novel *Groan of Mountain* by Japanese Kavabata and stories by American woman, Joyce Carol Oates who is the same age as I am. I did not like American woman's stories very much. As for Sillitoe it was rather interesting for me to read him not of the fact I like him as a writer but simply because the action of his novel takes place in modern England. It is very interesting to read of life in other country described by its habitant. As for Japanese he acted upon me like a hypnotizer. For some reason or other all Japanese writers bewitch me by their books full singularities and unlikeness of their life as compared with ours. But still I should not like to live in Japan.

I hope you will enjoy them.

With love, Your Lera

Kishinev
16.2.74

Dear Olive and Harold!

Surely you do not conceive how glad I was when yesterday I came home from office and got from the pillar-box a long waited letter from you.

We are very glad of the fact Harold is enjoying life and evidently you, Olive, too.

We both, Slava and I, sympathise with people, who whatever the situation is, are able to enjoy life and elicit the most pleasant from it while the others would only complain and would be full of claims as to their place under the sun.

Do you drive a car, Olive?

Even if we had such an opportunity we should not like to have a car because you will never be certain about the life of a man driving it.

Probably, you may enjoy the odour of driving only in such little town as your Newbury or in the countryside.

Yesterday we were at my mother's birthday party. She and her husband live in other part of the town. There she worked as a doctor and he was an agronomist. My mother's husband has grown-up children who live in other cities. We presented my mother with electric fire-place. Certainly it is far from being genuine English fire-place, but still it looks rather good. My mother was very glad of it.

Now we have beautiful weather in our places with no snow, it is dry, sunny and already smells with the spring. The weather makes a man walk and walk endlessly which we sometimes do on Sunday. Now I feel myself almost health and to my especial joy, did not gain weight at all. I hope that you both are well and safe.

Will be glad to receive your letter.

With love from us all,

Lera

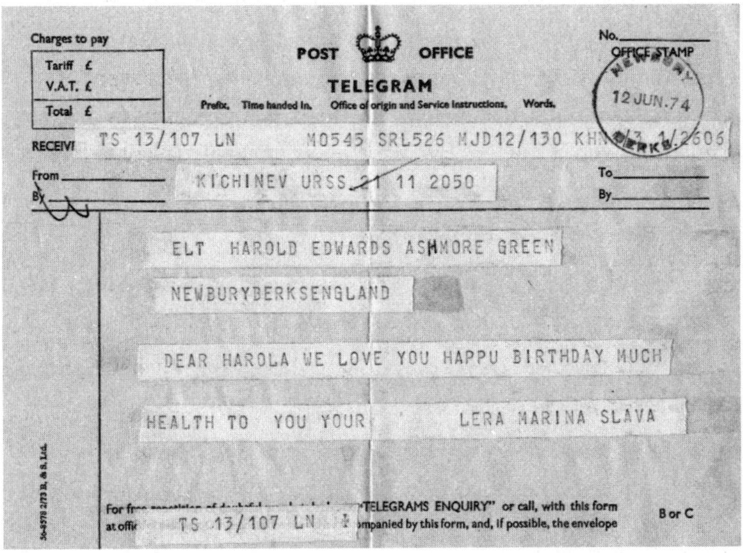

Charges to pay

Tariff £
V.A.T. £
Total £

POST OFFICE

TELEGRAM

Prefix. Time handed in. Office of origin and Service Instructions. Words.

No.

OFFICE STAMP

NEWBURY 12 JUN.74 BERKS

RECEIVED TS 13/107 LN M0545 SRL526 MJD12/130 KHN 8/3 1/2606

From KICHINEV URSS 21 11 2050

By

To

By

ELT HAROLD EDWARDS ASHMORE GREEN

NEWBURYBERKSENGLAND

DEAR HAROLA WE LOVE YOU HAPPU BIRTHDAY MUCH

HEALTH TO YOU YOUR LERA MARINA SLAVA

For fr... "TELEGRAMS ENQUIRY" or call, with this form at offic... TS 13/107 LN ...ompanied by this form, and, if possible, the envelope

B or C

56-8578 2/73 R. & S. Ltd.

Kishinev
September 28, 1974

Dear Olive and Harold,

It was ages since we have received your letter. I do not exaggerate – just judge yourselves – it was Olive's letter of March 7, 1974.

A month ago we experience a terrible heat here, but as you know we left it for mountains.

Still it is not quite safe for me to say that you know it in fact. It is a month that we returned from our trip in the Carpathians. It was there, in mountains, from more precisely in Lvov, that we sent you a parcel with souvenir – the Russian samovar. Do you guess what is it? Slava asserts it to be such a well known attribute of old Russian way of life that Harold will not puzzle too much over this wonder. Our Marina is already 11 old of age. It makes us sad to part with her childhood. She understands it clearly how wonderful it is to be a child; in her 10 years she cried bitterly because she has to part with childhood. Now she said that would invite nobody to her birthday party for it is very indecent in her age. Nevertheless it does not prevent her to be quite a perfect child both at school and home.

Now there is something in our family we try to keep a secret for the present and we succeed in it easily as yet. The point is that we are waiting for a baby in the end of March. And how you can conceive it all our present life is subordinated to this waiting. In this connection may I make a request for myself please? Would you send me a dress for this case? It is about four months more that I shall go to my work and I should like to have any winter maternity casual dress either suit of trousers suit – it is the same to me. It would be best of all if this dress were from not expensive heavy fabric with the white collar and the long sleeves.

Recently we spent some beautiful evenings at the TV-set when we saw multiserial TV-play *Dombey and Son* by Dickens. And now I make my acquaintance with modern England; I read the novel *The Black Prince* by Iris Murdoch. Next time I shall write you of my impressions.

How are Dylan, Barnaby and Daisy getting on? How are you personally? We hope that everything is all right at your home and that we shall hear some news of you in the nearest future.

Much love from all of us,

Your Lera

Kishinev

21.1.1975

Dear Olive and Harold

On the very eve of the New Year we received Olive's letter of December 17 and in 12 days, i.e. on the eve of the Old New Year we received one more Olive's letter of December 30. It may seem strange to you that we have yet such a phenomenon as 'The Old New Year'.* This day many people in our country congratulate each other with the coming New Year not confusing at all that they did the same a few days before. And what is more, many people meet the New Year once more at their festive tables on this day.

Many thanks for your parcels. We have received them just by the 7th January, i.e. the day of our orthodox Christmas. Your letters and parcels hitting the right nail on the head seems really fantastic. I think that even the Communications Minister himself could not reckon on a number of such good fortunes.

Slava's sweater suits him perfectly too and he wears it with great pleasure.

I do not work now and enjoy the great amount of spare time. I am walking more than usually, cooking and reading. In general my state may be called satisfactory, though it might have been better, but for my sick heart.† And of course these last weeks seem to be especially long.

I am reading Françoise Sagan now. People say she is very popular in

*In Russia and the former Soviet Union there are four main celebrations in December and January – 25th December, 31st December, 7th January for the Russian Orthodox Christmas and 14th January the Old New Year. When the Bolsheviks took power in 1918, they instituted a series of radical reforms of which calendar reform was one. (Previously Russia had followed the Julian calendar, which was thirteen days behind the Gregorian one used by Western Europe.) This is why there are now two dates, pre- and post-revolutionary for the same event referred to as Old and New.

†Lera suffered from heart disease, common among women of her generation in the former USSR, perhaps as a result of malnutrition during her childhood as she lived in Leningrad during part of the 900-day siege during the Second World War.

France. She has some admirers here, too. But as for me she does not move me as well as many other writers-women.

We have wonderful weather now. It is warm as in April. It happens probably only one–two times a century, not oftener. According to our orthodox calendar we should have the most bitter 'Christian frosts' now for Candlemas, Christ's christening. And so instead of this prescribed frosts we have warm spring weather, it looks as though the buds began to open and the gardens to blossom.

With lots of love from us all,

Lera

TELEPHONE: THATCHAM 2105 CABLES & TELEGRAMS DRYASDUST NEWBURY

H. W. Edwards (*Booksellers*) Ltd

DIRECTORS: H. W. EDWARDS · O. R. EDWARDS

Members Antiquarian Booksellers Association

ASHMORE GREEN, NEWBURY, BERKSHIRE, ENGLAND

13-3-75

Dear Lera

It is a very long time since I last wrote to you, so I thought I would try again. Perhaps my letter will not be so unlucky as the others and will reach you safely.

We are waiting to hear if the new baby has arrived? You must ask Slava to write as soon as he or she arrives.

No news from here except that we get older! I must not grumble, but of course I do. Seventy-five in June. Marina has a long way to catch up on me. When shall we see you all I wonder?

We are both reading a good deal. I still seem to be on my eternal Russians. There is a life of Gogol just published here by Troyat, a Frenchman who wrote a very good life of the great Tolstoy. One of the very first Russians I read – about 1916 – was Gogol's *Taras Bulba*.

Also we must thank you for the Lyeskov *The Enchanted Wanderer* that arrived quite safely. I read this about 1924 when it first appeared in English, and look forward to reading it again.

We are trying to obtain a kitten, but it is very extraordinary how difficult it is to get one. It would be quite easy if we wanted an expensive cat such as a Siamese or Burmese, but we only want a very ordinary farm cat. We have been without for a long time, and I miss them very much about the house and garden.

With much love to you three from us two,
Yours ever,
Harold

* * *

THIS IS THE LAST SURVIVING LETTER FROM HAROLD FOR 1975, and no letters remain from either him or Olive until 7 January 1978. That many letters and parcels were sent from England to Kishinev during this period is clear from the Aidovs' side of the correspondence which survives. Throughout his life, Harold was a prodigious letter writer, and as well as maintaining the correspondence with the Aidovs, he also wrote frequently to his family and friends; excerpts from this period follow, interspersed with correspondence from Kishinev.

During February 1975 he spent a day in London with Olive, returning 'much battered'. Olive went there again to go to the hairdresser, staying overnight with Sally. 'But really she is much better off here!' commented Harold. Olive, who had been diagnosed with arterio-sclerosis in 1971, had been told by her consultant that she must continue with cortisone for two or three years. This was a blow to her: she hated taking drugs of any kind, and had been trying to come off cortisone for a while as the side-effects were extremely unpleasant. 'She will never feel right whilst taking this stuff,' wrote Harold, 'but at least it keeps her going, and we are thankful for that.' Olive wrote to Lera lamenting that a parcel of baby wool had been returned to Ashmore Green; Harold retold this story in a letter to a friend sent on 14th March 1975.

Our friend in Kishinev is about to have another baby and asked Olive to send her some baby wool, unobtainable there. This she did, spending about £8. It was sent in the New Year and was returned to us yesterday with a stamp Entry Forbidden. What a bloody country. The only reason I want to vote for the Common Market is because the C.P.G.B.* is against it. Therefore I know it must be good.

Harold also wrote that the razor blades Lera requested for Slava had arrived successfully, and that his own new razor is 'quite the best breakthrough since Copernicus'. Comparing two recently deceased friends he revealed which one he preferred – the other being 'a typical Communist and, as such, best avoided'.

*The Communist Party of Great Britain. On 6 June 1975, Harold Wilson's Labour government held a referendum in the United Kingdom asking whether the electorate wished to remain part of what was then the Common Market. Sixty-seven per cent said yes.

Kishinev
28.5.75

Dear Olive and Harold

We have been very pleased to receive Harold's letter. A few words about our Andrei. He was born a properly big boy, weighting 9 pounds and measuring 21″. And now he is quite a grown up. Generally speaking our boy is a very good natured being. However he is a bit too serious. And still another thing is we believe he will grow up clever boy. Sure we are all enchanted by the little one!

We thank you and we both feel the same regret that the baby wool was returned by post.

The weather is wonderful here and our granny together with Marina take Andrei out for a walk so often.

Marina was in Moscow on her spring vacations with her ballet group, giving a concert.

Slava, Marina and Andrei send you their love.

With love,

Lera

* * *

IN MAY 1975 HAROLD WROTE THAT HE WAS SPENDING money 'mainly, of course, on books but also on the garden'. By August, though, he had become fed up with doing no business, and commented: 'I cannot take much pleasure in working in the garden . . . I like messing around with books.' Nevertheless, he enjoyed seeing the results of others working hard outside. 'What a blessing a garden is, in spite of all the toil and expense.' He wrote happily that Sally, Nick and Dylan had cut the grass with three mowers and gardened energetically during their visit for his seventy-fifth birthday.

Kishinev
6.10.1975

Dear Olive and Harold!

I hope you will grant us your Pardon for this lasting silence.

We were very glad to receive your Letter and the parcel for our Andrei. Those little shirts for the baby are just wonders, they are very becoming him.

Andrei is the greatest joy in our family for every one of us, he is the governor of our lives.

I do not go to work now, my lot is household and Andrei. And I find it a great pleasure. I think the pleasures of life will fail to compare with that one of the baby in your home. We just can not imagine our life without Andrei.

Andrei is growing up to give us a new surprise every day. He is just half a year old but some features of his future character are shaping very clear now, the boy is buoyant, cheerful, energetic, very kind and he really knows what he is driving at. Generally speaking he is altogether different from Marisha, he seems just a rioter and I think he will never allow us plenty of spare time to idle, he will have everyone employed.

Marisha loves her brother very much. She can not imagine she will live without him. She is in her sixth form this year and I admit it is much harder as compared with the last year and the complexity of her school work denies any comparison with my own experience I took 25 years ago, when I was in the sixth form. Besides of her English, comprising grammar, reading texts and speaking practice, she is taught geography in English. She has to learn lots of new English words every day, so I hope in a short while the girl will be able to assist me with my letters to you.

Recently we had been watching the British produced *David Copperfield* on TV. Sure it was a far cry from *The Forsyte Saga* but nevertheless we enjoyed much visiting the England of Dickens' times. Especially the aged actors were good. Have you watched the movie on TV?

Another good luck we had this summer was a number of theatre shows. The best theatres of Moscow and Leningrad came on tour in Kishinev and gave us plenty of joy and pleasure to meet their shows.

As for the things you kindly offered to send for our Andrei I would like to state that anything you send will be surely received with gratitude. So, I think you may send the boy anything for winter wear, as you choose it.

Slava and Marina send you their love.

Your Lera

* * *

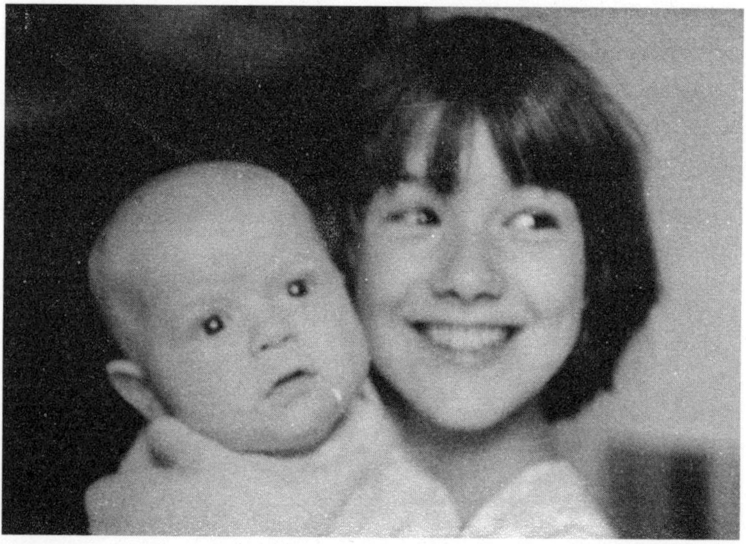

Marina and baby Andrei, twelve years younger than her.

OLIVE AND HAROLD STAYED IN SALLY'S HOUSE IN LONDON in October 1975 to look after their grandchildren. Olive found the stairs between its five storeys exhausting. They both concluded that London had become too much for them. Harold wrote 'the expense is so terrific that it is quite off-putting'. There was the added worry that business continued at a very low ebb, and money was in very short supply. He wrote that he couldn't see Mrs Thatcher standing up to the Trade Unions, 'the real rulers of the state' and couldn't see any government defeating inflation in Britain. Olive had to increase her dosage of cortisone and in November saw a homeopathic doctor about her rheumatism. For Harold rheumatism was 'something one has to expect over 60 and with our climate'. However, new kittens proved a good diversion from their worries, and Harold's enthusiasm for wine remained constant. 'We've been drinking a nice Burgundy lately, a Morey St Denis 1971. Extremely good. I bought 5 dozen so we have a couple of months drinking.' They usually drank a bottle of wine a day.

In 1976, Harold noted that *The Sunday Times* had 'deteriorated very much in quality as it has increased in quantity' and he stopped taking it. In the garden they planted bulbs, and Harold wished that they had started this years ago because they 'increase without effort'. They spent two or three hours each day in the garden and about the same in the bookroom.

Kishinev
June 1976

Dear Olive and Harold!

Every time at the beginning of June I remember the year when we have received your first post card. It has happened 5 years ago. Marina was still a little girl and Daisy was only born. Since so many events have happened in our life that it seem to me the ages flew by and we know each another almost all the life. And I consider you as my close relatives.

Dear Harold, we all together wish you many happy returns of the day and hope that you feel yourselves so well as it was 5 years ago and it will continue for a very long time.

Marina will celebrate her birthday in the train because just at the 13th of June she will be going to make a tour of the city of Kiev with her class. And now she is looking forward to such a trip.

As to Slava and me, I am afraid that we will not succeed to go somewhere this summer because of Andrei.

I fail to read now much with the exception of small stories. I have read some stories of Susan Hill *A Bit of Singing and Dancing*, which I liked much. I regret they publish few of her works.

Slava and Marina send you their love. On the 14th of June we shall drink for Harold and for the 5th year of our acquaintance.

With love,

Your Lera

* * *

BY AUGUST 1976, HAROLD CLAIMED TO BE DOING NO WORK at all and that he and Olive were more or less housebound. They spent little, apart from buying new books and magazines. He got fed up. Nevertheless, he commented, 'We are, happily, full up with wine and I keep it more or less so.' Harold shared a joke with an old friend about a journalist stranded in a small Russian town who asks a local journalist if there is any night life. 'Yes,' he is told, 'but she is ill to-day.' He admitted that Olive disliked that kind of humour, and added that he was looking forward to the excellent marmalade she would soon be making from their crop of quinces. Meanwhile, Harold's previously remarkable memory deteriorated – at least in regard to spectacles and keys. 'I find myself in a room without knowing what the hell I am supposed to be looking for,' he lamented.

Kishinev
30.11.1976

Dear Olive and Harold

What is a pity that the last time because of permanent disorders with receiving of letters the main content of my letters consists in continuous complaints and enumeration of received and not received letters.

We were glad to know that everything is all right with you and that the natural calamities* that fell upon England this year have spared your nice Newbury. There is a superstition that during the leap-year the greatest troubles occur on Earth. But now it is possible to hope that the Englishmen have received in full their part of leap-year troubles and that your idyll before Christmas will not become darkened by anything.

Yesterday on TV we saw the program about the history of apparition of the first car and steam-engine. Generally Marina and me have no interest in techniques but there was a film of English production and they showed much England. Everything about England rouses an interest extremely keen in our family.

Altogether now we put on the TV-set rarely. Our life is turned round Andrei and everything is submitted to him. And he, on his part, does not doubt for a moment that everything lives especially for his own delights and funs. The first word said by him was 'to give'. It is already some months that he needs something to be given – clock, meat-grinder, type-writer etc. Recently he needs the Moon from the sky. Everybody of us loves him so much that really we are ready to get him the Moon from the Sky.

The one thing that pains me is that he shows great interest for techniques. During whole hours he may take to pieces and assemble

*What calamity Lera is referring to here is unclear. She may be thinking of the extremely hot summer and subsequent drought earlier that year.

different mechanisms – clocks, phone, vacuum cleaner. But I should like to see him enjoying himself by drawing or listening to verses or music. It is fine that now he adores to listen fairy-tales. He grows so energetic and active that it is impossible to leave him sole for a moment and we have to devote to him all the time from the morning up to the evening. I indulge him more than everybody as I love him very much and cannot refuse him anything.

We hope you both are well.

With much love from us all,

Vasha Lera*

*Your Lera.

Kishinev
23.1.1977

Dear Olive and Harold!

I am given myself up because that our correspondence is not beginning to return to normal and I am fully powerless to do something to change it. And there are two months that we have received nothing from you.

How did you live the most unloved month of January? This year the winter is unprecedentedly cold and snowy. Everybody is pleased with it except me. I am prefer slush, fogs, rains and warmth to hard bitter frosts. I suppose your climate will suit me fully. Everything is all right with us, all events relate Andrei as usually. He knows already many words and we try to teach him to read these words. But we teach him to read by full words and not by letters. It turns out well.

In the same way, I have taught Marina to read and the results were perfect because at 4 years old she could read herself tales.

Andrei grows up as a general favourite of our family. Everybody allows him everything, particularly me. We shall see which results will give us Japan method of education. But generally Andrei is an exact antithesis to Marina. In his age Marina was like an angel, in contrary Andrei is very obstinate, wilful and needs our permanent occupation with him. You are right, Olive, saying little boys are more difficult for parents than girls. Nevertheless we all love him much though I think that if he was our first child and not Marina we would not have the second one because simply no forces would remain to us.

We hope you all are well. With much love from us all,

Your Lera

* * *

EARLY IN 1977, HAROLD RECALLED WHY HE AND OLIVE started drinking burgundy at home: a doctor had recommended it to Olive following Sally's birth in 1935. Later they transferred their allegiance to claret for a period, but they soon returned to the prescribed burgundy, which Olive preferred. 'There is no doubt we shall stay that way as long as we can afford to buy anything to drink of any kind,' Harold wrote. He added: 'Olive keeps going only owing to cortisone . . . I potter around, pretending to hear all that is going on.'

Harold and Olive in Brighton.

Kishinev

7.4.1977

Dear Olive and Harold

Thank you very much for your letter, cable and parcel with shoes for Marina and skirt for me. Shoes suit her well and she puts them on to go to school. As to skirt it is beautiful and once received it I has put it on immediately, sometimes I go in it to my plant where I work. And generally I must recognize that since you have sent us jeans I prefer not to put on other clothes than jeans and shirts, blouses or sweaters made by myself. And Marina and me we are looking forward to put on our skirts and dresses in vogue which I have sewed myself having used your perfect patterns. I love so to sew that Slava jokes proposing me to change my work of engineer for sewer's one.* Jeans skirts are now in vogue here and as soon as it becomes warmer I'll put it on.

Have you received our little present to Easter? I have made much efforts but did not succeed in getting a book better than that one which I have sent to you. Earlier these books were sold everywhere freely and now there are too much persons who desire to buy them and because of that it became impossible to procure them. The single way to have a book on icons consists in exchanging something of interest to a person collecting books for this one. I hope that I will be successful with your magazines doing such a change and I'll procure a book which will delight you much.

This year our Easter coincide with yours and falls on the 10th of April. We hope that it brings us warm weather as just before Easter the weather is cool and dull and everyone is sick of it.

Our Ksjuta-cat has won the own records for this time. She has 6 kittens. They are splendid but everybody of our friends has cats of Ksjuta, that we pity ourselves.

*Lera means 'sewer' as in someone who sews for a living, a seamstress. At the time she worked as a translator of German documents in the patent office of an engineering firm.

It is a pity we can not present our numerous kittens to your friends.

We hope everything is all right with you and soon we will receive your letter.

With much of love from all of us,

Your Lera

* * *

HAROLD WROTE IN SPRING 1977 THAT HE AND OLIVE HAD both become completely frustrated gardeners. 'Poor mutts for having thought that we would really, for the first time, give all to the garden', he wrote. Olive had produced so many plants that they could not get into the greenhouse. By June, she had planted all the available ground and was far too busy with her vegetable production, so Harold turned his reluctant hand to planting out the asters and dahlias, whilst Olive's kitchen garden flourished. Dylan, at a boarding school nearby, cycled over regularly to cut the grass with their various mowers. Meanwhile something was wrong with the flavour of Olive's best home-made chutney; Harold feared that his 'taste buds, like so much else', had 'just folded up'. Almost stone deaf, with only one eye functioning, and that with limited sight, Harold relied increasingly on Olive's company to keep him going. At that time he reordered *The Sunday Times*.

Kishinev
30-8-1977

Dear Olive and Harold,

Three months passed and we have received nothing from you except birthday telegram for Marina. I was going to send you telegram in this connection, but a few days ago we have received your three parcels with magazines, patterns, skirt and Olive's letters.

Now I send you a book on icons, on Bulgarian icons. I hope you will like it because reproductions are of quality, to my mind.

This summer we have not gone anywhere. But Marina was in Leningrad with her ballet group and brought a lot of impressions from this voyage. Then she passed 10 days on seaside with our friends. On the first of September she goes to school again, she is on the 8 form now. She became more grown up and we talk with her as with an equal. Now we are reflecting on her future: where shall she study after her 10 form. Though we have 3 years more to reflect but it is time to decide what subjects are to be payed more attention to. We would like that she enter to the University to continue her studies in one of two philological fields, Russian or English language and literature, but we have not yet come to an unanimous opinion.

I do not work as before, but I work at home doing technical translations from German on Russian and I receive money for it. Unfortunately I have not much time to translate but for a moment I am satisfied with my way of life. And that is Andrei who is satisfied with it most of all because he spends whole days with me and does not want another life.

Dear Olive, the last time I am enthusiastic about homeopathy. But I must say I have not enough of books and reference books on it. It is difficult to get them here. Could not you help me with it, provided it would not be too embarrassing for you.

We hope everything is all right with Harold and we shall receive letters one day.

With love from us,

Vasha Lera

Kishinev

7-12-1977

Dear Olive and Harold!

Thank you very much for your lovely letter on November 14th and for the parcel which is nice.

We are very moved that our correspondence has meant a lot to you. The same is with us, it means very much to all of us. As to your letters on vegetarianism we do not find them boring at all. You see now we are interested in this problem and it is spoken much in our family. I think I could tell about myself that I am vegetarian only in the case when I shall not only eat meat but I shall not also want to eat it. I understand well how it is immorally to eat meat to animals, but the smell of fritter stimulates desire to eat it. I suppose vegetarianism should became natural without violence with the man reaches the stage of emotional development at which the smell of roast or boiled meat should cause only detestation. But alas . . . I am only on the way to it.

I am sending you our Christmas gift. I hope you will like it.

Slava and Marina send you their love. Andrei sends you his love too and his thanks to Aunt Olya (he tells it so in Russian way).

With love,

Vasha Lera

* * *

IN DECEMBER 1977, OLIVE ORDERED OVER 200 PACKETS OF seeds. Harold was astonished: 'She started yesterday after lunch and is still at it, with the adding-up machine going like mad.' He concluded that 'there is nothing like a late beginner.' Increasing domestic comfort came in January 1978 with the installation of their first heated towel rail. 'I wanted it years ago,' Harold wrote, 'but you know what women are like.' He was pleased when a neighbour told Olive that he doubted there were six men in England who knew more than him. However, it worried him that he found it difficult to leave an open bottle of wine unfinished. He acknowledged that as he was no longer able to buy books with any hope of seeing a profit, there was 'no point in flogging round the shops when it is not really necessary for us to do so'.

Olive and her granddaughter Daisy.

TELEPHONE: THATCHAM 2105 CABLES & TELEGRAMS DRYASDUST NEWBURY

H. W. Edwards (Booksellers) Ltd

DIRECTORS: H. W. EDWARDS · O. R. EDWARDS

Members Antiquarian Booksellers Association

ASHMORE GREEN, NEWBURY, BERKSHIRE, ENGLAND

7.1.78

Dear Marina

First, to wish you all a very happy New Year. I am afraid that I am rather late, but must suppose that this is because of old age, about which nothing can be done.

And I must thank you very much indeed for the copy of *Treasures of Mediaeval Rus* which arrived at Xmas. I think this is quite the nicest produced book that you have sent. The typography is so clear, and the coloured plates so well produced. It is a great pleasure looking through it. It is first-rate.

Olive went to London last week to see Sally and the children. I stay here. It is all too noisy for me. Rather odd that when one is deaf, noise seems most unpleasant.

I am with you when you write about vegetarianism. I have always found it difficult not to enjoy meat. We have a chicken once a week, and other days Olive makes up various dishes all very good. Perhaps when I am 90 I shall free myself from these fleshly desires!!

What books are you reading now? I still read mainly the 19th century classics with one modern book a week. Have been reading George Eliot lately. I am sure she has been translated into Russian but is probably out of print. She is a magnificent writer, one of the best of the 19th century novelists. I cannot find any Russian writers (in English) that I have not read. When I look back, things appear to be so much better than now but I know that this is not really so. Everyone in England is now much better looked after in every way than when I was a boy. But I find that nostalgia still contradicts this.

We both now eagerly look forward to better weather so that we can start once again in the garden. Olive has ordered an enormous quantity of seeds of all kinds, far more than we shall be able to plant. But thanks to her, we are still eating fresh vegetables every day from the garden. And she makes wholemeal bread every week. This is so much better than the white bread that is sold here in the shops. But alas, I still rather like it. As the baker calls twice a week it is only too easy to buy it. I have it as toast every day for breakfast. I cannot recall ever having toast anywhere except in England and America. Certainly not in the USSR.

Very much love to you all from us both.
Yours ever,
Harold 'skromnyi knizhnyi cherviak.'*

*The modest bookworm.

Kishinev
18-2-1978

Our dear Olive and our dear 'skromnyi knizhnyi cherviak' Harold

I fail to make you know our joy due to receiving Harold's letter. There was a real holiday for us. What is a happiness to have dear men somewhere at the other end of the world! And before we have received a parcel for Slava and magazines for Marina and me (and my friends). Thank you very much for all that . Things are beautiful and as usually Slava has put on at once sweater.

As to jeans Marina is happy for they are very well for her (and for me), but a little small in waist and too bell-bottomed for Slava. Everybody of us has delighted with that Marina has new jeans as her last year's are and now worn out. She tried to repair them by sewing in leathern patches, saying there is a particular charm in it.

You ask when shall Marina begin to write letters herself. To my mind she knows English more better than me, but she can not write letters even in Russian. Like Dylan she is enthusiastic with pop music and is ready to hear her tape recorder during whole days.

As to me I cannot support TV, radio, play disks and even telephone. I regret to be submitted to noise by day. We live main street of the city and transport noise reaches easily our flat. I have an advantage at present not to work. I can permit myself to go to sleep late in the night and in silence when everybody falls asleep I am on the top of delight.

You ask what books are we reading now. To my regret I have little time to read as I am occupied all day long with Andrei asking every minute of my time. When Slava comes and begins to enjoy our son I start to work. Only in the night I can read something. Last time looking through the books on yoga that Slava was reading only I read a book. *My Autobiography* by Jagananda, which has impressed me literally. Since then, an interest to occultism but not to physical and respiratory exercises was born in me. Therefore I am taken by interest in this kind of literature.

As to artistic literature not long ago we have read with Marina *I am the King of the Castle* by Susan Hill. Marisha has had a great pleasure when reading it.

Though I am interested in occultism I can not refuse to sew and look through your fine Fashion papers.

With much love from us all,

Your Lera

Kishinev

[undated; possibly March 1978]

Dear Olive and Harold

I also write you a few words. First of all, I beg your pardon for a great number of mistakes that must be in this letter. It seems to me that Mum overrates my English. And I'd be very thankful, if you pointed out my mistakes.

We were very glad to receive your photo. You know, every picture is a real little window into your world. You can't imagine what details we are interested about. We look what sash you have there, what lamp, what mug and what not, whether they are the same as ours we have here. And we are always surprised with the perfect quality of the picture. They are really wonderful.

My best wishes to everybody.

Much Love,

Your Marina

TELEPHONE: THATCHAM 2105 CABLES & TELEGRAMS DRYASDUST NEWBURY

H. W. Edwards (Booksellers) Ltd

DIRECTORS: H. W. EDWARDS · O. R. EDWARDS

Members Antiquarian Booksellers Association

ASHMORE GREEN, NEWBURY, BERKSHIRE, ENGLAND

7.4.78

Dear Marina and all of you,

This is to thank you very much for the really beautifully produced book that you sent to me for Easter, and Olive. This is the book on Byzantine Miniatures. It must have cost a lot of money I am afraid. There is a very brief summary in English at the end, but the reproductions do not really need a text.

I am doing very little work now. Have got too old I think. Furthermore I have managed to twist a muscle in my back when gardening about a month ago. It has been very painful and has prevented me from doing garden work at a time of the year when there is most to be done. Fortunately Olive has taken over the vegetable garden, and we are lucky to have an old man in the village that comes along and does the digging. Together with the two cats, Mimi and Dolly, I watch them both at work. I find it impossible to bend, but can do some work standing up.

Reading, as usual with me now, is mostly 19th-century literature. I do not really enjoy modern fiction any more. Over Easter I read again the marvellous novel by Goncharov, *Oblomov*. A great pleasure. Also, Griboyedov *Woe from Wit*. I wonder if Marina has read these? But not really the kind of book for the young I think? I intend to read again Gogol's *Dead Souls*. I read this around 1920 at the time I was reading Dostoevsky.

Like you, at one time, during 1934–1950, I was very interested in occult works mostly on Buddhism, but my interest has almost vanished. I sympathise with you very much about noise, because although now very deaf, I find noise very difficult to endure. So I do not care to go to London any more, although I go there to the dentist. Rather foolish really to make the journey but I have been going to the same place for over fifty years and no longer want to change. In fact I hate all change of any kind, as it always seems to be for the worse and never for the better.

When does Marina start work, and what does she think of doing? And Andrei, when does he start Infant school? Sally began when she was four.

Much love from us both to you all,
skromnyi knizhnyi cherviak
Harold

Kishinev
17.5.1978

Dear Olive and Harold

Many thanks for letters, patterns, magazines and belt. We have delighted with everything. Surely I liked the belt because it is my weak spot, and they sell them very rarely here, I am glad to have your gift.

We are pleased you have delighted with our books. It is very seldom you can find them sold in bookshops and I am not free to choose what I like. I am obliged to buy every book being sold, therefore the production quality is not the same with each book.

You ask, Harold, if Marina did read *Oblomov* by Goncharov, *Woe from Wit* by Griboyedov, and Gogol's *Dead Souls*. Not only read but studied in detail at school though I am sure it is only an adult man who can really understand Oblomov. They study Russian classics of 19th century in detail and thoroughly. And as Marina goes to what is known as English school (a very great attention is paid there at English language and English classic literature) she studies English literature but not in such a detailed manner.

When does Marina start work? I believe not very soon. She will go to school 2 years more plus 5 years to study at the University if she successes to enter there. When she has 22 years old I think she'll start work. But if she fails to enter to the University it'll occur sooner just after she finish school.

As to Infant School for Andrei there are not here like this. We have only nursery school but I do not want he goes there when I do not work. He is better at home for the present he does not need the company of his age. Our boy likes to play with adults that takes all our free time.

Now I am reading Gurdjief. I am interested with everything he wrote but not sympathize with him as a man.

I am pleased, Harold, you hate all change of any kind. It is in tune with me. I am so conservative that I can not endure even a small rearrangement of the table or like it I do not mention more serious situations in life. (Surely it does not concern clothes there is my feminine origin which dominates I suppose.)

Dear Olive, we were very surprised to know Dylan and Barnaby are adopted. I supposed Dylan looks like Nick and Barnaby like Sally. They are so cared and domestic and you told always very well about them that it is difficult to suppose that. How brave is your Sally! I am not sure I could love adopted children as much as my own. What are relations between them and Nick? Does Daisy love them? Do boys justify hopes of Sally and Nick? Do they reciprocate their feelings? It is of great interest to us. Much loves from us all to Sally and Nick.

As my desire consists to have a raincoat or a rainjacket (I do not know how to name it) of any colour – brown, red, white, black . . . The fabric of raincoat looks like this one on picture, or like the piece of fabric applied here.

Everything you'd like to send for Andrei is beautiful.

By the way here we name him Andrujsha, it is painful to listen for you, is not it?

We are looking forward to your future letter.

With much love from us all,

Your Lera

Sally, Nick, Olive and Harold in the garden together at Ashmore Green.

TELEPHONE: THATCHAM 2105 CABLES & TELEGRAMS DRYASDUST NEWBURY

H. W. Edwards (*Booksellers*) Ltd

DIRECTORS: H. W. EDWARDS · O. R. EDWARDS

Members Antiquarian Booksellers Association

ASHMORE GREEN, NEWBURY, BERKSHIRE, ENGLAND

June 2, 1978

My dear Lera, Marina, Slava, Andrei

Today we received your parcel with the Turgenev works, birthday card for H. and lovely long letter. We were absolutely delighted to receive this as it is such a long time since we had heard from you, and we were beginning to worry. The Turgenev is such a nice edition and Harold is very happy to add it to his collection. We were very glad to have your news of Marina and her school and we are sure she will go to University as she seems so bright. H. was interested that you are reading Gurdjieff as he was very interested at one time, and he agrees with you that he was not a very pleasant man. If you read Katherine Mansfield, the novelist and poet and wife of Middleton Murry, you perhaps do not know that at one time she was a disciple of Gurdjieff and in fact died at his study centre in France.

Dylan and Barnaby both know that they are adopted. It makes no difference to them or us. Daisy is very happy with them both. Children do accept most things and as she is the youngest and a girl she is rather spoiled by them, and Barnaby especially is very sweet with her.

Thank you again for your lovely letter, one of the nicest we have had and we are so happy to have it.

Much love to you all from us both and H. will write to you soon.
Olive

Kishinev
28.6.78

Dear Olive and Harold

I am studying English for quite a long time and now I shall try to write you a letter myself. It is a bit hard for me, and I beg your pardon for the mistakes that you will find in my letter.

You wrote that I seem to be bright, but I am not sure that I shall success to enter the University, though I study quite well. It is very hard in our country to enter the University or Institute, besides I want to study in Moscow, Leningrad or Kiev. It is especially hard to enter to the University in these cities, because the degree that students receive in the Universities in that towns appreciated much higher, so a lot of very capable and well prepared boys and girls come to try themselves. Many of my friends of my age know already what profession they prefer. But I know only that neither mathematics, nor physics and especially chemistry don't attract me, and it is very pitty, because only two years remained before I shall finish the school, and it seems to me to be not very long.

I heard that people in your country begin to work in age of about 18, is that true?

Fortunately, I have my summer holidays, but now every pupil from 14 till 16 must try himself as simple worker, or go to village to help peasants to gather crops of something else. We must work for a whole month.*

*Marina remembers: *There was a requirement that at the age of fifteen all the students in high school should undergo some 'working practice', as it was called. In other words, the children were supposed to work somewhere at a factory or on a collective farm; the USSR was the country of workers and peasants, and they were the most important class – this was the ideology. When I was a student we were sent during the autumn time to help collective farmers to pick potatoes in the field. We didn't really study in September, but instead lived on a collective farm in barracks, and we would be sent to the field to collect potatoes. Often we were also sent there on Saturdays and Sundays in November and December. It wasn't only us. It was all urban Muscovites who worked in the universities, in research academies and so on: in other words all the intellectual workers and students. On these weekends, we'd be sent to huge barns where vegetable were stored. It was very cold and very damp and we had to sort out the rotten potatoes and cabbages from piles of vegetables, and pack the rest. It was disgusting work. We weren't paid, and if you refused to do it, you could be fired from your job or from your Institute.*

One year we were sent to work at a chocolate factory, for one afternoon a fortnight, helping to pack

And this rule is strictly followed by the administrations. Is there something like it in your country?

Olive, if it will be not very hard for you, could you write me how people in England enter universities. It is very interest to me as you probably know that entering institutions or Universities is one of most important that is thought about by children of my age. What does Dylan intend after finishing school?

Love to you all from me and Mamma will write you soon.

Marina

---

chocolates. So, from 8 am to 2 pm we had classes and lectures, and in the afternoon we had to glue cardboard boxes or put boxes of chocolates into big cases. We could not take any chocolates from the factory, but we could eat as much as we wanted whilst we were there. After we had worked there for four hours, the only thing we wanted to do was to eat some pickled cucumber. We had eaten so much chocolate that we couldn't even stand the smell of chocolate any more.

TELEPHONE: THATCHAM 2105 CABLES & TELEGRAMS DRYASDUST NEWBURY

H. W. Edwards (Booksellers) Ltd

DIRECTORS: H. W. EDWARDS · O. R. EDWARDS

Members Antiquarian Booksellers Association

ASHMORE GREEN, NEWBURY, BERKSHIRE, ENGLAND

17/7/78

Dear Marina

Delighted to receive a letter from you, and written in such very good English. Your spelling is without fault, and I noticed only two small idiomatic errors. Knowing how difficult English spelling is for English people, I think you can be very pleased with yourself. If you like I will correct any mistakes in grammar when you write again. It might help you, but I do not think you have much to worry about.

You ask me about University entrance here. Neither Olive nor I were able to go to a University for lack of money. Now it would be quite different and I think we would both go, as students are State supported when necessary. But entrance to all Universities is by examination. Our two best are Oxford and Cambridge, corresponding to your Moscow and Leningrad. These are difficult. But I believe all the other ones are much easier, but, of course without the kudos of the older ones. This, I imagine, is the same in every country.

School-leaving age is 16 here. When I was at school it was 14, but I stayed on till nearly 16 on scholarship. Olive left at 14, but went on to a Trade school learning for two years to become a milliner. She was very good at this, and I think it is a very nice occupation, even if quite useless. Perhaps because it is useless. Very few hats are hand made now.

You have my sympathy about not knowing what you want to be. I was exactly the same, and went into Lloyd's, the marine insurance people. I could not bear this, and left home and work when I was 17½. By great good fortune I managed to make my living as a bookseller. In those far off days not a lot of money was necessary for living.

We have no kind of work for school children as you have in the holidays. Dylan when he leaves school will, I think, become a farmer. He is not an intellectual, and is marvellous with machinery. He likes country life, and I feel sure that this is what he will do.

Did you receive our telegram for your birthday? I ask this, because when we sent it from our very small village here, we had a telephone call from Reading – our county town – asking what was the nearest large town to Kishinev. I said, Kishinev, and was told that there was not a telephone office there! A very bureaucratic young lady was most annoyed when I said that we had both received and sent telegrams. Finally she very crossly said it would be sent to London at our own risk. So I would like to know if it ever arrived? If not, I shall start agitating.

Olive sent some jeans to Slava and some things to you for your birthday. Hope these have arrived safely? We hope to buy something for Andrei this week. Tell Mamma that the raincoats do not come into the shops until the autumn. But we have not forgotten her!

And thank you for the two books that you sent us. We look forward to reading these, but my taste is for 19th century literature now. Old age of course. I am reading Thackeray's *History of Henry Esmond*. I expect that it has been translated into Russian long ago. And have just finished, with great enjoyment, Korolenko's *The History of My Contemporary*. Have you read it? It is very good indeed.

Let us know if there is anything you would like especially. I would send books but am never quite certain if these will arrive.

We are busy in the garden now. Olive has grown some marvellous vegetables this year. It is a great pleasure to go out and gather one's food. Very primitive but I think very human. This year, although the weather has not been very good, our trees and shrubs and flowers have grown a great deal more than usual. Especially the roses. I think it is because we had plenty of rain this spring.

Our love to you all. When are we going to see you all?
Harold

P.S. Have noticed one mistake. 'Pity' has only one t, not two!!

Kishinev
3.8.78

Dear Olive and Harold

We were very glad to receive Harold's lovely letter and your parcel with things for me. All things are very beautiful and fit me very well, and, or course, I began to wear them immediately. Generally, we always wear things that you have sent us. And now, I can wear the things that you had sent for Mamma, and thanks to you we are dressed very smart.

Of course I have received your telegram for my birthday and I ask you to excuse me for not thanking you in time for it. We were very surprised that they didn't want to take the telegram to Kishinev, because it is a rather large town (half million of people) and, of course, there is the telephone office. I think that it was the mistake of your bureaucratic young lady. The nearest large town to Kishinev is Odessa, but I think that it wouldn't be useful in future.

I am reading *Dombey and Son* by Ch. Dickens now, and I like it very much. After 5 days I will come to Leningrad to our friends. I will go by train and during two days of my travel (the distances are too large) I am going to read *The Idiot* and *Brothers Karamazov* by Fyodor Dostoevsky. Now I am in pleasurable anticipation of my travel. Now I have not any definite plans. I want simply to walk about this beautiful town from morning till evening and look at its wonderful buildings. And, of course I shall go to every famous museums of Leningrad. And at the same time it will be the entrance examinations in all institutes and Universities and I want to look how it is passing. We do not pay for education, so there are a lot of people who want to enter the institutes and Universities. And the entrance competition is great not only in the famous institutes of higher education but almost in every town and even in Kishinev.

Dear Harold, I quite agree with you that the literature of XIX century is the best one. So, as you see, our tastes are same, in spite of the different of ages. I think that it would be very useful for me if you corrected my English mistakes, because I know exactly now that I shall never write 'pity' with two 't'.

Your letter was very interest for everybody of us. Mamma and Pappa send you their love.

With love,

Vasha Marina

P.S. Dear Olive and Harold. And when are we going to see you all?

Your Lera

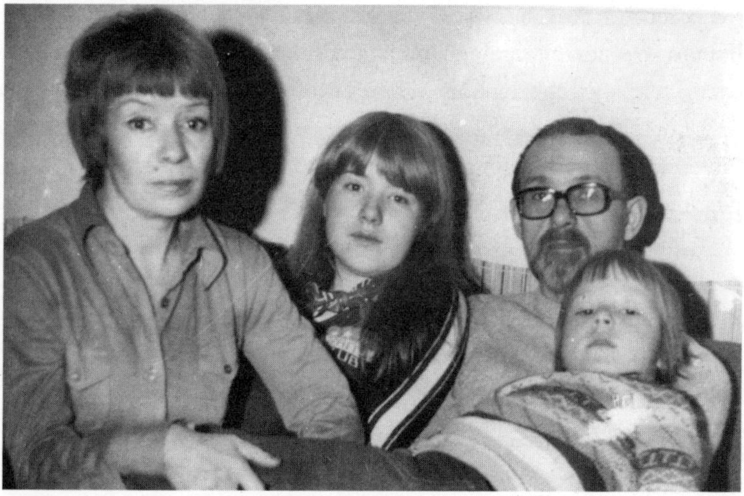

Lera, Marina, Slava and Andrei in their apartment.

Leningrad
[undated; possibly 12.8.78]

Dear Olive and Harold

Leningrad is the most famous town in Russia after Kiev and Moscow. So, as you understand, my life is very interesting here. There are a lot of foreign tourists here and Englishmen are among them, of course. And by chance, I talked with Englishmen (they asked me the way to the Russian museum and then we fell into talk). At the first moment I couldn't say a word in English. I was like dumb. After a few minutes I could connect words somewhat and after 15 minutes I spoke English rather easily.

So, after this case I satisfied myself that one of the most important factors in studying foreign language is colloquial environment. By the way, I managed to go to the University to look at the students and find out whether they know English so well, as I was told. When I heard them, I wondered why they want to study English, what more they want to know. It seems to me that they speak English as real Englishmen. I think that those who go to study at the English faculty want to study mainly English literature. Otherwise I can not understand them.

The weather is typical for this place, neither cold, nor hot, approximately 17 degrees centigrade every day, and I like it.

Hope that you are healthy and happy,

Much love, your Marina

TELEPHONE: THATCHAM 2105 CABLES & TELEGRAMS DRYASDUST NEWBURY

H. W. Edwards *(Booksellers)* Ltd

DIRECTORS: H. W. EDWARDS · O. R. EDWARDS

Members Antiquarian Booksellers Association

ASHMORE GREEN, NEWBURY, BERKSHIRE, ENGLAND

7.9.78

Dear Marina

Many thanks for your letter of Aug. 3 and the nice postcards from Leningrad. I ought to have answered long ago, but have been busy in the garden, as far as the most horrible summer has allowed me. As far as any I can recall.

Your letter, as always, is very good. NO spelling mistakes at all. And our spelling is very difficult for all of us here. Your main trouble is that you do not use the definite or indefinite article 'the' and 'a'. This is because you do not have these in Russian. How you manage without I fail to understand. How do you differentiate between 'Bring me the book', and 'Bring me a book'? Two quite different things.

You make quite clear what you wish to say. And I am sure you will soon be writing as an English girl. What you really need is to spend six months in England we think.

What heavy reading you have taken with you on holiday! I mean the two novels by Dostoevsky. The Dickens is much easier. I read the two Russian novels before I was twenty, which is much too young I think. But I have of course read them again. One of the few advantages of being old is that one forgets what one read when young, so that we have the pleasure of reading them all over again. I have read all the novels of Dickens during the last few years, and some of Thackeray. Also the short stories of Chekhov. I failed to read Tolstoy's *Childhood, Boyhood* etc. But I think *Anna Karenina* is almost perfect. Have you tried the novels of Jane Austen, and the Bronte sisters, both very good indeed.

How nice that you were able to talk to that English tourist when in Leningrad. I envy him. Your postcards brought back memories of my first visit to Russia in 1932. I had to spend over a week there with my wife (not the present one) as we arrived (very fortunately for us) a day late for the return by ship. We stayed in a Sailors Home on the Vassilievsky Ostrov. In one of the former grand houses on the Neva. As we had no money we used to walk about all day. Leningrad was practically empty with very few people and all shops closed. I remember well the Sennaya district which was the scene of Dostoevsky's *Crime and Punishment*. Now, alas, all destroyed. Of course, it is one of the most beautiful cities on earth. Perhaps Venice is better. I certainly preferred it to any other in the USSR although we liked Kiev. But that was before it was destroyed by the Germans. Not long after we returned to England we agreed 'to divide the samovar' and then I married Olive. But I believe that it is the woman that marries the man.

Also I liked Nijni Novgorod, and Kazan. And Simbirsk. But I like almost any place in Russia. Rather like I do any cat. Do forgive this long letter. Give our love to all the family, not forgetting Andrei. And write soon, giving us all your news.

Have you tried the novels of Thomas Hardy? Very fine, as is his poetry. I am reading the Shukshin volume you sent. His *Collected Works* have received very high praise here in our literary journal. A whole page and a half. And his film also. I expect you have seen it?

Harold

Kishinev
9.10.78

Dear Olive and Harold

Forgive me not to reply in time to your letters. It is because of that your letters and parcels took a long time to arrive – 1.5 months nearly. And when they had arrived at Kishinev we were away – Slava, Andrei and me. At last we got back into our routine. I have laid your letters out and answer them.

First of all I want to thank you greatly for clothes sent to us. The jeans fit me very well. Now I think I would not like to put on skirts until the jeans will be worn out. As to lipsticks our fashion is years behind the English one, we use up to today red lipstick (it is difficult to procure too). I suppose next year we will follow you and I shall be the first possessor of pale lipsticks in Kishinev. So I shall use one soon.

Slava, Andrei and me during last weeks have traveled to the Crimea, to Yalta where live my elderly aunts, my dead father's sisters. We were given a hearty welcome and have passed two nice weeks on the seaside. Almost everyday there are in Yalta touring foreign motor-ships with tourists. It was a pity you were not there on them. We imagined what would be like. Marina stayed at home alone and liked it. She had a pleasant rest from us and Andrei. But she said that 2 weeks passed and she missed her family.

Where will she go to study? Only such a thought occupies her mind now. This year she entered the courses where they study English literature. Now she is preparing the report on the novel by Iris Murdoch *The Black Prince*. To my mind it is impossible to understand the novel in 15 years age but it is not her mind.

Have you read *Life after Life* by Raymond Moody.* I should like to know your opinion on this subject. Some time ago we have read a very short story by Richard Bach *Jonathan Livingston Seagull*. Have you read it? It is not a long book but some pages impress us much.

*Published in 1975, the book recounts the near-death experiences of one hundred people.

Now Slava is a vegetarian man. It was not too difficult for him as he never liked meat and fish. I think we all will finish to become vegetarians.

Dear Olive, we are proud of you your successes in growing your vegetables, and envy you a little. All of us send you their love. I enclose the two cards.

With love,

Your Lera

TELEPHONE: THATCHAM 2105 CABLES & TELEGRAMS DRYASDUST NEWBURY

H. W. Edwards *(Booksellers)* Ltd

DIRECTORS: H. W. EDWARDS · O. R. EDWARDS

Members Antiquarian Booksellers Association

ASHMORE GREEN, NEWBURY, BERKSHIRE, ENGLAND

27.11.78

Dear Lera and all the family

Forgive me for not writing before this to thank you for your letter and the two books. These arrived quite safely, and we are very glad to have them. My collection of books on Russian Art & Architecture is now quite large, thanks to the Aidovs.

It was nice to have a long letter from you after all this time. I know how much time it must take you writing in English. The two photographs are very good. Poor Andrei looks very serious, but perhaps that is because of the dark glasses, I see that Marina has changed her hair style. I liked it more when it was long and showed her ears.

Let us know what you would like for the New Year for all of you, and we will try to get it. But we no longer go to London – too old – so we are restricted to Newbury. But it is a good little town for shopping – about 20,000 people live there and the villages surrounding it. I buy all my clothes there now, although at one time I always went to London.

Yalta must be very nice, but I think I should prefer Odessa – home of Katayev and Paustovsky. How grown-up Marina must now be, staying at home by herself, and looking after herself. It's not long ago she was almost a baby. I wonder where she will go to study?! Suppose she would prefer Leningrad or Moscow, as people here prefer Oxford or Cambridge to the other Universities.

It is Olive's birthday on Dec. 2nd and Sally & Nick will be here we hope. I must remember to ask them about the remedies. As far as I can tell Homoeopathic treatment has not made much difference, but at least it does little harm. I feel that if it was so efficient there would be no other kind of doctor? After all, it has been going for about 150 years.

I do not know the books you mention in your letter, *Life after Life* and the other one. I have no belief whatsoever in any future life, but of course I do not know, nor does any one else. To me it appears quite childish to wish to live for ever. Horrible thought. But I am sure that it is a great comfort to many people, especially the idea of meeting again those they have loved – and perhaps a consolation for those whose lives have been unhappy. You will find it all in Shakespeare. In my 79th year I have turned to Shakespeare as you might turn to Pushkin.

Please tell Marina that Iris Murdoch has just won a very big prize for her last novel, *The Sea, the Sea*. We have not read it yet. Could I send you a copy? I never know what books can be sent, if any. In yesterday's *Times* she says about her own reading: Not much contemporary fiction; but around the giants of the 19th century from Austen and Dostoevsky to Proust and Henry James. And, of course, Shakespeare is God: Everything comes out of Shakespeare, pure romance, melodrama, marvellous characters, poetry, and wisdom about life.

I am sorry that Marina has stopped writing to me. Her letters are so good, and we enjoyed them very much. But at her age, who wants to be indoors writing in a foreign language?

I must stop, as lunch is ready. Also, I must tell you that I no longer am working seriously as a bookseller I am 'as idle as a painted ship upon a painted sea'. After 63 years I find it too pleasant and begin to feel guilty.

Love to you all,
Yours ever, Harold

Kishinev
15.12.1978

Dear Olive and Harold

Has Olive received our birthday telegram and perfume 'Krasnaya Moskva' (Red Moscow). We have send for her birthday? I am afraid it is arrived too late.

Every thing is all right here. Slava works, Marina studies at her courses of English and goes to School and I am keeping my house and Andrei's delight. We are not alone because every evening we have some guests. I do not feel myself uncomfortable not going to work at any distance. There is no lack of dealings and contacts.

As you can notice I am very interesting in medicine more and more, especially in this one connected with homeopathy, yoga, magnetism, Chinese massage. Maybe it is a past for you. I imagine Harold's laughter when reading my letter and saying 'They are still children'. But everybody must pass through all his interests and desires to find something of determinate. I am looking for it yet. At this time our family and friends take no remedies but homeopathic ones. Results are good. If in some time I realize technics of Chinese massage I hope everybody of us should be healthful. Are you laughing again, Harold?

On receiving your letters we can not help surprising at your breadth of knowledge. It is hard to believe that an Englishman may know what is the hometown of Katayev or Paustovsky.

All of us (Andrei included) send you our very sincere love and the best wishes for Christmas and New Year.

Yours,

Lera

TELEPHONE: THATCHAM 2105 CABLES & TELEGRAMS DRYASDUST NEWBURY

H. W. Edwards (Booksellers) Ltd

DIRECTORS: H. W. EDWARDS · O. R. EDWARDS

Members Antiquarian Booksellers Association

ASHMORE GREEN, NEWBURY, BERKSHIRE, ENGLAND

January 22, 1979

Dear Slava, Lera, Marina and Andrei

The lovely box of two bottles of perfume arrived safely last week, in perfect condition and beautifully packed. There was no card or letter though. Thank you very much and it is very kind of you to go to so much trouble for me. It is lovely perfume, and I was very pleased to have it. We are well, but rather fed up with the weather and we will be glad when January is over. Sally and her family are well, and the boys are back at boarding school, and Daisy back at her day school. She was very proud last term as she was chosen to play the part of Mary in the Nativity play which the school does each year.

Harold will be writing to you and will answer your questions about medicine. As you have guessed he has gone through enthusiasms for various 'cranky' types of cures, but not to my knowledge Chinese massage or homeopathy. I pin my faith in 100% wholemeal bread made by me, and lots of fresh vegetables, grown by me. Also red wine, preferably Burgundy, but this is now becoming too expensive to drink very often. I do not care to take any drugs if it can be avoided and Harold is the same. At least your cures should do no harm, and if you really believe in them could possibly do good, and we do not laugh at you, but approve your interest in all these things.

We do love your letters and your friendship has made a lot of difference to our lives and all for the better.

Lots of love and a Happy New Year,
Olive

Kishinev
13.7.79

Dear Olive and Harold

Thank you very much for your parcel with cosmetic. Now I am the happiest possessor of the best and unique cosmetic first existing here in Kishinev. Some of the things like pencils I saw for the first time. So it has taken me a lot of time to do experiments before mirror to practice their use. The results are good, I believe. As to creams they are exquisite. I can safely say I am completely provided with cosmetic for the future.

Would you forgive me not to answer your letter. During the days I was absent, having a trip to Moscow and Leningrad to say goodbye to my friends leaving our country for ever. I am not likely to see them again. It is a pity to farewell for good.

Being in Moscow and Leningrad I tried to procure the books with icons but I failed to do it because of the said books are sold only in free shop.* There is a book stall near the Tretyakov's Gallery where beautiful books are sold. It's a dream of books! But they are sold only for foreigners. I regret much not to procure anything of them for you. But I'm not stopping to cherish the hope to complete in the future your collection of books on old Russian art.

It's a pity we cannot come to general opinion on occultism and life after life. To my mind it's due to lack of our personal contacts and the difficulties in English. It doesn't mean I should force my opinion upon you, but surely we'd draw closer to one another when discussing the said problem. And now it seems to me we speak different languages like people from different planets. Surely that such a misunderstanding concerns the subject which are not very important in real life. As to other things you, dear Olive and Harold, are more closer to us than hundreds of people living beside us.

*These were shops only for those who had foreign exchange, but effectively it meant they were only for foreigners since it was a crime for Russians to carry any foreign currency.

Harold, please don't apologise to write long letters. How wonderful to receive and read them, feeling dealing with intimate friends. As longer is your letter, more we enjoying with it.

With much love from us all,

Vasha Lera

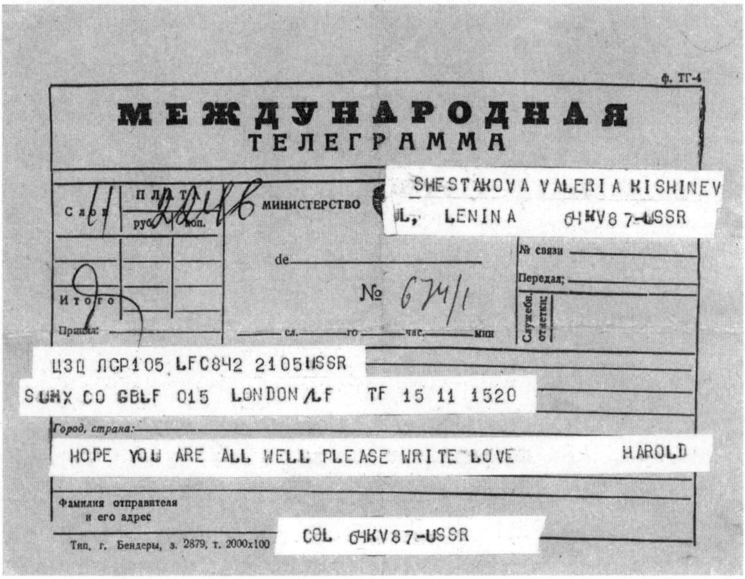

ф. ТГ-4

МЕЖДУНАРОДНАЯ
ТЕЛЕГРАММА

SHESTAKOVA VALERIA KISHINEV
UL, LENINA 64KV87-USSR

Слов | Плата руб. коп. | Министерство

de

№ 674/1

№ связи
Передал:
Служебн. отметки

Итого
Принял: сл. го час. мин

ЦЗЦ ЛСР105 LFC842 2105USSR
SUMX CO GBLF 015 LONDON/LF TF 15 11 1520

Город, страна:

HOPE YOU ARE ALL WELL PLEASE WRITE LOVE HAROLD

Фамилия отправителя и его адрес

COL 64KV87-USSR

Тип. г. Бендеры, з. 2879, т. 2000x100

Kishinev
October 4, 1979

Dear Olive and Harold

Many thanks for your letter and the parcel.

Will you forgive me a so long silence. I was going to write you after receiving the book on Astrology sent by Harold, but I regret to say that up to day it has not come to us. Somebody liked it much or maybe made mistake considering it as a political one. It is a very pity.

Slava has gone for a holyday to see his mother who lives in Saratov. He likes to go to the places where his childhood has passed during the war.

During the winter we must earn a lot of money as Marina's trips and entering the Institute will need great expenses. I am not sure Marina shall enter a Moscow Institute but she had better try and have no grievance against her parents.

Dear Harold, I was lucky to buy verses by Anna Akhmatova, a book with plenty of her beautiful portraits which I admire greatly every minute. Anna Akhmatova is for me a divine woman to say nothing of her poetry. It is difficult to imagine it in English, but in Russian it is wonderful.

Not long ago I have read *Marry Me* by John Updike. To my mind it is pointless. The same about of the Durrenmatt's play *Play Strindberg* seen in the theatre. The single desire I had after the play was to take a fresh shower. You are right, Harold, preferring literature of 19th century.

Dear Harold, there is long ago I asked your opinion on Evelyn Waugh but received no answer. Suppose they lost this letter. To my mind his humour is black and unreadable. But the most of readers are almost chocking with excitement when reading him, I am interested to know your opinion on this.

As to Marina's wish about Christmas present, she would like to have a pretty party dress. This not for Christmas, but for her leavers' party which will take place just after finals, in June. This is a gala-day, like a wedding. Being in the 10th form girls begin to dream on their dresses a year before this day. Any light colour is well, Marina prefer beige or white with flowers, and without decollete.

September is the finest month in Kishinev. There are a lot of fruits, vegetables, it is impossible to eat them all at once. I have preserved many vegetables for the winter, especially our favourite aubergine paste and sweet red pepper. I regret not having a lot of time to read books. But I am doing some mechanical jobs, when doing it I can meditate on many things or listen to music. I used to switch on the tape-recorder and listen to Bach or Mozart my favourite composers.

You ask, Harold, where all the visitors will sleep during the Olympic games. In Moscow they are not planning to erect houses in connection with this event. But without Olympic Games I think Moscow of 1932 has no connection with now days Moscow when you were last here Harold. I suppose foreign travelers are enjoying with their rooms and service in Moscow hotels. Time flies.

Let Sally to know our admiration as to her notepaper, it is wonderful.

With much-much love from us all,

Yours ever, Lera

TELEPHONE: THATCHAM 2105 CABLES & TELEGRAMS DRYASDUST NEWBURY

H. W. Edwards (Booksellers) Ltd

DIRECTORS: H. W. EDWARDS · O. R. EDWARDS

Members Antiquarian Booksellers Association

ASHMORE GREEN, NEWBURY, BERKSHIRE, ENGLAND

16.10.79

Dearest Lera

Your two books and long letter came this morning safely. Thank you very much indeed. Thanks to your kindness I must have one of the best collections of Icons in England! I am very sorry to know that so far the very nice book on Astrology has not arrived. Perhaps someone thinks it is to do with religion. I hope it comes back to me. The post office here say that it is a waste of time making enquiries, although it was registered. They say they get no reply. But this may not be true of course.

Glad to have good news of Marina. I hope that she is successful in her efforts for the University next year.

And I hope that Slava has enjoyed his holiday in Saratov. I believe that I have been in Saratov. If it is a town on the Volga then I have, but I cannot recall it. The one town I liked was Simbirsk. We spent a day there. The thing I remember most vividly was walking back to the steamer, we met a detachment of soldiers who had been on a route march and were returning. It was a beautiful summer evening, and the soldiers were singing those marvellous Russian songs. It was most moving. It seemed like the real Russia.

I hope that you manage to get a copy of Bely's *Petersburg*. I am going to try this again. But feel that you have to be a Petersburger to really understand it. I quite agree with you about John Updike. A waste of time. Once long ago we saw a play by the Swiss writer Durrenmatt and liked it. And a short novel also. Anna Akhmatova I have in translation, but you will agree that generally it is impossible to translate poetry. A great and brave woman like Marina Tsvetayeva.

To get back to Mother Earth. I am glad that you have been enjoying the good things of life in Kishinev. We do not like aubergines being too oily, but like peppers very much, which we grow in our greenhouse. Olive has been very busy – as she always is – in making tomato and pepper chutney. But we had a very large crop of damsons this year. We gave a lot away, and Olive has made for the first time damson chutney. And now we prefer it to the usual tomato one. Now busy making Quince marmalade. We have a French recipe for this, with oranges. It is very very good. Quinces grow well here and are beautiful to look at on the tree. Apples were a very poor crop this year. Raspberries fair only. Our ground is too heavy I think. Not one of our best years in the garden, the weather being the usual English difficult one. Very cold spring, then in the summer not enough rain. But gardeners always grumble about the weather. It never is quite right.

You must forgive me for being so talkative. Write soon.

Love to you all including Ksyuta from us (including Dolly and Mimi).

Yours ever,

Harold

TELEPHONE: THATCHAM 2105 CABLES & TELEGRAMS DRYASDUST NEWBURY

H. W. Edwards (*Booksellers*) Ltd

DIRECTORS: H. W. EDWARDS · O. R. EDWARDS

Members Antiquarian Booksellers Association

ASHMORE GREEN, NEWBURY, BERKSHIRE, ENGLAND

3.12.79

Dearest Lera

Many thanks for all the things that have been arriving from Kishinev. First & foremost the really magnificent two volumes of the Kievan Psalter. Beautifully produced and very interesting for me to look at. It must have cost you a small fortune! And the vol. of Chekhov arrived safely with the two photographs of Slava. Alas, we do not like his beard. He looked so much nicer without it. I grew one once during the war, but found I could never wash my face properly! It was also red in colour and that didn't help. What a relief when I shaved it off. It was nice to see him with his mother, both looking so happy at the moment. And finally your birthday telegram arrived in time. Thank you once again.

We had a very pleasant birthday. Sally & Nick came down on Friday, together with Daisy & Dylan. Barnaby is at school. Olive had many presents and on the day we had a great vegetarian dinner beginning with tomato salad. Then a potato dish, with red cabbage cooked in the Polish manner, and parsnips. This followed by fresh pears with ice cream and hot chocolate sauce and a sponge cake made by Sally. Two bottles of wine. Hope you can translate all this into Russian?

Your mention of music was rather sad for me. Bach & Mozart were my favourites also, together with Haydn. And I liked early Church music very much, especially Polyphonic. I had some fine records of the great singer Boris Chaliapine singing Russian church music. Alas, all gone. We had about 800 long playing records. Sally and Nick now have these. I always used to think that when I was old I should listen all day to music. And now owing to deafness I cannot. Such is Life.

Evelyn Waugh. We have read all of his books I think. There is no doubt whatsoever he was a great writer, and some are very funny. But the man himself was so horrible in almost every way that I have never kept one of his books. He stood for everything that is unpleasant in the English character. And also I always have difficulty in reading novels by Roman Catholic writers. This is why I do not read Graham Greene, although Olive likes him very much. The problems that these writers deal with have no interest for me.

The question you ask about prices and wages I cannot answer because I really do not know. Some workers earn very high wages of course. And there are many state benefits for those that need help. But I think that generally speaking most people manage. In this tiny village almost everyone has a car, and there are certainly no poor people. But in the great industrial regions of the North things may be different. Inflation is certainly a problem with us now. And I see no end for this.

I have been rather sad of late. My oldest friend died a week ago. He was almost 85 and we first met at the end of 1918. I first went abroad with him to Berlin in 1922, and he became a bookseller through me, and a very good one. He was also a good writer on bibliographical topics. We wrote twice a month, he lived in Norfolk a good way from here. I miss him greatly.

We are going in to Newbury to-morrow. Is it possible to send you things like toothpaste, soap, etc. etc. which we understand here are in short supply in the USSR? Difficult to know.

Happy Christmas to you all and also the New Year. Write soon.

Love from us both,
skromnyi knizhnyi cherviak
Yours ever, Harold

Kishinev
29.12.79

Dear Olive and Harold

Many-many thanks for your kindness as regards us. There is nobody who would be so kind to us. It is hard to believe we are not relatives and have never seen each other.

We have received your Xmas gifts for Andrei, Marina and for me. Sizes are choosed perfectly, everything is beautifull.

Don't you worry about troubles we have to procure books, they are pleasant for us. As to their prices I think they are lower than this ones for clothes, it's not bothering about it. You see this book sent to you as Christmas gift is two times cheaper than jeans. The more so that kind of jeans is not sold in stores. Sailors making trips abroad sell them at prices more higher, as you can suppose. That's why I repeat: don't worry about our expenses, that we can do it. As to the books on Art I'm sending you they don't cost much, for example, this book costs one rouble 70 copeks (price is written on cover or at the last page where the printing-house notes are printed). You can see it in all the books.

Dear Harold, thank you very much for *Petersburg* by Bely, you suggested me that I read it. I liked it very much. I've read it avidly like a detective story. I couldn't tear myself away from the book so it was filled with its arome and beauty. It's impossible to translate into other language, to my mind, it's written only for Russian people. Even between them only one in a hundred will read it. But of course he will do it with great pleasure. This one is myself. I've delighted it thank to you.

I'm satisfied with that your opinion as to Evelyn Waugh coincides with mine. There are some difficulties to discuss it in letters.

As to music, believe me I had no intention to hurt you. Simply I like classic music so much that I can't stop to speak about it. The music means for me much more than pictures or poetry. Like you I am enthusiastic about Polyphonic Church music. We have a lot of playing records I used to listen to them very often with my friends. I feel myself so related to my favourite music that I can listen to whole symphonies or concertos in my head walking along the street or standing in a queue. I am sorry for men who do not understand and do not feel music.

Dear Harold, we feel for your grief as to your friend. There is nothing for it but to think that this life is not done only to die and that is all. I suppose it must be something else of unknown and this life is not only but preparation for this unknown. There are many problems I should like to discuss here they are so complicated that it is impossible to express each of them clearly in one letter as each problem requires many hours to discuss it.

Now I return to something of earthly. I forget to tell you that Andrei loves very much your Panda though he has a lot of toys. He sleeps with it 'nurses' and treats it giving him preference.

Once more something of prose concern soap and shampoo to wash hair (greasy or normal). Can you send us quaker instant oats for Andrei? Once our friends have given us a tin. Andrei has eaten it with great pleasure. I suppose it is not too much trouble for you. Up to day we have no frost. It is raining slushy, misty. Everybody complains of weather. As to me I am completely satisfied with it. The weather is warm. There are no frosts. I think I was an English woman in my past birth: this kind of weather does not depress me.

We are sending you our sincerest love and best wishes in New Year.

With love, your ever,

Lera

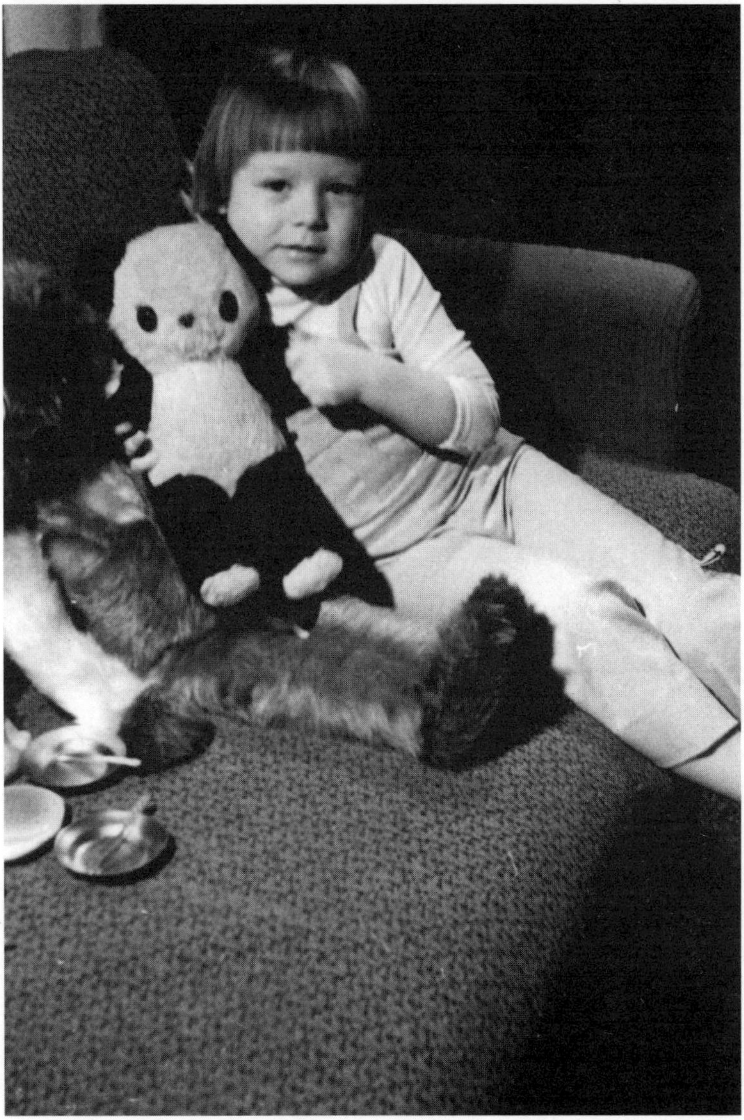

Andrei with the favourite panda bear Olive had sent him.

Kishinev
27.3.80

Dear Olive and Harold

At last I sat to write you a letter. I'm having spring holidays now, but in a week I'll start the last term at school. In June I am to pass through 6 exams to receive my General Education Certificate. And in August I'll be trying to enter the Moscow State University. This horrible time is coming nearer and nearer but I can't choose between the Russian Language and the English Language Departments. Fortunately the exams are the same at the both faculties. Composition on the Russian Literature, Russian Language, Russian History and a foreign language. But there are some pupils in our class who don't know whether to choose the humanities or natural sciences.

I understand very well that I have few chances to enter the Moscow University, but I've made up my mind to try. (It's very difficult for me to explain in English.) I know for sure I'd blame myself in case I entered the Kishinev University right away after school. I'll reproach myself that I had such a good opportunity to study in Moscow (even forgetting that they admit only one pretendent from 20 who'd like to enter) and I've lost it. I would blame myself that I had spoilt my best years in the stagnant dull town. But if I try to enter the University and fail (to enter would be a scream!) I return to Kishinev and enjoy life as it is, it can be marvelous everywhere, everything depends on a person, doesn't it?

And I have an advantage – I am a girl. Our boys can't do such experiments. If failed, they are going to the Army for two years, and only after being demobilized may make another try.

You see, I'm far from being confident that I'll be a success. That's why without giving an account to myself I'm looking through the advertisements about some temporary physical job. I'm so tired of this endless mental work (sometimes, after long hours of study, smoke seems getting out of my head) that I dream of some physical job. I think that to be washing up somewhere in the museum, or an interior decorator in a shop is a very good thing.

Oh! I become too egotistical with all my troubles, I chat exclusively about my own person. I am ashamed. Hope that in the future my letters will be more interesting and not so monotonous.

We had a lot of snow yesterday if you can imagine at the end of March, and we have large snow-drifts, unbelievable.

Hope that you are healthy and happy.

My best wishes to your grandchildren.

Much Love,

Your Marina

TELEPHONE: THATCHAM 2105 CABLES & TELEGRAMS DRYASDUST NEWBURY

H. W. Edwards *(Booksellers)* Ltd

DIRECTORS: H. W. EDWARDS · O. R. EDWARDS

Members Antiquarian Booksellers Association

ASHMORE GREEN, NEWBURY, BERKSHIRE, ENGLAND

15.4.80

For Marina

Detochka moya*

Your letter has arrived safely, and we have enjoyed reading your news. It is written in such good English, and your spelling is so good, that I should think that you should choose the English dept. where the competition would not be so great as in the Russian?

I am absolutely certain that you are quite right to try for Moscow University. We have a saying – and I expect you have also – Better to have loved and lost, than never to have loved at all.

And we are sure that you would be right: to take on some physical job, thus giving your brain a rest. You can study too much so that when the great day arrives, you are what we call 'stale'. As I think can happen to athletes.

I have read over once again your letters. Your command of English is, it seems to me, remarkable. I know that Russians are fortunate enough to be able to learn languages in a way that we English cannot. So you have an inborn advantage. And we have always found that by speaking nothing but English in a firm loud voice we can go everywhere! Do write again dushenka.†

Love from us all,
Harold

*'My child'.

†'My soul' – a nineteenth-century term that is a tender endearment.

Kishinev
10.6.1980

Dear Olive and Harold

We have enjoyed receiving your photographs. As usually we were touched by your Russian words chosen very much to the point.

I beg your pardon not to answer your letters at once. This year is very hard because of Marina. I was very busy. Marina is passing her final exams. Up to now everything is all right. She has passed the easiest ones for her: Russian literature (composition), English language and English and American literature. Technical translation. She has received excellent marks – five, our best mark. But the most difficult exams are yet to be passed – physics, chemistry and algebra. She is dreaming to say them good-bye for all her life. One more difficulty to overcome – University entrance exams in August. There is a lot of troubles for us this year.

I can not miss your remark that 'Andrei is too young for the gun'. I agree completely with you. Most of all I hate everything concerning war.* From now I am frightened by the time when Andrei must go to military service. I dream he should never take the gun. It is a pure chance – Andrei with a gun on the card. These 'war' toys belong to his friend. Never we buy such toys for him. Fortunately he is not interested in them. Most of all he likes animals – both real and toy – and small cars.

Will you forgive me for such a boring and prosaic letter? I have caught cold and am running a temperature. But I feel awkward to postpone the reply for a week or more. That is the reason my letter is so dull. Once I am recovered I shall write you.

Yours ever,

Lera

*The Russian invasion of Afghanistan had happened the year before, in 1979, and at the time of Lera writing this letter, young Soviet men were being called up to fight there.

Andrei and Lera walking together in Kishinev.

TELEPHONE: THATCHAM 2105 CABLES & TELEGRAMS DRYASDUST NEWBURY

H. W. Edwards (Booksellers) Ltd

DIRECTORS: H. W. EDWARDS · O. R. EDWARDS

Members Antiquarian Booksellers Association

ASHMORE GREEN, NEWBURY, BERKSHIRE, ENGLAND

9.7.80

Dear Lera

First, as usual, to thank you very much for the little collection of the Faceted Chamber in the Moscow Kremlin. Very nice to have, beautifully reproduced.

I cannot remember whether I have written to you since my birthday? There is one of the things I notice very much about old age – forgetting.

However all went well on the great day and I now feel truly patriarchal.

I hope that two parcels arrived safely for Marina? You have made us feel quite worried about her in respect of the examinations. You must let us know at once if all goes well. It must be very worrying.

We are very sorry to learn that you have been ill. I do hope that by now you are recovered? A cold in the summer always seems so much worse than one in the winter, when you at least expect one. Living as we do, about 400 feet above sea level, and with plenty of fresh air, we usually manage not to get cold.

Yours ever
Harold

Kishinev
5 July 1980

Dear Olive and Harold

On the 22nd June Marina has finished her school studies. In her General Education Certificate (paper given on finishing school) there are three good marks (algebra, geometry, physics) and the others are excellent. As you see she has made good progress in her studies, but to our regret it does not mean anything when one passes this entrance examinations to the Institute. So the real difficulties are in future.

We have had the leavers' party on the 24th June. I have made her a dress myself from a simple Holland cotton. It was done by hand and looked rather beautiful on. The parents were invited to the ceremonies of handing in General Education Certificates. Everybody was dressed very well. As to me I have put on your dress from Laura Ashley. It suits me well, I was completely satisfied. At midnight the adults had gone away and the children (17-years-old girls and boys) continued to dance till the morning. Then they went to the lake to see sunrise. In the morning they were seen in all parts of the town – well dressed children. It is a beautiful picture – schoolchildren at leavers' party – nice, young, fearful and sure simultaneously of their happy future waiting impatiently for the adult life. It was a pity Slava was absent. Being in Saratov for two weeks to see his mother. And on the 13th June Marina had her birthday party, more than 30 boys and girls of her friends went to wish her many happy returns. Surely it was very crowded in our two rooms, but Marina has enjoyed much. Andrei and me, we were in my mother's house. The children enjoyed till midnight. When returned home, I found our flat like Russia after Tartars invasion. But everybody was satisfied with this evening and decided Marina's parents are the best ones.

On the 30th June I had my own birthday. By this time Slava has arrived and we have gathered our friends from Kishinev and Leningrad too. It was turned out well. They do not eat much at table, the intellectuals, they rather speak and discuss a lot of problems. So I managed not to be very tired neither on the 13th nor on the 30th. Cake, different sandwiches, fruits and wine – that was all. I was in your dress from Laura* once more as for a moment I prefer it most of all. It fits me better than Marina. It suits me perfectly. As to Marina, she has no grudge against that, what is more she is perfectly content: her mother looks well and calls everybody's attention.

I have given you a detailed account of almost every day in June. How it was for you? How was Harold's party? On this day we have drank his health, told much of you, of our extraordinary acquaintance, of the best you have done for us as morally so materially.

Dear Harold, how do you feel yourself on your remarkable age? You remember you once said Cato started learning Greek at 80. Have you started to learn Russian? However I know it myself for you have found out this very fine and much to the point word 'neskazannyi'† that it can be considered as your first successful step in learning Russian.

Marina and me, we enjoy every time with your letter plenty of humour despite the fact that your has written it in 80. I have met no one perceiving the life in a so good manner at this age. It is a dream for another one.

You make fun of me smoking in a nice manner too. Really I do not smoke mahorka§ nor St. Moritz, I was presented with twice in my life. Surely these are not so good but enough acceptable for a civilized woman. I must say it is my weak spot, but I am not persuaded completely it is necessary to stop smoking. I hope I will be one day.

I had once more event in June – University graduates meeting. Earlier I have written you I had graduated from the Physics and Mathematics department in 1960, 20 years ago. My fellow students have arrived in Kishinev to celebrate this date. We have not seen each other for twenty years; it is difficult to recognise some ones. We had a pleasant party in the restaurant. I enclose here one card where I am with my

*Laura Ashley.
†'Ineffable, unknowable.'
§Inferior rolling tobacco, traditionally smoked by sailors.

fellows. Everything put on me is made with the aid of your patterns by myself.

We are impatiently waiting for the photos taken on Harold's birthday party. We are looking forward to your letter. With much love from us all,

Tselouem*

Lera

*'We kiss you'.

Kishinev
17.7.1980

Dear Olive and Harold

At last I sat down to write you a letter. Thank you very much for your parcels with the white dress and skirt, with top for me. Though, they're come two weeks later the Graduating Ball took place, I was very glad to receive them. After all, the life doesn't end after finishing school and I wear the dress now with great pleasure. The skirt is just up to the point and I like it very much. It's very nice, and especially comfortable for our sultry summer. Once again I do thank you very much for your concern for us.

At the end of June we had the Graduating Ball. Mum, Granny came there. Andryusha danced till 1 o'clock at night, when Mum had to use force to take him away from there.

I still live the school life. When with my former classmates we talk exceptionally about our school problems. It seems to me that not only me, but everybody of us can't imagine we'll never come to our beloved school again as pupils with schoolbags in uniforms which we hated while at school, by the way. And I'll be very glad if you send me some photos of your grandchildren at school (if there are such, of course) or simply write something about their school studying. I am still boiling in that pot of school life and can't imagine my life without those school problems and interests.

But, anyhow, I have to prepare for my entrance examinations. Though I try to do my best, I lose hope with every day the examinations approach. And I prepare my parents, relatives, friends to be ready for my failure. I try to face life bravely and not to be in despair in front of difficulties and faults, but I still have a great deal of jitters.

How are you? How did Harold's birthday party go. It seems to me that you, Harold, at 80 are much more optimist than me at 17.

Looking forward to your letter and the news about you, your children and grandchildren. Your every letter is a real holiday at our place. I will write you as soon as I have the results of my exams. Sorry for my clumsy English

Much love

Your Marina

TELEPHONE: THATCHAM 2105 CABLES & TELEGRAMS DRYASDUST NEWBURY

H. W. Edwards *(Booksellers)* Ltd

DIRECTORS: H. W. EDWARDS · O. R. EDWARDS

Members Antiquarian Booksellers Association

ASHMORE GREEN, NEWBURY, BERKSHIRE, ENGLAND

6.8.80

Dear Lera

Your very long and welcome letter has arrived safely together with the book by Bunin and the colour photograph.

I was delighted to have the Bunin, a writer that I have enjoyed long ago. I am surprised to see it is published, as I thought he was not regarded too well by the powers that be.

When Olive gave me the parcel, I was still in bed. I looked at the photograph and said, Good Lord, she has dyed her hair! But Olive wisely replied, You have never seen her hair. For some quite extraordinary reason I have always thought that you had dark hair. It is just one of those odd things one thinks without reason. But it was very nice to see you with your friends looking so well. If only we could see you in the flesh. But now that I am turned 80 it is most unlikely.

I think I gave you an account of my birthday festivities in my letter of the July 8th. I am sorry that so far we have not seen any of the many photographs that Sally took. I hope I will get them some day. But our daughter is disorganised and takes on far more than she can manage. Two houses in London and one large one in the country which is more than 250 miles from her home in London. The second house is where she works with Nick.

Olive has gone to London to have lunch with her, leaving me in care of our two cats. The garden is a great source of happiness for us, and in spite of the very worst weather for about a hundred years, is looking very beautiful. And Olive still manages to grow her vegetables.

You must forgive me for mentioning your smoking. I have seen so much misery caused by this habit among my friends as they became middle-aged. Olive found it very difficult to stop, but she did finally some eight years ago. She used to smoke little cigars. It is very easy for me to talk about giving it up, because really I never liked it. I used to smoke a pipe to make myself look more important, and large cigars for the same reason. But that was a long time ago. I never liked cigarettes. But I drink too much and cannot give that up.

An early Christian mystic, a Kempis, said, Be not angry you cannot make others as you wish, as you cannot make yourself.

I wonder if you have seen a new novel by Fyodor Abramov called *Home*? I should think it was very interesting, about the future of the Russian village. Something I am interested in myself, having left London to live in this tiny hamlet.

There is a new translation of the works of Anton Chekhov just appeared in nine volumes. Very well translated, better than the old edition. I have been re-reading the stories again. One of his very best, *The Steppe* I was pleased to note that one of the characters suddenly burst out singing

Here's to good old Mother Russia
Finest nation in the world.

I think that things have not changed so much in the last hundred years?

About Barnaby. The reason he isn't mentioned is that we so seldom see him. For that matter, we hardly see any of them. This is because they are always going to their country house, and I do not go to London now. I find it too difficult. The noise and the people are all too much.

I am interested that you are a mathematician. A few weeks ago we suddenly had a small book sent to us by a Russian we used to write to. It was very nice to be remembered. But the book, apart from the text being in Russian, was entirely mathematical symbols. We were very impressed. He gave no address so we have not been able to acknowledge it. But it was very heart-warming as you can imagine.

And this reminds me that 64 years ago I took the usual school leaving examination. The only subject I failed in completely was maths! This was a compulsory subject, but I did so well in everything else that I was allowed to pass with Honours as I had distinctions in five subjects. I have made many attempts to understand this subject, but alas, no use. I was a little more successful with Philosophy. And this reminds me of a story (true) in the Life of our great Dr Johnson who compiled our first dictionary in the middle of the 18th century. He was walking along Fleet Street one day and met an old school friend, oddly enough, named Edwards. He got talking to Johnson, and at last said, I have tried to be a philosopher, but cheerfulness keeps breaking in. This is my case. Tell Marina I have her letter and will write next week.

Love to all from us both,
Harold

TELEPHONE: THATCHAM 2105 CABLES & TELEGRAMS DRYASDUST NEWBURY

H. W. Edwards (Booksellers) Ltd

DIRECTORS: H. W. EDWARDS · O. R. EDWARDS

Members Antiquarian Booksellers Association

ASHMORE GREEN, NEWBURY, BERKSHIRE, ENGLAND

1.9.80

Dear Marina

At last I am answering your letters which have been on my desk for far too long. I think because, partly, we have had good weather for a week or two (now gone as usual) and also because I know you have been in Moscow on your most important visit and that Slava may have been away also.

I do hope that all went well for you? When will you know the results? We both hope good news, but if not, remember it is not the end of the world for you.

Were you able to go to the Taganka Theatre* when you were there? I think that is now the fashionable place for Muscovites.

Before I go any farther, Olive asks me to thank you all for the marvellous gift of the crepe de chine that Mama sent. It arrived safely, as did the Turgenev book. And the little book of the Kiev Mosaics which I saw long before any of you were born. I liked Kiev very much. It had very good food for the time – 1932.

*Marina remembers: *The Taganka theatre had a very important place in Moscow's cultural life in the 1970s and 1980s. It was run by a very famous director named Yuri Lyubimov. He staged such plays as* The Master and Margarita *by Bulgakov and* The House on the Embankment *by Trifonov, both of which were implicit criticisms of Soviet Communism. Moliére's* Tartuffe *was even staged in such a way that it was possible to read references to the USSR between the lines. It was such a famous place that every intellectual wanted to go there. It was very difficult to get tickets, and everyone spoke constantly about what was on at the Taganka. The famous ballad singer Vladimir Vysotsky was an actor there. It's strange that the Taganka was tolerated by the authorities: people have different answers as to why; maybe somebody in the Politburo liked its plays. For some reason the Soviet authorities left this one place where you could still feel some fresh air. It was like Tarkovsky's films, which – like the Taganka plays – were an awakening for people. I remember going to his films and the cinema was so full I had to squeeze on to the staircase in the gangway to have a space. Perhaps the authorities couldn't stop everything, and so just gave people a little titbit to keep them going.*

I have the complete works of Turgenev here, 12 vols. Some time ago I read the first 10 and then stopped at the last two, *A Hunter's Sketches*, as I detest Hunting in all its forms, except hunting for books. I do not mind mushroom hunting!!!

I shall now read your volume. And a request from me. If you see another copy of the Lermontov book I should like to have this for a friend. Does not matter if now unobtainable of course.

Now to answer your letter. Your spelling is excellent, I see only one error – 'percieve' for 'perceive'. This is a very common mistake. The rule is (I shall have to go and ask Olive what the wretched rule is). The rule is 'i' before 'e' except after 'c'. So it is 'perceive' and not 'percieve' as you have written and I have typed. I am writing this in the morning so do not think that I have been at the vodka bottle, although it looks like it. As I wrote before, only some of the idiomatic phrases are a little wrong.

You ask me about photographs of my 80th. Well, at long last Sally has sent us a very nice album with these placed in position. But we are still trying to get some from her to send to you. Alas, I have no 'blat'* where our daughter is concerned. Parents seldom have I'm afraid. And you probably know how difficult life can be without 'blat'.

We greatly enjoyed having the photos of you and your friends on the great school-leaving occasion. Olive said to me that the fair girl with the flowers looked interesting. Alas, my opinion is of no value at all. For some reason, which I do not understand, I find all girls interesting!

I am amazed at the number of subjects that you have to study – 19. This seems far too many. I am happy to know that you are 'impetuous'. At your age surely a very good thing to be.

*I.e. clout or influence. Marina remembers: *During the Soviet times there were shortages of everything – books, food, clothes, furniture, carpets, cars, everything. All these things were relatively inexpensive, and practically everybody could afford them, but they were not produced in sufficient numbers. 'Blat' was a special connection that could help. A woman would say, 'Oh, I have blat in the carpet shop' – meaning that she knew the director of the carpet shop and could buy things under the table. Everything was done like that, and you had to pay extra – sometimes double – to obtain these things. It meant that the people who had this blat everywhere were highly successful because all doors were open to them, but those who didn't could get hold of very little. Blat ruled our lives. In 1992, when prices were liberalised, the cost of living sky-rocketed and goods were available but unaffordable, so blat was no longer useful.*

I am glad to read about all the festivities and parties that you have been enjoying. But, I ask myself, Where is the sad Slav soul about which I read so much when I was young? Where are the Gypsies singing sad songs while the troikas dash along? 'Where are the snows of yesteryear'? You will see that I have been reading Chekhov again.

I think that it is quite usual to be pessimistic at your age. One tends to get more optimistic as one gets older. Always remember that we worry far more about the things that do not happen, than about the ones that do.

Olive tells me that lunch is now ready. I have a glass of Sherry first, then we have – nearly always – cheese with home-made wholemeal bread, butter and home grown tomatoes. And biscuits. And sometimes I have very small onions which Olive grows for me. I must confess that I am passionately devoted to the Onion Family, especially Garlic. And of course we finish with the inevitable cup of Tea, without which life would hardly be worth living.

Much love to you all from us both.

Yours ever,
Harold

Harold at his eightieth birthday party.

TELEPHONE: THATCHAM 2105 CABLES & TELEGRAMS DRYASDUST NEWBURY

H. W. Edwards (*Booksellers*) Ltd

DIRECTORS: H. W. EDWARDS · O. R. EDWARDS

Members Antiquarian Booksellers Association

ASHMORE GREEN, NEWBURY, BERKSHIRE, ENGLAND

22.9.80

Dearest Lera

At long last I am answering your letter of the 28th July. I have delayed, partly because I hoped that Sally would send on the photographs, partly out of sheer laziness, also work in the garden; finally a bee sting on the hand last week gave me a further excuse.

Now the photographs have arrived and are enclosed. These for some reason are not nearly so good as the first lot which Sally sent enclosed in a small album. The colour is not so good, nor the impression so sharp. But you can see me in all my glory on my 80th.

We are anxiously awaiting news of Marina's examination. Have you heard the result? We do hope satisfactory.

How was Moscow when you were there? I liked it so much when I was there in 1932 and the old town still existed. Alas, in 1965 it seemed to me to have lost all its native characteristics. The same has happened in the little town of Newbury. When we came here to our dacha in 1937, it was as it was in the 19th century. Now just horrible office blocks. And nearly all the little shops have disappeared owing to the supermarkets.

Times change, and seldom for the better. In spite of the terrible summer, our garden has done well. At present I am sweeping up dead grass. The apples look most beautiful on the trees – all lovely colours. Far, far too many. We give most away. I have baked apples with cream almost every night at dinner. Unfortunately Olive does not enjoy them as I do. No pears, but we did have three peaches! Chutney and tomato chutney. Forgive all this about food. Old age I think?

Yes, the film you mention made by Tarkovsky has been shown in London, and has received enormous praise from all the critics.

I like Bulgakov too, especially *The White Guard* which was very sympathetic Have you read it? A silly question perhaps.

I hope that you have been able to go to the Crimea? We too like the sea very much. Olive and I once spent a whole month on a ship, only spending three hours on land in all that time. We came back from America via the Panama canal. Happy days.

Olive is sending separately some patterns for you. Now lunchtime so must end.

Love to all four of you, and to both grannies. I think that you both have a grandmother alive? One of my grandfathers was born in 1835. Seems a long time ago.

Harold

TELEPHONE: THATCHAM 2105 CABLES & TELEGRAMS DRYASDUST NEWBURY

H. W. Edwards *(Booksellers)* Ltd

DIRECTORS: H. W. EDWARDS · O. R. EDWARDS

Members Antiquarian Booksellers Association

ASHMORE GREEN, NEWBURY, BERKSHIRE, ENGLAND

15.10.80

Dear Lera

Very many thanks for your letter posted from Moscow, which arrived safely. As you know, I expect, Marina had written to tell us of her success, and I hope that our telegram of congratulations arrived at Kishinev? No need to tell you that we look forward to hearing from her, when she has managed to find a place to live. It will be good for her English to write, but I can fully understand that she will find many other things to do in the great city.

I am very sorry to learn that your father was killed in the war. Do you remember him, or were you too young? And of course the hair dye question is utterly unimportant. Olive used to darken hers but left off about four years ago. We think when one gets near to 70 it is better to accept the inevitable.

By the way, I feel some anxiety when you tell me that we had some influence over Marina's choice of English. When you write to her, will you tell her that any books she might like to have I will send if it is possible to get them. I might be able to help in this way as I am sure the books she would want would be scholastic. Alas, I do not know the ballad singers you write about. Once I think I should, but I have not been able to listen to music for about 12 years.

Enclosed a photograph of Daisy and Barnaby. The words on her T-shirt are: If you love animals do not eat them. But I am afraid that we do eat chickens here. A black mark of course.

Weather now turning cold. Olive has planted winter lettuce and cabbage in the garden under cloches. I spend my time trying to make the place look tidy, but without much success. Too large of course, just 1 hectare. It did not seem so large forty years ago. Have just finished reading *Great Expectations* by Charles Dickens. Wonderful novel. He is our one writer that can compare with Dostoevsky and Tolstoy. Perhaps also Jane Austen.

All good wishes to you all. Write soon.
Love from us both,
Harold

TELEPHONE: THATCHAM 2105 CABLES & TELEGRAMS DRYASDUST NEWBURY

H. W. Edwards (Booksellers) Ltd

DIRECTORS: H. W. EDWARDS · O. R. EDWARDS

Members Antiquarian Booksellers Association

ASHMORE GREEN, NEWBURY, BERKSHIRE, ENGLAND

29.10.80

Dear Marina

Many thanks for your letter of the 9th Oct. which has been waiting for an answer far too long.

First of all, it is very good indeed, just as usual a few idiomatic errors. You will not mind if I point them out I know. There are NO spelling mistakes at all, and I know only too well how difficult our spelling can be. I often have to ask Olive how to spell a word. For the rest: At last I sat to write. This should be At last I sit to write. Present tense. When everything calmed down a little. = when everything has calmed down a little. OR with everything calmed down a little. And there must be much more mistakes, should be And there must be many more mistakes. I hope that in the nearest future should be, I hope in the near future. I am still homesick greatly, should be I am still greatly homesick. I begin to understand what parents are in real for their children, should be, I begin to understand what parents are in reality. That is all, and I hope that you have remembered to bring your 'dushegreychka'?*

That very useful word 'blat'. Well, I picked it up from reading about it in *The Times*. We do not have quite the same thing here, because, as I understand it, it mainly refers to things that are difficult to get. There is no shortage of any articles of any kind here, so that it is not necessary. I should add however, that this does not apply to MONEY. That gets more and more difficult, and no amount of 'blat' will find it. But of course something like it appears among those that were at school or university together in social things and in work. It is

*The archaic word for a warm winter jacket.

known as 'the Old Boys Act', or also as 'Buggins's turn'. Difficult to explain, but I think you will understand it.

I have been going through a Russian phase once more in reading. Have read a book of stories by Elena Militsina (have you heard of her?) and Saltikov and also by V.I. Nemirovitch-Dantchenko. All very readable. Also a very good biography of Pasternak. Apart from these, as always, Charles Dickens. I think this is old age.

I never receive news of Ksjuta. Our two cats, Dolly and Mimi are very interested.

As you can very well see, I am running out of things to write about. Do look after yourself in Moscow, wrap up warm, and be sure you have plenty to eat, but not too much dairy and meat fats!!!

Love from us both,
Harold

TELEPHONE: THATCHAM 2105 CABLES & TELEGRAMS DRYASDUST NEWBURY

H. W. Edwards (Booksellers) Ltd

DIRECTORS: H. W. EDWARDS · O. R. EDWARDS

Members Antiquarian Booksellers Association

ASHMORE GREEN, NEWBURY, BERKSHIRE, ENGLAND

21.11.80

Dear Lera

We must thank you very much indeed for the beautiful table cloth that you sent us from Moscow, and which arrived yesterday. It is very nice and so full of colour. It will lighten up our meals. It got unwrapped on its journey, but our post office very kindly repacked it.

I suppose that Marina will be home for Xmas, but perhaps Christmas is no longer observed in the USSR? And of course, Easter is the really important time. Here a great deal of fuss is made about Xmas, and we hear from many people once a year only at this time.

I have been re-reading Chekhov once again in a very good new translation just published here. What a marvellous writer. And once again, I will try Bely's *Petersburg*. I do hate being defeated by a book. I have also an enormous novel by A. Zinoviev who now lives in Germany, titled *The Yawning Heights*. But alas, I cannot get through it. Over 800 pages and all a fantasy.

The film named *The Run* by Bulgakov has been running in London, but as I never go there if I can avoid it, I shall not see it. But it has been very successful I know.

I now come to your letter from Moscow. It must be very odd for Marina to be living in the next room to someone born in 1893. Imagine being 21 in 1914 when all our troubles began. I was 14, just beginning to live.

I am so glad that she is studying Latin, because it has been such an important language for civilisation. I like the poems of Horace very much, and Seneca's *Letters*. Alas – once again – I now have to read them in English. But I still remember a lot of Latin from my school days.

No need for me to tell you how much I sympathise with your idea;

about life in a gigantic city. But I think for the young it is something to be experienced. We go, I hope, to London for a day on Olive's birthday, the 2nd of December, when we shall have lunch with Sally and Nick at a French restaurant. Olive will then begin her 70th year. She was 15 when we first met. It is strange that you are younger than Sally, who is now 45.

An hour's journey is a long time for her to get to the Institute. As you know, I was fortunate to have been born in the very heart of London, and always lived there except for a short time when Sally was a baby, and we moved to one of the suburbs.

I did know that the famous singer of the Taganka theatre, Vladimir Vysotsky had died at a very early age. When you are next in Moscow and the weather is fine, I hope that you will both go one Sunday to the Vagankovskoye cemetery and pay homage at his grave. At the same time, you might visit the grave of a great Russian poet buried there – Sergei Yesenin. I do not think he is forgotten in Russia. There is a very nice church in the grounds of the cemetery where you might go to see the fine Icons, and to light a candle in my name!

I fear that I am rambling on as old men do, and will exhaust your patience. It is a sad November day here, but thank goodness it is quite warm, which is why I am writing such a long letter.

As always, we look forward very much to hearing from you. I know what hard work it must be for you to have to write in English. And I must tell you that we are very proud that we have been able to direct Marina's studies to England and the English. I do not think that she will ever have regrets.

Greetings and much love from us to the four of you and to your friends also.

Yours ever, Harold
Staryo pokupayem*

*'Rag and bone man', a term used in nineteenth-century Russian literature. The literal translation is 'We buy old stuff'.

TELEPHONE: THATCHAM 2105 CABLES & TELEGRAMS DRYASDUST NEWBURY

H. W. Edwards (*Booksellers*) Ltd

DIRECTORS: H. W. EDWARDS · O. R. EDWARDS

Members Antiquarian Booksellers Association

ASHMORE GREEN, NEWBURY, BERKSHIRE, ENGLAND

21.4.81

Dear Lera

Delighted to have received your long letter of the 2nd March, and the book by Vassilyev which looks interesting. I have already thanked you for the Moscow Icon book with French text which is quite all right for me. It is very good of you to take so much trouble. And the photographs we liked, especially the one of Andrei's birthday party. How marvellous the children look.

Very glad that all the letters have arrived after all. I wonder why everything was delayed. But, as we say, Better late than never.

I am sorry to hear about your friends in Canada who feel so homesick and don't have any sympathetic friends to talk to. But these are national characteristics. It is far worse in England I think. We just do not indulge in heart-to-heart conversations.

I never have in the whole of my life. Nor of course, do we find it very easy to mix and be helpful when the occasion arises. It is just the same in travelling, one says 'good morning' or 'good evening' and not very much else usually. It is a form of shyness I think.*

I agree with you absolutely about the pleasures of travel. Of course

*Marina remembers: *When Harold wrote this to us, it always seemed so strange to me, and later on my experience of travelling was very different to his. While studying in Moscow for five years I regularly visited my parents who lived 2,000 kilometres away. The train trip lasted for twenty-four hours and I made this Moscow–Kishinev, Kishinev–Moscow trip at least thirty times. I do not remember a single time when in the evening, when it was getting dark, four absolute strangers doomed to being together in the same compartment, would not start sharing their food and drink. Then they would begin to talk. Eventually two passengers would fall asleep and I would sit in the corner of my berth listening to the fourth one telling the story of his life. There was something special about those night talks. You would meet an absolute stranger, and you knew that after bidding farewell to him at the railway station at the end of your trip you would never meet him again in this country with hundreds of millions of people. So I would sit in my dark corner in a swaying carriage and listen to these stories above the noise of clattering wheels. Sometimes I felt like a priest listening to confession.*

in itself it brings neither happiness nor sorrow, but one's life is much enlarged in every way by seeing other lands and peoples.

We did not receive the postcard from Marina. How is she? It must be rather lonely for her in Moscow?

You will be amused to learn that yesterday I pulled out one of my teeth, which was loose through old age. This is the third I have dealt with. I suppose I could set up as the village dentist?

I was sorry to read that Yuri Trifonov has died. Not very old. Two of his books are appearing in English this year, and we look forward to reading him. Have you had the pleasure of seeing his play at the Taganka? *The House on the Embankment* I think? I was reading a very nice novel written by an Englishman called William Gerhardie. He was born in St Petersburg and lived there until 1920. The book is called *Futility*. And another book I am reading for the second time is a book by Prince Peter Kropotkin called *Memoirs of a Revolutionist*. I read it first in 1916 when he was living near to me in London. I should have loved to have knocked on his door and to have seen him. But this was quite impossible for me as I did not know him! All this in my far off Anarchist days. But I did once meet his daughter in the 1920s. She was very nice, and I think went to America.

I really must not go on in this rambling way. Old age as usual.

Your Harold

Marina with Andrei walking down the street in Kishinev.

SPRINGFIELD ASHMORE GREEN NEWBURY BERKSHIRE

TELEPHONE THATCHAM (0635) 62105

September 23rd, 1981

My dear Lera

The arrival of your telegram today has inspired me to write to you. We have been receiving your letters and parcel. The last letter in two copies, but separate envelopes came together last week. Harold has been writing to you and thanking you for the books. I expect you will get the letters eventually. They were all registered.

The reason for my not writing (which Harold has written to you about) is that I have been ill. About the middle of July I had some kind of heart trouble and the consultant diagnosed a leaking valve in the heart.

This has been very worrying for all of us, as I am normally very healthy and active. Luckily I am now feeling much better although I shall never be the same again, and I am living very slowly and quietly. In fact I have hardly left the house and garden since I was first taken ill, and have not been to Newbury for 10 weeks. We are giving up the car as I have been advised not to drive, and Harold stopped driving some years ago.

Harold is being pretty marvellous through all this worrying time, and he does all the shopping by taxi once a fortnight, and our neighbours have all been very kind. Some of the ardent church goers have offered up prayers for my recovery which touched me very much.

Harold is very well, as are Sally and family. Dylan has started school, a boarding school 8 miles from here, and for the last two Sundays has cycled over for lunch which was lovely for us. For him too, as the food here is much better than school food. He likes the new school, as well as being near us, and we think he might do well there.

Harold is writing a short note to you, so I will stop but I did want you to know that I am going on all right and as soon as I feel able to go to Newbury hope to be able to get something for you all.

With lots of love,
Olive

TELEPHONE: THATCHAM 2105 CABLES & TELEGRAMS DRYASDUST NEWBURY

H. W. Edwards (Booksellers) Ltd

DIRECTORS: H. W. EDWARDS · O. R. EDWARDS

Members Antiquarian Booksellers Association

ASHMORE GREEN, NEWBURY, BERKSHIRE, ENGLAND

10-10-81

Dear Lera

We are delighted to have your letter of – alas – it is undated, but it arrived at the week end. I am sorry that I did not take copies of the letters that did not arrive. But from this one I will do so in future. I find dealing with the carbon paper not easy. I expect you realise that I have no practical sense at all, and that Olive does all the things that I should do.

To answer some of your questions I am very pleased to write that Olive keeps going and is quite cheerful. But she has not yet left the house since July, except once to the hospital for a blood count, and once last week with me for a hearing test. I am to get a new hearing aid. But was told that for my age my hearing is quite good. But music etc. I can never hear properly.

For housekeeping. Olive does all the cooking. I do all the housework, filling up the stove, seeing to feeding the two cats. We have a machine, a very efficient machine that does the washing-up. We do not have a clothes washing machine because of having to do the ironing, so send things to the laundry. But Olive washes the small things such as socks, vests etc. I go into Newbury once a fortnight and do all the shopping. I enjoy this, because I think I am good at it; I have a taxi there and back. The bus service is not very good. You know we live in a very small village without a shop or even a public house. It did not matter when we were young and were using a car. We also have a very good girl who comes in twice a week and really cleans up the place properly. Also two men once a week for the garden. So you see we manage very well. By the way, our hospital service and medical service is quite first class, and all of course, as in

Russia, quite free of any payment. Olive had three doctors when she was first ill.

Before I forget. Olive wants you to know that she has made a very beautiful dress for Daisy to wear at Christmas with the silk that you so extravagantly sent to her from Moscow. I hope that we will have a photo of her, but knowing Sally I am not very hopeful.

I am so glad that Andrei has decided not to eat animals. It is for that reason we have all become vegetarians. And the fact that we think it is a much better diet. I have been reading a lot about Moldavia in articles in *The Times* and it seems you are living in a land of milk and honey. And the wine sounds excellent. So you have no excuse! I hope that Marina likes her new apartment and is doing well? I am sure she will be a great success.

I have left myself no space to tell you what I think about life. Briefly, I think it is something to be enjoyed and not to be worried about. None of us knows the answer to your question. I think about it often, but never come to any answer about whether there is any life after death. Two very devout Irish friends of ours have been on a pilgrimage to Lourdes in France and have given us a lot of thought. We like the idea of this very much. And we thank you also for thinking of us.

How is Slava? And yourself? You never say. We have been watching a nice travel film of Russia on television. Yalta, Samarkand, Irkutsk so far.

We like the South very much. Plenty of sun and light. But we are OLD.

Love to you all,
Harold

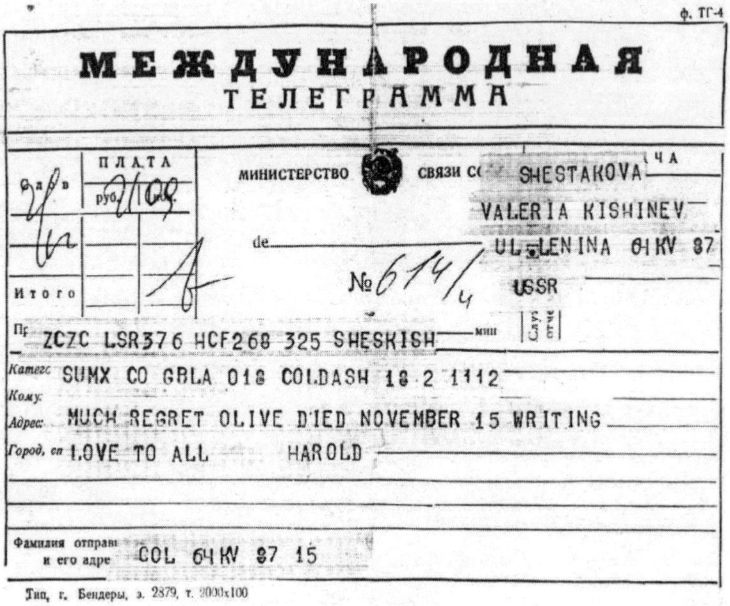

ф. ТГ-4

МЕЖДУНАРОДНАЯ
ТЕЛЕГРАММА

МИНИСТЕРСТВО СВЯЗИ СС

ПЛАТА
руб.
Итого

de
№ 614/4

SHESTAKOVA
VALERIA KISHINEV
UL LENINA 64 KV 87
USSR

ZCZC LSR376 HCF268 325 SHESKISH
Категс SUMX CO GBLA 018 COLDASH 18 2 1112
Кому:
Адрес: MUCH REGRET OLIVE DIED NOVEMBER 15 WRITING
Город, ст LOVE TO ALL HAROLD

Фамилия отправи и его адре COL 64 KV 87 15

Тип. г. Бендеры, з. 2879, т. 2000х100

Apart from cups of Keemun tea throughout the day Olive's daily routine included a glass of whisky or two – always Ballantine's – before dinner – and in her later years a siesta in the afternoon. She had a drawling, exaggerated way of speaking which only leaped into fast tempo when she was riled. To the end she was a devoted grandmother, always sewing and knitting beautiful clothes for her grandchildren.

TELEPHONE: THATCHAM 2105 CABLES & TELEGRAMS DRYASDUST NEWBURY

H. W. Edwards (*Booksellers*) Ltd

DIRECTORS: H. W. EDWARDS · O. R. EDWARDS

Members Antiquarian Booksellers Association

ASHMORE GREEN, NEWBURY, BERKSHIRE, ENGLAND

2.2.82

Dear Lera

At long last I am writing to you. You will forgive me for my long silence, caused as you know by the sad event of last November.

I will not answer your long letter of the 27th Nov this time, but will later in the week. The Tvardovsky book arrived safely, and your kind telegram also. I appreciate very much your thoughts.

I have answered about 50 letters of condolence from friends, nearly all of course bookseller friends. These letters have been most helpful, and I am very glad that I have written also in these sad circumstances.

The end was quite unexpected, sudden and peaceful. Sitting in her armchair in front of the fire. Thank goodness whilst I was there. Her last words were, 'When you come in we will have a drink.' I like that.

The family had been to tea that afternoon (it was a Sunday) and had only just left a quarter of an hour before.

It was exactly the kind of end that Olive would have wished, as indeed I should myself.

A very quiet cremation in Oxford with a simple service that was very moving. I am enclosing a note that appeared in the *Antiquarian Booksellers Newsletter* written by a very old friend who lives near Oxford.

The clergyman was most kind and consoling, and there were many flowers.

One other sad thing is that her eldest sister, who was there, has died just a month later. All the sisters so far have died from a heart attack. Two are left.

You four are often in my thoughts, and you know that I shall always be here until my time comes.

Please write as soon as you get this. The photograph is of Daisy's 11th birthday party. I will send more later. The party frock of green silk that you sent – do you remember – was made by Olive.

No more for now.
Your Harold

TELEPHONE: THATCHAM 2105 CABLES & TELEGRAMS DRYASDUST NEWBURY

H. W. Edwards (Booksellers) Ltd

DIRECTORS: H. W. EDWARDS · O. R. EDWARDS

Members Antiquarian Booksellers Association

ASHMORE GREEN, NEWBURY, BERKSHIRE, ENGLAND

13.3.82

Dearest Lera

Your most welcome letter, dated Feb. 2nd, arrived yesterday the 12th. I may say that reading it over an early morning cup of tea brought tears to my eyes. It is so sympathetic and warm-hearted, and I thank you much.

I hope that before you get this, you will have received a letter I sent with some photographs of Daisy's 11th birthday and the extract from the news letter of the *Antiquarian Booksellers Association*. I regret that I cannot find the registration slip, so do not know when I sent it. But in future I am taking a note of everything that I post to you. Let me know if it arrives please. You mention a parcel. Was this the one containing Olive's last present to you?

In that letter I gave you all the events that were Olive's last moments on earth, and do not wish to repeat them unnecessarily.

I am enclosing separately Sally's address both in London and the country, so that if you get worried about not hearing from me, you will be able to write to her. It is difficult for me to describe my emotional state. I just feel that there is a complete blank in my life. We were together for over fifty years, and it is entirely owing to Olive that any success in life has come to me. I never had much, if any, common sense (else I would not have been an Anarchist in my youth). She always seemed to have the right answers to any problems that we had, both domestic and business. So now, as I say, everything is a blank.

There is a very famous line by John Donne, one of our greatest Elizabethan poets. 'No man is an island.' But when a man has no one to share a laugh with, a simple meal, or a glass of wine, or a piece of news, he is indeed an island. But I determined when all this happened, that I would do what I knew Olive would have wished me to do, and to go on living to the best of my ability. So I take care to have proper meals, not to drink too much, and keep the garden going. When one is old, it is very easy to start living in squalor, and to be too self-indulgent. I think being aware of these things helps to avoid them.

Of course, the two cats have to be looked after, and this gives me something to do apart from myself. I am also very fortunate in having a very nice girl that comes in 3 days a week and cleans etc. Also she does my shopping if I do not want to go into Newbury. But alas, she is going to have a baby in September. But above all, Sally and Nick have been everything they could be. They come down very often to see me, and Sally always comes with much food that she has prepared, and bread that she has made. Cheese and vegetable dishes. At Christmas they bought me a deep freeze. I doubt if you have these in the USSR. It freezes food quite solid, and it will keep many months. This means that I do not have to worry in case I have not any food in the house. It is quite remarkable, as she brings soup that is a frozen ball, and bread to go into the machine. The odd thing is that it tastes exactly as if it were fresh.

Dear Lera, you ask me about my emotional state and all I seem to write about is my physical state. And what do I think about life. I find this almost impossible to answer. Two things are inevitable, birth and death. To me, the best thing to do is to enjoy the interval in between. There is so much to enjoy in life. Flowers, trees, the sun, fresh air, love, music, pictures, and, above all, books. I do not think that this is the answer to your question, but I cannot pretend to think otherwise. I have forgotten the most important thing. Do you know the Russian proverb 'Better to have a hundred friends than a hundred roubles'? Am happy to think that you remember us in your prayers, and that you are not the only one that does so. Please give my love to you and Marina, Slava and Andrei. And write again soon.

Yours ever, Harold

Olive

TELEPHONE: THATCHAM 2105 CABLES & TELEGRAMS DRYASDUST NEWBURY

H. W. Edwards (Booksellers) Ltd

DIRECTORS: H. W. EDWARDS · O. R. EDWARDS

Members Antiquarian Booksellers Association

ASHMORE GREEN, NEWBURY, BERKSHIRE, ENGLAND

27.6.82

Dear Lera

First and foremost, to thank you for your birthday telegram, and the two books, one from you and one from Marina. Believe it or not, all arrived exactly on my birthday. It is really most kind of you, and I appreciate it very much. And especial thanks to Marina in Moscow.

All went well on the 14th. Sally, Nick and Daisy and the very nice girl that helps came down for the weekend. Dylan came over from school, and two very old bookseller friends, one age 79, the other 84, came over from Oxford.

Sally and Lynne (the girl) cooked a beautiful vegetarian lunch – and we had Sherry, two bottles of red wine, and one of white, and a bottle of Muscat. All enjoyed themselves. We all thought of Olive who I am sure was there in spirit.

The book on the Great Palace of the Moscow Kremlin is magnificent. Thanks for your generosity. I have a very fine collection of books on early Russian Art and Architecture. The Dostoevsky short stories I am happy to have, and think of Marina in far away Moscow when I read them. What a writer he was. I sometimes wonder who was the better, Dostoevsky or Tolstoy. Very difficult. What do you think?

You say in your letter that only the women smoke. It is very strange, but it is exactly the same here. We only have one friend that smokes, she is Olive's younger sister. Olive used to smoke a great deal, but gave it up. I think the damage to her heart had already been done as she smoked for about 45 years. Your conversation is very Russian. We never discuss such things in England. Our talk is about books or politics. To talk of religion would be too difficult in England. One respects other people's beliefs, or non-beliefs without comment.

You ask me about our family life. All are vegetarians as you know. I think that you will become one as you get older. I no longer have any difficulty, but you will be amused that I first tried in 1917 under the influence of the poet Shelley, and the great Russian Prince Kropotkin.

All happiness for your birthday dear Lera. I hope all goes well.
Love to you all, and write soon.
Harold

* * *

AFTER OLIVE'S DEATH, HAROLD'S LIFE CONTRACTED greatly. His diminished hearing and partial blindness magnified his loneliness. His friends, like him, were unable to travel any longer and he missed their conversation about the world of antiquarian books. As he became increasingly detached from his immediate surroundings, letters, more than ever, became his lifeline. He continued to correspond with a handful of lifelong friends, with his daughter Sally and her family and, of course, with the Aidovs. But the letters Harold wrote to the Aidovs grew more scarce as his energies and health failed.

His mind was alert, and his knowledge and humour remained unaltered. In practical matters, this not very practical man reluctantly modified his habits to cope with his changed and changing circumstances. He was self-disciplined, and maintained a sensible domestic routine. He wrote that it was some consolation to him that Olive did not survive him to bear her accelerating disability alone. But he admitted to friends and family that he was lonely.

TELEPHONE: THATCHAM 2105 CABLES & TELEGRAMS DRYASDUST NEWBURY

H. W. Edwards (Booksellers) Ltd

DIRECTORS: H. W. EDWARDS · O. R. EDWARDS

Members Antiquarian Booksellers Association

ASHMORE GREEN, NEWBURY, BERKSHIRE, ENGLAND

15.12.82

Dearest Lera

Your letter from Moscow never arrived I regret. But I am glad that the parcel that I sent on the 7th July reached you safely. So glad the jeans are all right, the secret in shopping is that you must be an old man, and look helpless. It is as easy as that. I go to one of the nice girl assistants and simply ask for what I want, and leave it entirely to her. When I say that it is for a very dear friend in Russia great interest is aroused, for Russia is quite as unknown to nearly all as was Tibet or Japan at one time. I greatly enjoy going into Newbury once a fortnight as everyone is very helpful. On the 16th November I sent a parcel containing jeans for Andrei, two little books to make him laugh and a pattern book. As soon as I know you have received this, I will send jeans for Marina. After that, poor Slava. Will you remind him that it says in the Bible that the first shall be last, and the last first. I only wish it was not so difficult to send things, but one never quite knows what is allowed and what is not. There is not the slightest chance of my sending you the book you would like on astrology. As you know I sent a very fine book with large coloured illustrations which you never got. One must accept the inevitable.

Congratulations on the autumn weather. Ours, as usual, has been very mixed, but generally on the cold side. But we have had a marvellous apple crop this year. I have thrown away thousands, no one wants them.

Being a vegetarian. How well I know the difficulties. I have been one now for nearly two years and think that I have conquered. As the Buddhists say, only the Self can conquer the Self.

One item of news for you. I have taken up walking, and now walk for 3/4 of an hour every day. I realised, after the anniversary of Olive's death, that I had taken almost no exercise at all. I find gardening too difficult now, and leave it to others. So, unless we have snow and ice, I set out each morning. We are half way up a steep hill otherwise I think I should stay longer. I look forward to the spring when it will be more pleasant.

Now that I know a little more than I did about Russians and Russia, I have begun to re-read Dostoevsky. I could not read *A Raw Youth* when I was young. Now I think it is most interesting. I can never make up my mind between Dostoevsky and Tolstoy. But I prefer Dostoevsky – usually.

It is Dylan's 18th birthday today, and Sally is coming here with Daisy and their girl Jane to make a large dinner for him. Nick will bring him along. All stay overnight. Then come along the next weekend for a Xmas party for me. I do not now wish to travel to Yorkshire for Xmas itself. Too far for my old bones. Nor do I like leaving the two cats.

Forgive the dreadful typing, partly me, and partly the machine itself.

Christmas will be over long before you get this, but I wish you all a very happy New Year. Write when you can. We all keep well, and I hope you all do the same.

Much love,
Harold

* * *

HAROLD WAS ALWAYS CHEERED BY FAMILY VISITS, BUT conversation was inhibited by his deafness. Whenever Sally was abroad, Nick made the almost daily phone call to Harold himself. Although by now Harold could hear very little of what was being said, he recognised the voice on the telephone, and spoke about what he had been doing, and asked for things that he needed. He often joked about his misunderstandings of what had been said to him. He recorded in his diary 'Phoned Markham Square [Sally and Nick's London home] last night, got Barnaby. No one seems to know where the two [Sally and Daisy] are, nor when they are returning. Nick either in Hackney or Hyne-high (Sinai?). And a few days later: 'Better day today. Another long letter from Sally not delivered. The post is not like it was when I was a boy. Joke made me laugh: Three half-deaf men (like me) touring the Midlands. As the train slowed down, one asked, 'Is this Wendesbury?' 'No,' said the second, 'Thursday.' And the third man said, 'I could do with a drink too.'

Harold relied on Sally or Nick to bring cash and special purchases – 'petits fours from Harrods to make a change from ice cream' – and to collect books he wanted sold at Sotheby's, to keep himself in funds. The books he bought were for him to read, or to send to his grandchildren. His grandchildren wrote to him and he to them. He reported that he now relied on an electric bar fire for heating in the sitting room: the open fireplace, beside which he and Olive had spent many winter evenings reading with their drinks next to them, had been boarded up.

No letter remains from either side of the correspondence for 1983. In 1984 Harold warned his friends that he could no longer keep up a regular correspondence; he intended to send only a 'still alive' letter once or twice a year. Except for Sally and her family, he did not want visitors and to his younger friends – in their seventies – he had become a hermit. His friends in their eighties accepted his need to withdraw and conserve his reduced energy. He continued to read prodigiously; a friend wrote to Sally that five books a week was nothing unusual for him. In his last years he turned to Shakespeare again, whose works were among the 164 books he listed as having been read in 1985. Also included were Hammett's *The Glass Key*, Gaskell's *Sylvia's Lovers*,

Davenport's *Memoirs of a City Radical*, Bone's *Seven Years Solitary*, Agate's *Ego 7* and Kilvert's *Diary Vol II*.

* * *

Kishinev
13.02.84

Dearest Harold!

It is long to me since we have received your letter except the New Year telegram and we have not even received the answer on my letter sent in November.

Have you received the book for Christmas?

We known nothing about you and we are very worried.

We had a very hard and grievous time, my mother died on the 28.12.83. She had cancer, we knew that she had little time to live, but we still believe in a miracle.

We shall write to you as soon as we receive your letter.

We hope that you are well and everything is all right.

Much love from us all.

Yours ever,

Lera

HAROLD W. EDWARDS

ASHMORE GREEN, NEWBURY BERKS, RG16 9ET, ENGLAND

3.4.84

Dearest Lera

I hope that by now you have received my long letter which I sent on 3.3.84. In accordance with this in which I promised to write every month even if I had not heard from you, I send you this.

I am so glad that the books arrived safely so that I feel I can send you many more. I should like very much to know what Marina thought of my selection? Not very modern I know but perhaps better for that?

I note that your mother was born in the same year as Olive. It must have been a great comfort having her living in Kishinev.

You say that you like poetry when it sounds beautiful. Some years ago we had on television a programme that was taken entirely from one that had been televised in Moscow for Russian viewers. One item was a Russian that recited poetry. It was absolutely beautiful, his voice was marvellous and Russian in my opinion is one of the most beautiful languages. I have never forgotten this, although I did not understand a single word. I only wish I could recite one fiftieth as well as he did. I have not read the book by Aitmatov but hope to. I do not know of the work of Bella Akhmadulina, but do not think any has appeared in English.

Sally was very pleased with your remarks about her. She was born in September, but I can assure you that she is not in the least Libran. I think your belief in astrology is because you want to believe in it. A very common human failing. Recently a French scientific journal offered to send free to anyone a 10 page horoscope. To all those that replied an identical horoscope was sent. The receiver was asked to comment. Of the first 150 replies received 90% said that it was quite accurate. I may say that the horoscope was one that had been cast for a very famous criminal.

I think this is enough, so am going to make myself a cup of tea. My love to all of you,

Harold

HAROLD W. EDWARDS

ASHMORE GREEN, NEWBURY BERKS, RG16 9ET, ENGLAND

22.11.84

Dearest Lera

Many thanks for your letter and photograph which I received about two weeks ago. I think that Andrei looks very bright.

I am sorry not to have replied before but have been having trouble with my back. I think that I have sprained it lifting up all the books from the floor after the decorators had finished. Believe it or not, I have been dealing with all these domestic problems since last May. First I had to have the roof repaired as the rain was coming in. Then I had to have the whole place rewired for electricity, as the old wiring was in a dangerous state. This included the bookroom. After that, two bedrooms and the kitchen had to be repapered and painted. After that, the bedrooms had to be fitted with new carpets. This was all for Sally's benefit. I think we have now finally finished. Of course, none of this would be much worry if Olive was still here, and if my hearing was better than it is. All this from being nearly 85.

Am now working in the house, as the bookroom is very damp and cold in the winter. This affects my typewriter which is electric.

So glad that Marina likes Jean Rhys. She is a great favourite of mine. Died not long ago. Her reputation is growing in this country. I do know the work of Adrian Mitchell, and rather like it. Some of his poetry is excellent.

I am not surprised that you enjoyed the film, *Moscow Does Not Believe in Tears.** It is very good in spite of its title.

I agree with you very much about the type of film that is shown on television here. In fact, I think that television is a great mistake. Here people have it on nearly all day. The programmes get worse and worse. Radio was quite a blessing. But no use grumbling. Tell Andrei

**Moscow Does Not Believe in Tears* was directed by Vladimir Menshov in 1979. It tells the story of three women living in Moscow in 1958, it then fast-forwards twenty years to see what has become of them. It won an Oscar for Best Foreign Language Film.

that I saw one of Conan Doyle's plays *The Speckled Band* about 74 years ago, and it frightened me I must admit. Have never forgotten it.

I do not think that Daisy has developed any interest in Russian literature. She is not yet 14. She reads a great deal, likes the theatre and music. Has not been to the Ballet I think. She likes and writes poetry. I find T.S. Eliot rather difficult to understand, but Emily Dickinson is very fine. Forgive this very dull letter. Old age again.

Much love,
Harold

HAROLD W. EDWARDS
ASHMORE GREEN, NEWBURY BERKS, RG16 9ET, ENGLAND

01.05.85

Dearest Lera

Many thanks for your nice letter and the photographs of Andrei, the two cats, and yourself.

I like the idea of your farm on the balcony. I suppose the birds have flown away by now? Can I have a photo of Marina please? How I should like to see her in Moscow or even in England, but all impossible alas.

I spend my time reading far too much, and doing far too little. But I enjoy the garden, the trees, the birds, and especially my two guardian cats.

But oh for the touch of a vanished hand
And the sound of a voice that is still. (Tennyson)

Next life. Who can tell. In the meantime I believe live one life at a time, and worry about the next when you get to it.

Glad that Andrei has read *Robinson Crusoe*. A great book, read by nearly all English children. Daisy still plays the piano. She is also doing very well at school, even in Mathematics.

Much love as always,
Harold

Kishinev
15.06.85

Dearest Harold

It is still difficult to put in words how happy I was to receive your letter and to learn that you are getting on well, and that your sense of humour does not fail you.

Unfortunately Slava does not recover quickly after the operation because his spleen disease was the consequence of the blood disease, which still remains after the operation and of which he knows nothing. So you'd better write as if nothing happens, but of course, this is the most important problem for us nowadays. And as you can imagine our life is not so joyful and pleasant now.

In a month Marina graduates from the Institute. Now she writes her diploma paper which is called 'Semantic analysis of phraseological units belonging to phraseo-semantic field of "disapproval" in Modern English'.

It seems to be rather heavy stuff for me, and I have a rather vague notion of what she is doing. I only know that she has selected all phraseological units expressing 'disapproval' from the idiomatic dictionaries. The total number of units selected was 96. And then she tried to analyse them. But how she analyses them and what for she does all this work I cannot understand. I know only that her room is piled with numerous books on semantics, on problems of imagery, metaphors and so on, and that she is working hard now.

Not long ago she read *A Summer Bird-Cage* by Margaret Drabble, where she wrote about Oxford students and it was very interesting for Marina to read how they work on their graduation essays, about their life and their problems which appear to be common for all students.

Andrei is having his summer vacations and is very happy. He spends all his time outdoors busy saving fledgelings who fall down from the nests. Unfortunately, he does not read much fiction, mainly informative literature about nature. But yesterday he saw a wonderful film over TV about Tom Sawyer after Mark Twain and today I found him reading this book. So now may TV be useful sometimes. We are waiting for your letters very much.

Much love from us all,

Vasha Lera

Kishinev
7.12.1985

Dearest Harold

Many-many thanks for your parcel with jeans, photos, pens and the letter. We liked Sally and Daisy very much. Daisy looks an already grown-up lady. I wonder what is she really like. And, of course we were very glad to receive your letter.

We feel awfully sorry for not writing to you for such a long time. The work at school turns to be not so easy to get used to in several months. It seems that since the first of September there wasn't a single day we didn't talk about our school problems at home.* Slava considers it abnormal to think about other people's children so much. You say that Daisy is getting more difficult to manage. I recall with horror the difficulties I had with Marina at that age. It seemed irremediable then. But, thanks God, when she was 17 everything was over and she became quite a normal, easy-going and sociable girl. Now, when I remind her about certain misunderstanding which has remained especially firmly in my memory she even doesn't remember that such things ever happened in her life. So, I think Sally can be not in despair, for these problems must come to an end, as Daisy is already 15, isn't she?

And you can imagine what difficulties a teacher face when he teaches 30 such teenagers as Daisy is. Marina gives lessons in the 9th form where children born in 1970 study. Now you can understand why every evening we have our 'home deliberations on the problems of children managing'.

But fortunately, we still have some pleasant moments in our lives. We are glad to let you know that on the 8th of February Marina marries. Her future husband is a painter, he is 30, his name is Dmitry (Dima as we call him). He lives in Moscow. They got acquainted 2 years ago

*When Marina came back to Kishinev after finishing her degree at Moscow university, she lived with her parents and she and her mother both found teaching jobs at the same school. Marina taught English, Lera mathematics.

They'll have their marriage in Moscow. But there'll be no marriage in the proper sense of the word. It will be a civic ceremony in a registry office and then they'll invite their closest friends (not more than 15) to his studio where they'll mark this event. I hope that I'll have the good fortune to be present there too. So, if they let me go from my work, Andrei and I shall go to Moscow. After that they'll return back to Kishinev because Marina must work at school till the end of the school year. When we thought of a dress for Marina we faced some unexpected problems. First of all, she said that there would be no 'clouds of drifting tulle, no veils' and so on and so forth. Frankly speaking, I was afraid they were going to get married in jeans. So now I rack my brains over her dress. It's a pity there is no *Burda** magazines which could help me greatly. But these problems are very agreeable, I must say, and to solve them is a real pleasure. Is it true that in England a bride must wear 'something old, something new, something borrowed, something blue'?

Dear Harold, could you write us about your present way of life. Has your girl born a baby? What about your new girl?

Not long ago we have seen over TV an English film *The Invisible Man*. They showed a little English town and we thought of you all the time.

I fully agree with what you say about TV. People are really ready to look into this box as if hypnotized from morning till night. Old teachers say that since television became popular, children's literacy fell down to a very low level, for they have neither time, nor wish to read. And it's Andrei who watches TV most of all in our family. Thanks God, he likes to watch different educational programmes on history and biology, but it's a real trouble for us to switch off the TV when they show a silly film with a lot of shooting and firing. But this summer he got a real present from our television when they showed an English film *Robin Hood*. He is simply crazy about *Robin Hood*. He even doesn't resist when Marina makes him read the adapted variant of this book in English.

**Burda* is the name of a well-established and popular German sewing-pattern magazine.

Alas, I have to finish for an English film *The Evil Under the Sun* after Agatha Cristie with Peter Ustinov in the leading role is beginning over TV.

Hope that everything is all right and you successfully spend winter in your wonderful house.

Much love from us all.

Yours ever,

Lera

P.S. Marina is very thankful to you for the correction for mistakes, for you are probably the only person who can help her now in her language problems.

HAROLD W. EDWARDS

ASHMORE GREEN, NEWBURY BERKS, RG16 9ET, ENGLAND

10 July 1986

Dearest Lera

Was delighted to have your letter of 15th June, as always. I do hope that you had a nice birthday, and received my cablegram?

Congratulations to Marina on becoming a teacher. I would like her to come here and teach me Russian, but I am sorry to write that my poor old brain no longer really does its duty.

Please give Slava my very best wishes for his recovery from that big operation he has had. I am sure it will take a long time, but that it will be all right in the end.

Interesting about Andrei and Mark Twain. He reads this in Russian of course? It is a great book.

My 86th birthday was spent very quietly here with Sally & Daisy. Nick was in Hong Kong, Dylan in Australia and Barnaby at school. Dylan was away for six months in Australia where he has been sheep farming. Nick on business. Both I am glad to say now safely back in London.

The weather has been very bad here for the last six months. Now it is summer at last. My garden has far too many weeds, I can no longer do much work in it. But the trees and shrubs are most magnificent. It is nice to think that Olive and I have planted all of them. We started 50 years ago, a very different world from now.

There is a Chinese saying: There are three things that every man should do before departing from this life. Build a house, plant a garden and have a family. I rejoice that I have been able to do all three.

I think of you all each evening when I have a glass of red wine. This is about 7 o'clock. It is about 10 in Russia, so I like to think you are having the same.

Much love to you all,
Harold

LIFE IN NEWBURY WENT ON AS IT HAD DONE FOR NEARLY fifty years. Harold continued to feed the birds in winter and took over Olive's responsibilities in the greenhouse, watering each plant with the delicacy of a sommelier pouring wine. An elderly part-time gardener now kept the garden from becoming a wilderness.

One night Harold fell on his way to bed. An early-rising neighbour noticed that the lights were on in his cottage and found him lying where he had fallen. An ambulance took him to hospital. Harold hated it there and Sally arranged for a private nursing home to care for him until he recovered. Harold contracted pneumonia and died on 6 October 1986.

An independent-minded scholarly bookseller who, in his seventies, had responded spiritedly to a distant family's loss of freedom, Harold approached the end of his life with characteristic fortitude. In 1983 he had written to Sally, 'I have no desire whatsoever to leave here. It answers its purpose very well, and I am used to the place & to Newbury.

A little house
A garden plot
And I am content
With what I've got.'

Harold as a young man.

Kishinev
October 1986

Dear Sally

We received your telegram of October 10 and immediately sent you the telegram in reply. We sent it to Newbury to Sally Gray.

Not long ago we were informed that it didn't reach you because the address was not complete enough. Perhaps we should have written the name of Edwards.

Dear Sally, I can imagine what you think of us, having received nothing from us. But we didn't know your London address. And how happy we were when I found at last your address in one of Harold's letters.

I want to tell you what your parents meant to us. We considered the acquaintance of them as a real gift of fate. We received their first letter the same year Daisy was born and the last one in Summer of 1986. We even forgot the time when we didn't know Olive and Harold. They were our close friends, beloved relatives of us.

All this time we admired their philosophy of life, their love of life especially at their age. In the most difficult periods of our life we felt their constant support and help.

And we don't know what profession Marina would have chosen, but for Olive and Harold. We wanted greatly our contact to last forever. It always seemed to us that Olive and Harold would live as long as we, but . . . alas!

Dear Sally, we would be very glad if you wrote to us. Once Harold wrote, he'd like his collection of Russian books to be passed to Daisy. We would be very glad if it were so, too.

I hope this letter will reach you at this address, and our contact won't stop forever.

Much love from us all,

Yours, Lera, Marina, Slava, Andrei

Marina's Afterword

A year and a half after Harold's death, in early 1988 when perestroika was transforming the Soviet Union, we received a letter from Sally and Nick explaining that they were coming to Moscow the following summer, and asking if we could meet. June passed and then July, and we still had no news from them. We had to plan our holiday and didn't know what to do. Reading their letter for the hundredth time, I suddenly noticed a telephone number at the top of it, and I decided to phone them. For nearly twenty years every letter from Harold and Olive had their telephone number at the top, but it never occurred to us to phone them – I don't really know why – perhaps it was because to us it was a miracle to receive the letters, coming as they did from some parallel world.

I took my courage in my hands and decided to telephone England. Lera watched me as if I was performing black magic as I dialled the number of the telephone operator. A serious girl answered, sounding very self-important.

'Excuse me, can I call London, please?' I asked her.

'London? What country is it in?'

'Well, Anglia,' I replied, calling England by its Russian name.

'Just a moment.' And a moment later she said, 'Such country as Anglia does not exist, there is Algeria, Angola, and no Anglia.' She hung up.

My mother and I gazed at each other, stupefied, in complete silence – what if she's right, and it really doesn't exist?

Later we tried again, and I asked for Great Britain and London. The sulky operator told me we would be connected within two hours. I remember so clearly those dreadful two hours; we stared at the telephone and chain-smoked. Sometimes we forgot to light our cigarettes, and simply moved them to our mouths and back with shivering fingers, shaking off non-existent ash into the ashtray.

At last the telephone rang. I grabbed the receiver and heard a young female voice saying 'Hello'. My tongue was frozen, and with great difficulty I manage to squeeze out, 'Can I speak to Sally and Nick, please?' 'They are not at home. Can I take a message for them?' I started explaining that I am Marina, from Kishinev, when the voice interrupted me: 'Oh, hi, Marina. This is Daisy. Can you wait for a sec. I will close the door.' She went away and I could hear cars driving past, the noise of a London street. It was incredible.

Sally and Nick called us that evening and explained that with perestroika, Moscow had become the fashionable tourist destination, and its hotels were booked up a year in advance. They had written to tell us this, but these letters never reached us. They hoped to come in January 1989 instead. Three months later, I was woken up at midnight by a telephone call.

'Hi, Marina. This is Nick. We're coming to Moscow in January, and I'm off to the States tomorrow. Do you need anything special from there that I could bring out to you in Russia?' He emphasised the word 'special' as though we should both understand what we were talking about.

'No thank you, I do not need anything,' I said.

'Are you sure?' he insisted. 'Maybe you want me to meet some of your friends and to bring back something from them?'

'Oh, no, thanks,' I kept saying, hardly realising what was going on.

The next morning, I was sure it was a dream, but when I checked with Lera, she confirmed that Nick had called, offering to bring us back something from the States.

Finally, on a cold winter's day in 1989, we ran across the snow to meet Sally and Nick in front of the Cosmos hotel in Moscow. It was one of the most emotional days of my life. There was much hugging and kissing and crying and then we talked for hours and hours. I remembered that strange telephone call, and apologised to Nick for sounding half-asleep. Nick looked blank and said he'd never rung me in November in the middle of the night. He looked at me and said,

'Marina, did the man you talked to sound like me? Did he speak good English, or did he have an accent?' We realised what had happened. Even then, in the fourth year of perestroika, the KGB were still up to their old tricks.

We took Sally and Nick to our friends' homes, and we had real Russian parties with lots of drinking and talking about life and death, love and art. When, as usual, we would run short of drink, my friends would go out to find a taxi in the middle of the night and buy a bottle from the driver. Sally and Nick could not understand why this scheme was so complicated, and why we didn't just go to a bar. We took it for granted that there were no bars open, and it was common knowledge that taxi drivers had second businesses as dealers in black-market vodka.

At our final dinner in Moscow Sally and Nick asked us if we could come to England. They explained that they would cover all our costs and that they were insisting on that because if there was any small hole in the sky through which Harold and Olive were looking at us, they would be really happy.

So in the Summer of 1989, my mother, my brother and I boarded the Moscow–Hook-van-Holland train, which took twenty-four hours to cross the USSR and Poland and to enter East Germany. The scenes behind the window became very different, and in the middle of the night, as our train slowly passed under a bridge, I saw the Berlin Wall. East German border guards woke us up, asked us to go out into the corridor and pedantically searched through every inch of our compartment while we stood there in our nightgowns.

At three o'clock in the morning we arrived in West Berlin. While the train was standing at the station I pulled down the window and leaned out of it. I wanted to smell freedom. I was smiling idiotically from happiness, like someone who had thought they were sentenced to a life term but had been suddenly released.

On the platform near my window, a few teenagers were standing and speaking rather loudly. Sipping beer from their cans, they were very drunk and could hardly stand. One of them noticed me. He looked at the plate on our carriage saying Moscow–Hook-van-Holland, stared directly into my face and said 'Russische Schwein' (Russian swine). I did not take offence. At that very moment I realised that for these people in the West I am not Marina Aidova, who as a child always expected KGB searches at home, who felt humiliated for not being able to speak out about what she really thought. For these people I wasn't the representative of the Russia Harold loved so much. For this boy and many others, I was the embodiment of Soviet power that dominated the world for seventy years. It never occurred to me that someone could possibly associate me with this Soviet Russia, but being Russian, and being proud of being Russian, I have to accept this too.

For the first few days in London I felt as if I were in a film. Nothing felt real. On the first morning we woke up rather late and Sally and Nick had already left for work. Sally had left a packet of muesli on the table, a bottle of orange juice and some milk for breakfast. She had left a note with her office number, and told us to eat whatever we could find in the refrigerator and the cupboards. We examined the muesli thoroughly, but couldn't decide how we were meant to eat it, so in the end we had to telephone.

'Can I speak to Sally, please?' I asked a friendly receptionist who answered the telephone.

'Sorry, but we have no Sally here.'

'Don't you have Sally Gray here?'

'We have Mr and Mrs Gray. But Mrs Gray's name is Amanda.'

I was stunned, and wondered whether they allowed polygamy in the United Kingdom; how could Nick have two wives, one called Sally and the other Amanda? My head was spinning when Nick picked up the phone, but I dared not ask him about his second wife. He explained that muesli didn't have to be cooked, but was eaten with milk or juice.

We followed his instructions and took the first spoonful. 'Goodness gracious,' I thought, 'in England, where they've never had food shortages, they eat this strange stuff as if they were canaries or hamsters.'

Initially, I was really worried about the mysterious Amanda, and feared I had discovered Nick's secret double life by accident: I had stumbled on, as English people so vividly put it, 'a skeleton in the cupboard'. Finally, I plucked up my courage and asked about this

Amanda person. Nick burst into laughter and explained that when Sally had begun her career as a model, her boss felt that she needed a far more glamorous name and chose Amanda. Only Harold and Olive kept calling her by the name they had given her at her birth, and wrote to us – the friends they had never seen – so much about his daughter Sally and her family.

The person who was probably most put out by our stay in England was poor Daisy, who was seventeen at the time. She still lived with her parents and had to deal with these crazy Russians who had invaded her house. What really shocked me about Daisy were her clothes. She wore jeans that were full of holes and a sweater that was probably ten sizes too big, with her fingers hidden in its sleeves. 'How come,' I thought to myself, 'Harold and Olive sent us so many beautiful clothes for so many years, and couldn't even get something decent for their own granddaughter?' Sally caught my astonished glance and explained that these were the most fashionable jeans – Levi 501s – and that they were also very expensive.

'Are jeans without these holes cheaper than the ones with them?' I asked.

'Oh yes, much cheaper!'

'But why can't you buy cheap jeans and then make your own holes?'

'Because then they wouldn't have this tiny red label saying "Levi 501" on them.'

I looked at her in complete silence and asked no more questions.

As I write this, my sixteen-year-old son Anton has come home from his computer class. He's wearing a sweater that is very similar to the one that Daisy had so many years ago and huge jeans that would fit his father. But I must admit that I bought them myself, and that now I find this style rather attractive.

The gulf between my childhood and my children's is huge. When I was in England for the first time in 1989, I went to Madame Tussauds and I recognised most of the waxwork figures, such as Charles Dickens and Margaret Thatcher, but there was one everybody was taking photos of, and I had no idea who this was. I asked a Japanese woman who this was, and she looked at me and she said, 'This is James Bond.' I had never seen a James Bond film. When Nick and Sally heard about this, they took me to one and I found it so scary that I was sat with closed eyes through half the film because I couldn't stand all the scenes with sharks. We didn't watch these types of film in the Soviet Union.

How can I explain to my children what it was like to live in the country called the USSR, a country no longer to be found on any modern map of the world? When they watch films about the Soviet Union – films about children being Young Pioneers, Young Komsomols – they just cannot imagine how it was. They can't understand how we could have had those parades, and demonstrations for May 1st or commemorating the October Revolution. 'Why did you join in?' they ask, and we try to explain that you could not avoid it, you had no choice. It is very difficult for them to understand how we lived. When they were younger and we would tell them about the Soviet Union sometimes they'd say, 'And did you see Lenin?'

Once, when he was eight, we asked Anton where he would like to travel to if he had a time machine. He thought for a while and then answered, 'I would probably go to the Soviet Union.' We had expected all sorts of answers – ancient Egypt, the times of knights or dinosaurs. Why the Soviet Union?

'All of you lived there: Mum, Dad, Grandfather and Grandmother, everyone except me. And I would be curious to see what it felt like,' Anton replied.

Oh, what it felt like to be there. I remember when I was eight, walking home from my ballet classes on a warm spring evening. I wore the red Marks & Spencer suit with bell-bottomed trousers that Olive had sent to me; its golden buttons sparkled in the fading sunlight. I probably looked rather bizarre, and people turned round to look at me because no one else had anything like it in Kishinev. A car pulled up and a young girl ran out and asked me to stop for a minute so she could examine my suit and remember the pattern. Mum waited for me at home, faced with the decision of what to buy with the fifty kopeks she had left that week – a loaf of bread or a bottle of milk.

How right was the Russian poet, Tyutchev, who once said:

Blessed are they who sojourned here
In this world's fateful hours.

How blessed are we who in those fateful hours were found by a modest bookworm from the small town of Newbury in England. He thought that most of all he loved books, but it turned out that he loved life and people much more than all the books of this world put together.

Marina Aidova, Chisinau, 2006

CATALOGUE NUMBER 100

BOOKS IN ENGLISH PRINTED ABROAD

H. W. EDWARDS BOOKSELLERS LTD.
ASHMORE GREEN, NEWBURY, BERKS.
ENGLAND

WHEN LERA, MARINA AND ANDREI went to England in 1989 they visited Harold and Olive's house. Lera wrote:

My fingers trembled and my heart ached because our beloved friends were not any more in that house and in this world. I sat in Harold's library and imagined how many years ago he wrote there a short postcard:

With love from Newbury
Berks
England

Postscript

Slava and Lera are still living in Kishinev, now Chisinau. Lera works full-time in a school teaching mathematics, and Slava continues to pursue his interest in philosophy and religion. Marina has two children, Anton, aged sixteen and Liza, aged fourteen. Marina is an English translator in Moldova and throughout Eastern Europe working for the World Bank and IMF among others. Andrei moved to Moscow in 1992. He is married with two children, and runs a business there. Sally and Nick live in Scotland, London and France. They have seven grandchildren, and maintain close links with Marina and her family in Moldova.

ПОЧТА СССР
ПОЧТА СССР
20 КОП
ПРОЛЕТАРИИ ВСЕХ СТРАН, СОЕДИНЯЙТЕСЬ!

NEWBURY
6 30PM
8 MCH
1974
BERKS.
5P

Chronology

1900	Harold is born.
1912	Olive is born.
1917	7 November: Bolshevik coup d'état.
1932	Harold goes to the Soviet Union for the first time.
1933	Slava is born.
1938	Lera is born.
1940	Bessarabia is invaded by Soviet troops following the Molotov–Ribbentrop pact and becomes the Moldavian Soviet Socialist Republic, one of the fifteen republics of the USSR.
1953	5 March: Stalin dies.
1956	Nikita Khrushchev denounces Stalin at the Twentieth Congress of the Communist Party. Thousands of Stalin's victims are rehabilitated and start returning from the Gulag. The full extent of Stalin's terrors becomes known.
1963	Marina is born.
1964	Khrushchev is overthrown by Leonid Brezhnev; there is increased KGB activity once more.
1966	Slava is arrested.
1967	Slava is tried and sentenced for five years for anti-Soviet activities.
1971	April: list of names of children of political prisoners appears in the *Chronicle of Current Events*. June: Harold sends the first postcard to Kishinev. December: Slava is released.
1970–74	Edward Heath, Conservative Prime Minister, clashes with the unions.

1973 The miners' work-to-rule policy leads to power cuts and three-day working week.

1974–6 Harold Wilson's third term as Labour Prime Minister.

1975 Referendum over entry to the EEC causes a bitter split in both Labour and Conservative parties.

1978–9 Widespread public sector strikes culminate in the Winter of Discontent under Labour Prime Minister James Callaghan.

1975 Andrei is born.

1979–90 Margaret Thatcher is Prime Minister.
March 1984: the miners begin a year-long strike but are outfaced by Thatcher.

1981 Olive dies in November.

1982–4 Yuri Andropov leads the Soviet Union for fifteen months.

1984–5 Konstantin Chernenko, at 74 the oldest of all Secretary Generals, rules for thirteen months and promotes his young successor, Mikhail Gorbachev.

1985–91 Mikhail Gorbachev, General Secretary of the Communist Party, introduces democratic reforms; glasnost (openness) and perestroika (restructuring) result in the end of Soviet Communism.

1986 Harold dies in October.

1989 January: Marina meets Sally and Nick for the first time in Moscow.
Summer: Marina, Lera and Andrei go to England for the first time to stay with Sally and Nick.
November: fall of the Berlin Wall, the most potent symbol of the end of the Cold War.

Excerpts from Slava's Amnesty International case file

15th May 1970

Vyacheslav AIDOV USSR

Investigator case
Date of birth unknown.
Occupation unknown.

Probably arrested in 1967, but could be as early as 1966.
Tried in 1967.
Attempt to organise an 'illegal underground printing press'.
Sentenced to a period in a labour camp, length of term unknown.

Article 70 of RSFSE Criminal Code, see attached sheet.
BSSE, Mordovskaya, USSR. st, Barashevo, uchrazhdeniye Zh/Kh 385/3.
State of health unknown, but see below.
Family details unknown.
Nine-yr old daughter, Marina
J. Kishinyov, Ul Lenina 64Kv.87.

Very little is known about the circumstances which led to Aidov's arrest and conviction in 1967. We do know that the affair involved a printing press. It is worth mentioning that in the Soviet Union today it is extremely difficult, or even impossible, to obtain a private Xerox or duplicating machine of any kind. A few organisations such as universities, libraries, etc., do have them, but only the most reliable employees are allowed to use them. Therefore, anyone who is found to possess an unauthorised machine, or who is caught using an official machine for an unofficial purpose, is immediately suspect.

Whilst we do not know a great deal about Aidov's case, we do have some details on what is happening to him in the labour camp to which he has been sent. He is mentioned in issue No. 11 of the Moscow underground journal called *Chronicle of Current Events*, December 1969. Here there is an article about the political camps in the Mordovian Republic, east of Moscow. A great many political prisoners are held in these camps, and there is much dissatisfaction and unrest, often leading to the organisation of hunger strikes and protests by the prisoners.

Vyacheslav Aidov is in Camp 3, and he has participated in several recent protests in this camp. For example, a fellow-prisoner, Berg, who was arrested and convicted in the same case as Aidov, was recently sent unjustly to the camp punishment block. Aidov and other prisoners organised a hunger strike which forced the camp authorities to release Berg from the punishment cell. After this hunger strike, Aidov was apparently summoned to an interview with the camp authorities, but he was too weak to attend – we are told that he was unable to walk. For his failure to obey this order, Aidov was himself immediately put into the punishment block. His friends organised another hunger strike, and Aidov was released from his punishment cell. Among the strikers was Berg, the prisoner convicted with Aidov in the affair of the printing press.

Soon after this Berg was removed from the camp altogether and taken to Vladimir prison – a prison with a notoriously severe regime. Aidov and other prisoners in Berg's former camp protested at this by declaring yet another hunger strike which lasted three days. While all this does not shed much light on Aidov's case, it does show him to be a man of principles and a campaigner for justice inside the prison camps. Prisoners like Berg and Aidov are obviously a source of considerable embarrassment to the camp authorities. It is therefore not surprising that many camp prisoners who are active in strikes and other forms of protest are eventually removed from the camps and put into solitary cells in some other prison so that they should not influence other convicts. This is what happened to Berg, and it is quite likely that Aidov will suffer the same fate if he goes on protesting and organising strikes in the camp.

Amnesty has no information regarding the length of Aidov's sentence. But convictions under Article 70 are considered very serious, and often mean long sentences, the maximum being 7 years.

We are treating Aidov as an investigation case at the moment, since not enough is known about the circumstances of his arrest and conviction. But it is significant that he was sentenced under Article 70 (see attached sheet), one of the Articles most frequently used to justify the arrest of prisoners of conscience in the Soviet Union.

Ideas for Action

Groups might like to inquire into the reasons for Aidov's arrest, since we know only that the case involved underground printing (see above). It would appear that Aidov had committed no offence whatsoever, and was merely using his human right to freedom of expression – guaranteed, incidentally by the Soviet Constitution itself. We do not know anything about the content of the material Aidov was alleged to have printed, or to have intended to print.

Groups should stress also that Aidov is apparently being victimised for his quite reasonable protests and demands for justice within the prison camps, and his loyalty to his friend and fellow-convict, Berg.

Letters could be sent to as many Soviet authorities as possible (see attached list of addresses), and also to the camp authorities at Aidov's camp in Mordovia, address:

SSSR,
Mordovskaya SSR,
St. Baraschevo,
Uchreshedeniye Zh/Kh 385/3
Lagernoi Administrataii.

'During all the time I spent in the labour camp and prison, I felt completely isolated, hardly any information penetrated our cell and we all thought this system would go on for thousands of years. I had absolutely no awareness that the outside world was interested in Soviet political prisoners. I'd heard about Amnesty International – but I didn't think it could possibly have any effect on my life or my family.'

Harold believed that everyone is entitled to the widest possible freedom to make his own way in life. He was scathing about the inhumanity of religious and racial intolerance and being himself an ardent free-thinker, he readily identified with people persecuted for their beliefs or deprived of their freedom of speech. What Amnesty International stands for, he and Olive believed in all their lives.

Amnesty International

Amnesty International is a movement of ordinary people from across the world standing up for humanity and human rights. Our purpose is to protect individuals wherever justice, fairness, freedom and truth are denied. We work in two main ways: we try to make people aware of human rights and we oppose abuses of human rights. Campaigning on behalf of victims of human rights abuses has been central to Amnesty International's work since we started in 1961. Through Amnesty International there are many ways you can protect individuals at risk of violations of their human rights – including prisoners of conscience, human rights defenders, the 'disappeared', and those at risk of unfair trials, torture, abuses perpetrated by companies, and denial of the right to education, for example. One simple but effective way to take action, at the heart of Amnesty International's work, is writing letters. Letters do make a difference: whether they bring hope and support to prisoners of conscience and their families, or put pressure on governments and countries to change their policies. As Lera said:

'It is difficult to explain how greatly our life changed after that first post card. I never felt lonely any more . . . Harold and Olive's letters changed my life – they gave me hope.'

To join Amnesty International, and to find out more about our work and how you can get involved, please contact:

Amnesty International UK
The Human Rights Action Centre
17–25 New Inn Yard
London EC2A 3EA
Tel: 020 7033 1500 Email: sct@amnesty.org.uk
Or visit us online at: www.amnesty.org.uk.

Acknowledgements

We would like to thank Nick and Amanda Gray for their enormous help and encouragement in editing the letters; for finding the original material, for writing commentaries about Harold and Olive where letters were lost and for providing so many of the photographs. This book would not have happened without them. We would also like to thank Natalia Cebotari, Donna Edgerton, David Edmonds, Richard Haas, John Horsbrugh-Porter, Vanessa Howe-Jones, Nick McNulty, Nadezhda Novikova, Nicky Parker, Maggie Paterson, Allan Slipher, John Sutcliffe and Mark Sutcliffe, who all contributed greatly in individual ways to this book, and whose help was invaluable.

* * *

The excerpt from *Fat Sasha and the Urban Guerilla* by David Bonavia was reprinted with the kind permission of Judy Bonavia-Boillat.

* * *

Our grateful thanks to all those who contributed illustrations but especially Amanda and Nick Gray (photographs on pages, x, xv, 17, 58, 71, 82, 90, 137, 142, 172, 200, 216, 217, 222, 241, 250 and 261), and the Aidov family (photographs on pages xiii, xix, xx, 2, 27, 35, 42, 50, 55, 75, 92, 98, 113, 121, 130, 158, 181, 186, 191, 204, 211, 260). Thanks also to Amnesty International (page 40) and to Scala for permission to use Vincent Van Gogh's painting, *Prisoners Exercising* (page 44 copyright Scala, Florence).

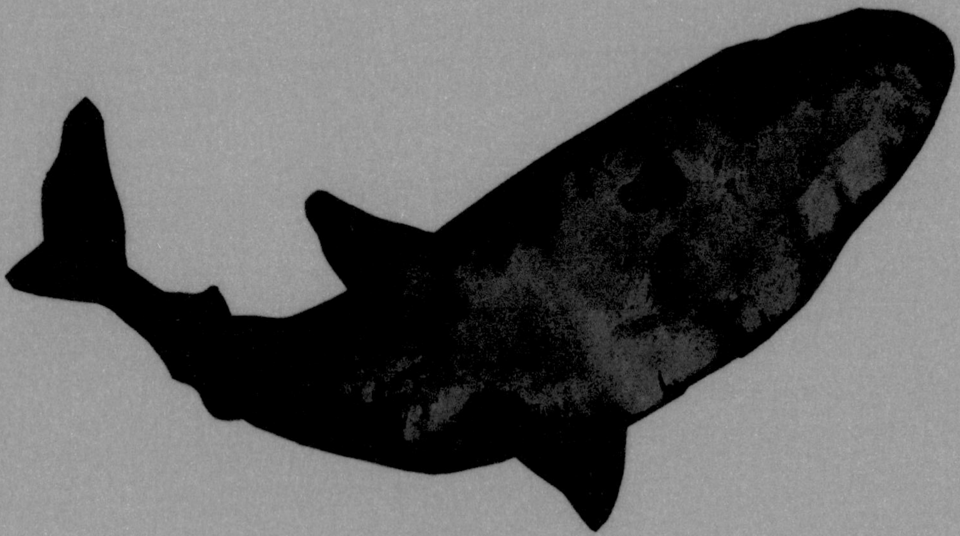

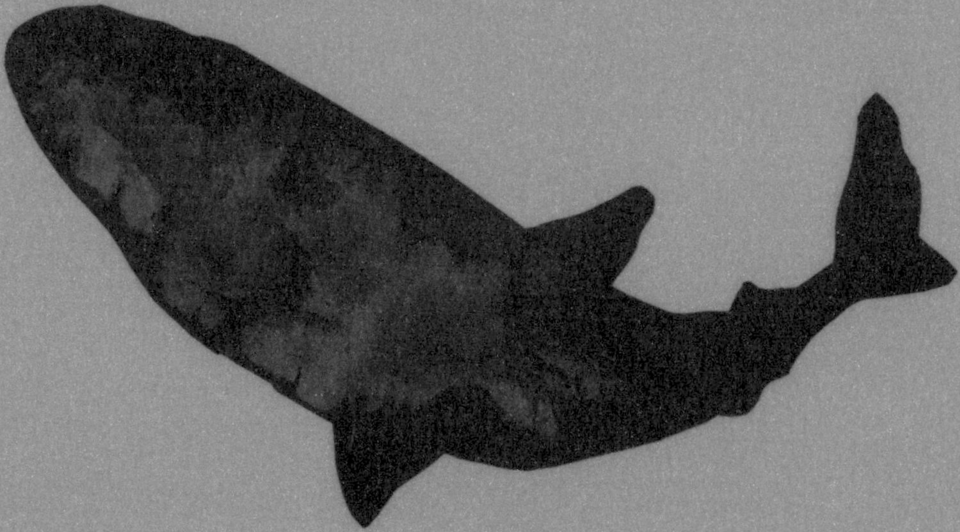

Praise for
JULIA AND THE SHARK:

'Tom de Freston's stunning illustrations perfectly complement the poetry of Kiran Millwood Hargrave's story'
Cressida Cowell

'A rich, immersive and wondrous journey, through deep darkness to hope and light'
Sophie Anderson

'What a gorgeous book – calm, funny, heartfelt, wise, full of the quiet and force of the sea'
Ross Montgomery

'I fell in love with the tale itself, the setting (I do love a lighthouse!), the characters and the little details – it's a beautiful, forceful storm of a book'
Emma Carroll

'There are no wasted words in this book. Like a seashell, or a flying bird, it is uncluttered and vital. The illustrations, by Tom de Freston, are mesmerising. I loved it.'
Hilary McKay

'INCREDIBLE. Poignant and lyrical and beautiful, it's my favourite of Kiran's books so far and that is saying something. Tom's stunning artwork just brings it to a whole other level'

Cat Doyle

'Truly extraordinary ... it will redefine what a children's book can look like, in a way that adults will ooh and ahh over, and children will love because the story is wonderful and the art is amazing. It is the kind of book that you will want to have on your shelves and treasure. I can't wait for the world to fall in love with *Julia and the Shark*!'

Katherine Webber Tsang

Praise for

KIRAN MILLWOOD HARGRAVE:

'Hargrave has a real and rare talent for combining poetic prose with compelling, page-turning storytelling'

Guardian

JULIA AND THE SHARK

Other titles by
KIRAN MILLWOOD HARGRAVE:

The Deathless Girls

The Girl of Ink & Stars

The Island at the End of Everything

The Way Past Winter

A Secret of Birds & Bone

AND FOR ADULTS:

The Mercies

Kiran Millwood Hargrave

JULIA AND THE SHARK

with
Tom de Freston

Orion

ORION CHILDREN'S BOOKS

First published in Great Britain in 2021 by Hodder & Stoughton Limited

1 3 5 7 9 10 8 6 4 2

A CIP catalogue record for this book is available from the British Library.

ISBN 978 1 510 10778 6

Printed and bound by Livonia Print, Latvia

The paper and board used in this book are made from wood from responsible sources.

FSC www.fsc.org MIX Paper from responsible sources FSC® C104740

Orion Children's Books
An imprint of
Hachette Children's Group
Part of Hodder and Stoughton
Carmelite House
50 Victoria Embankment
London EC4Y 0DZ

An Hachette UK Company
www.hachette.co.uk

www.hachettechildrens.co.uk

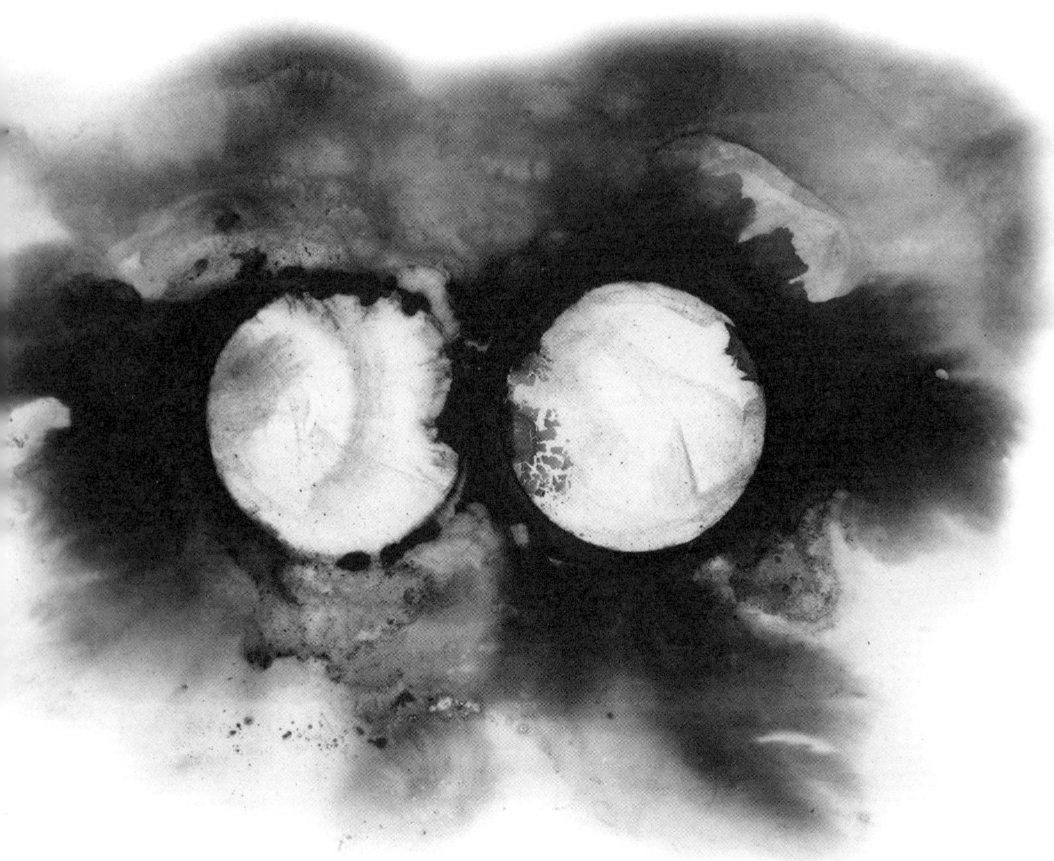

for Rosemary & Lavender,

who made possible all that comes after

ONE

There are more secrets in the ocean than in the sky. Mum told me when the water is still and the stars prick its surface, some of the sky's secrets fall into the sea and add to its mysteries. When we lived in the lighthouse, I hauled my long-handled crab net over the balcony railing and tried to catch them, but I never did.

Other nights, when storms turned everything upside down and hurled water and sky at each other, the spray from the waves reached the beam. It came through the grates at the high windows to scatter across the floor of Dad's office. I listened to the puddles in the morning, but I never heard anything. No messages fallen from the clouds. Perhaps the secrets drowned in the night, like a fish in air.

My name is Julia. This is the story of the summer I lost my mum, and found a shark older than trees. Don't worry though, that doesn't spoil the ending.

I'm named after my grandmother, who I never met, and also after a computer program that my dad likes. I am ten years and two hundred and three days old. I had to ask my dad to work that out for me, because numbers are not my favourite. Words are. You can make numbers into words, but you can't make words into numbers, and so words must be more powerful, mustn't they?

Dad disagrees. He works all in numbers. That's why we ended up at that old lighthouse in Shetland. He went to program it, to make it work automatically. A lighthouse keeper used to live there, and the flame was made of gas and sparks, not a one thousand watt tungsten light bulb. Gas and sparks, like stars.

It's closer to Norway than England, there. Closer to Norway than Edinburgh, even. To find Shetland on a map, you start at our home in Hayle in Cornwall and you move your finger diagonally up, up and to the right, until you find islands scattered out like ink splatter. That's Orkney. You go even further and there's another scatter. Shetland. It's an archipelago, which means a group of islands, and we went to one called Unst.

Unst, Shetland, Scotland.

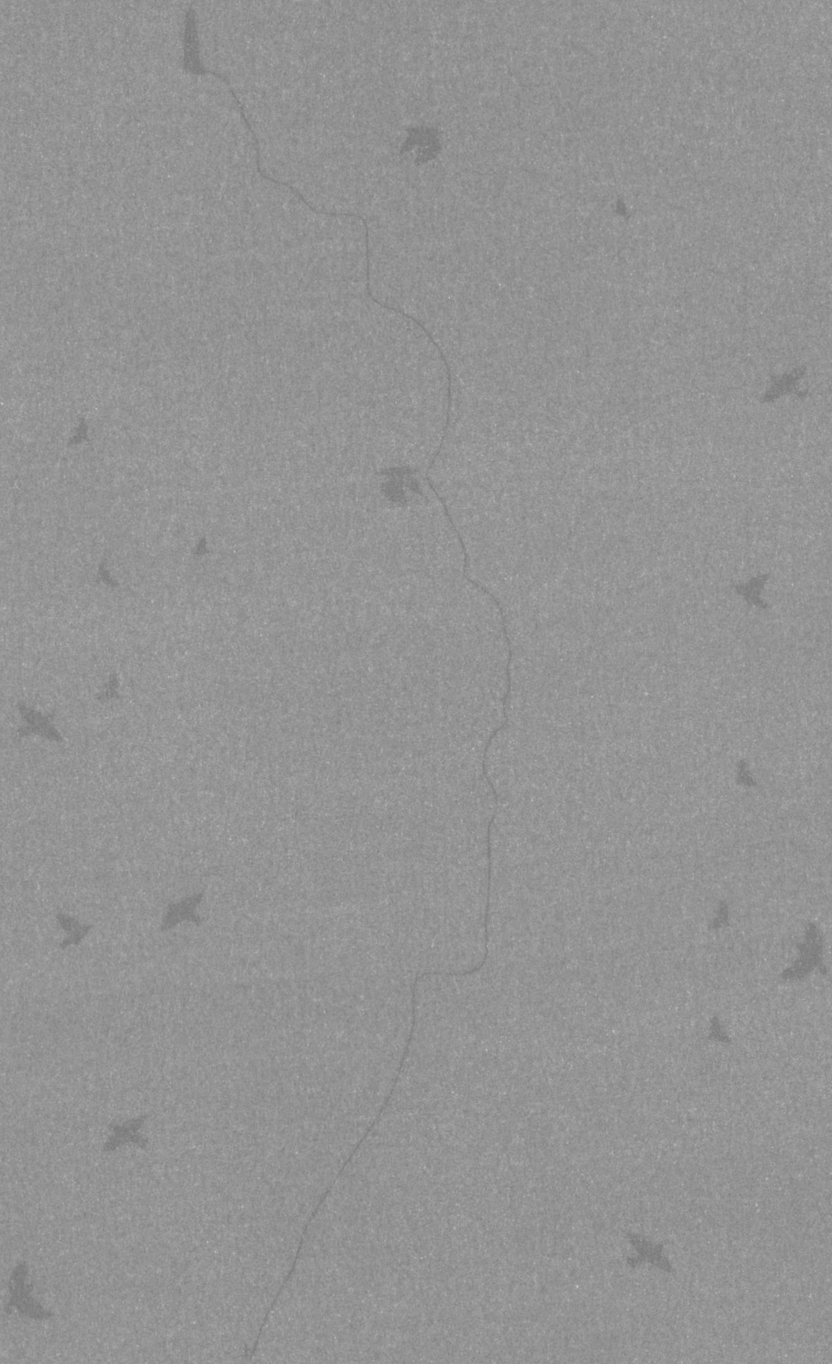

I like how people there say it like it's got a whole other bunch of letters in it. Sco-awt-lund. That's another thing about words: there's space in them. They change according to whose mouth they're coming out of. Sometimes they change so much in mine they become something else entirely, but Dad says these are called lies.

There's no room for that with numbers. Even the 'language' of numbers, which my dad works with, is called 'binary code'. If you look up 'binary' in the *Oxford English Dictionary* it says:

(adj.) Relating to, composed of, or involving two things.

Two things. Right and wrong. True and false. Where's the space in that?

Mum works with numbers too, but words are her favourite. She's a scientist, which means you need to like both. Numbers help you keep track of things, but only words can help you explain them.

In Cornwall she studied algae, a special kind that cleans the water of any bad chemicals and perhaps one day even breaks up some kinds of plastic. You've probably seen the footage of turtles with plastic up their noses. I did once and it's still there in my head. I wish I could forget it, but perhaps it's fair I can't. Closing your eyes doesn't make things like that go away.

When Dad got offered this job in Shetland it was Mum who suggested us all moving there for the summer. Because while her algae work was important and good for the turtles, moving to Unst meant she would be closer to what she really wanted to study: the biggest things that lived in the coldest seas.

She studied whales at university, and wrote a very long essay about a whale that goes around the world alone because it sings at a different frequency to other whales. It can hear them, but they can't hear it. I understand a little how that whale feels. Ever since Mum got ill, I feel like I've been screaming inside. Yet her favourite animal in all the world wasn't a whale, but a shark. A Greenland shark. And because it was hers, that summer it became mine too.

I like how words are gentler than numbers. I could make everything go back to how it used to be, if I didn't care about this being a true story. If I had to tell you in numbers about my mum, I would have to tell you the most important numbers about her now are 93875400, which is what's on her hospital bracelet. But 93875400 doesn't tell you anything about Mum. Only words can do that. And even they fail me sometimes.

I'm getting tangled. That's the problem with words, and it's the same as the best thing about them. They can mean so many things,

and each word has so many branches, so many roots, if you're not sure of the route you can get lost like Little Red Riding Hood in the wood. So I have to go back a bit. I have to remember where I'm trying to get to. And where I'm trying to get to, is Mum.

Reaching Shetland took four days. That's longer than it takes to fly to Australia, which is the other side of the world, and back again. Twice. I didn't think it was possible for anything to take that long now that we have aeroplanes and bullet trains, but we had to travel there by car because we have books that are too heavy to take on planes, and a cat called Noodle who is too loud to take on trains.

She's called Noodle because she was so tiny when she was a kitten she fitted in the empty instant noodle pots Dad ate for lunch. My mum washed them and kept them to plant tomato seeds in because she hated throwing away plastic. You've probably heard of pirates having ship's cats and that is what Noodle is. Mum used to take her out to the algae farms and she'd sit at the front of the boat and hiss at the sea.

There was no question of leaving Noodle behind in Cornwall, so we bought her a special crate to travel in. It was made for dogs and took up nearly all the back seats, so I was squashed to one side with the tomato pots by my feet. Dad fitted out the crate so

that it had levels for her to climb in, and a litter tray in its own little compartment so she would have privacy when she needed it.

'I hope she doesn't poo,' said Mum. 'It stinks when she poos.'

'It stinks when anyone poos,' said Dad fairly.

I'm sorry that the first time you're hearing my parents' voices they're talking about poo.

Noodle was too busy meowing very loudly to use the litter tray much. This is a superpower cats have: they can hold their wee a really long time. They are unlike humans in this, and other ways. We stopped loads for toilet breaks and for Mum and Dad to swap driving. They put an audiobook on. It was called *The Crowstarver* by Dick King-Smith and it was very sad and soon we were all crying.

I traced our progress on the road map my parents didn't use any more because they have a TomTom. Maps are more interesting than screens, I think. They show you the whole picture and make roads look like veins or rivers.

We spent the first night in the West Midlands, at a B&B run by a fussy couple who allowed dogs but not cats. It was too late to find anywhere else, so Dad stayed with Noodle in the car while I slept with Mum in the big bed. It had a mattress made of water, which apparently was popular in the olden days.

'It's like sleeping in the belly of a whale,' said Mum, shifting around. 'All these gurgles and grunts.'

'You think?'

'I know. I've heard inside a whale. One swallowed a transmitter we were using to capture them singing. It was louder than the sea in there.' Her breathing went all calm like it always did when she talked about the sea.

'Are you excited for the whales in Shetland?'

'Yes.' I could hear the smile in her voice. 'There are so many kinds. *Balaenoptera musculus. Physeter macrocephalus, Monodon monoceros, Delphinapterus leucas.*'

'Blue whales, sperm whales, narwhals and belugas,' I reeled off, translating her Latin words into ones I could actually pronounce. 'It sounds made for you.'

'Yes. And for you. It's going to be the best summer ever.'

'Will we see otters?'

'Unlikely, but possible.' Mum never answered questions like that with 'yes' or 'no'. She was a scientist, and that meant leaving room for the impossible. 'Though I'll be travelling north, out to the Norwegian Sea. There's rumours of a Greenland shark around there.'

I hoped for a story, a story about the Greenland shark. She's been telling me about sea creatures since I was little, and I've collected them in this small yellow notebook with a daisy on the front, strung them on a thread like a necklace, each fact shining and precious. But she yawned again, and I could tell from her not

using fancy words any more that she was close to falling asleep.

I rolled over and all I could see were her teeth glinting in the dark. It was like the rest of her face wasn't there and I touched it just to make sure. I can remember her face that night, feel it under my fingers. Words can be time travel, too.

We didn't stay for breakfast at the stuffy B&B, and Dad was very grumpy because Noodle had pooed and it made his pyjamas smell. Mum hung them outside the door and closed the window to hold them in place but they escaped on the M5 just outside Birmingham and flew under the wheels of a lorry. They had a little fight, which took us to the M6 to Manchester, then the M62 past Manchester, then the M6 again.

By this time I was very bored of the M6 and also of the names roads have. Wouldn't it be better if they had names like in books? 'Elven-way', 'Old North Road', or 'Yellow Brick Road'? That would have made the last paragraph a lot more interesting for you and me both.

TWO

'Is that it?'

We were sitting in the car on the quay in the village of Gutcher, on the island of Yell, looking at the tiny boat that was going to take us to Unst.

By now we had driven nearly a thousand miles, and had taken one long ferry ride from Aberdeen to Lerwick, a town on Mainland, Shetland. If you still have your map about you, it'll probably be a speck. But it's the biggest speck in Shetland, so that's where the ferries from mainland Scotland arrive.

What I had seen of Shetland so far was very green and very wet, the clouds hanging so low over us I felt sure I could have touched them. Dad unfolded himself from the car as soon as

we stopped, and began doing these squat bounces he does every twenty minutes when he's working at the computer. I slid down in my seat, but at least there was no one my age around.

'Sausage roll?' Mum twisted round, holding one out to me. She had a tub of them on her lap, the size of a paint can. She said it's best to buy in bulk if you have to buy plastic. She liked the really cheap, dry sausage rolls where the meat is pink or grey and occasionally you find a little lump that it's best to spit out. Dad says they're made from all the bits they can't sell in a butcher's. He won't eat them.

I took one while Mum stretched in her seat. I heard her neck click. She was used to being outside and moving. She had this really heavy-duty yellow mac, the kind oil rig workers wear, and she went out in all weathers. Even when she was on her computer she rested it on the kitchen counter and typed standing up.

'The Greenland shark,' I said.

'Mmm?' said Mum, her mouth full of sausage rolls.

'You said about the Greenland shark, at the B&B. Will you find one, do you think?'

Mum chewed thoughtfully, then checked her watch. 'Want to stretch your legs?'

'As long as we don't have to stand with Dad.'

Now he was swinging his arms from side to side so they hit his bum and legs. I could hear him making little huffing noises even

over the wind. Mum snorted with laughter. 'Agreed.'

We got out and Mum fetched our coats from the boot. Mine is red, and next to her yellow and Dad's green we look like a set of traffic lights.

The wind nudged us in the direction of a small, drenched bench on the stone quayside. Mum plonked herself down. She doesn't mind being damp: it comes with the territory of being a marine biologist.

'How you holding up, my J?'

'Fine.'

'It's been a long journey,' she said.

'I know,' I said. 'I was there.'

She looked around and jumped when she saw me, pretending surprise. 'So you were!'

I giggled. 'The Greenland shark.'

'*Somniosus microcephalus*.'

'I've been reading more about it on Dad's phone.'

'How did you get signal up here?'

'It says that they live to five hundred and seventeen years old.'

Mum shook her head.

'It's not true?'

'It's not proven. It could be true, but they've never found one that old. I think the oldest was about four hundred.'

I stared at her. 'Four *hundred*?'

'Yep.' Mum often did this: dispensed amazing facts like she was reeling off a shopping list. Her knowledge was something she wore as easily as her coat. 'There's room for error. Normally with sharks it's easy to age them. Their bones grow rings, like trees. But Greenland sharks, their bones are too soft for that. So they dated the crystals in its eyes.'

My brain felt like it was stretching, and I made myself remember these facts to put in my yellow book. 'But that's mad!'

Mum flinched. She hated that word. She said mad people were only misunderstood. 'It's clever.'

'How do they get so old?'

'They're slow,' she said. The wind was blowing her hair across her face but she didn't brush it away. I still remember that, how it was loose though usually she tied it back. That day it half-hid her from sight, so that I thought she looked like a seer from a story, giving prophecy.

'Slow?' I wrinkled my nose. 'So?'

'So they move so slowly, they age slowly. They sort of cheat time. They grow one centimetre a year. You know that's this much?' She held up her hand, her fingers nearly touching. 'It's not much at all.'

'Do you think I'll live a long time, even though I'm growing fast?'

Mum laughed and pulled me to her. She smelt of the rubber of

her coat, and of fresh air and sausage rolls. 'Of course you will.'

'Mu-um.' I pretended to try to wriggle free, but really I didn't mind her hugging me. The ferry horn sounded. The boat went very low in the sea once all the cars were onboard, and I tried not to look, taking out my yellow book to distract myself from the idea we might sink. I've been writing in it since I was nine, over a year, and it's full of facts about sea creatures. I turned to a fresh page, titled it *Greenland Sharks*, and added the thing about the crystals, and soft bones.

History isn't my favourite, but I know enough to know that shark was alive before Napoleon was born. Before Mozart, who we learned about in Ms Braimer's music class. And Napoleon and Mozart were alive a really, really long time ago.

The village of Belmont arrived out of the grey sea and grey clouds, low grey buildings slumped on the shore. I don't mind grey. My favourite animals, other than Noodle, are grey seals. But it did make me feel a bit heavy in my chest, leaving sunny Cornwall and arriving to rainy Unst, even if it was only for the summer.

There was more driving. We were all very quiet, even Noodle, and I wondered if she felt the same as I did. There was one road out of town, and the other cars mainly peeled off until there were two left ahead of us, but they turned right when we forked left at the end of the road, following a print-out of directions Dad had

been sent by work. There were no signs, and it got bumpier and bumpier.

The rain tapped on the roof like fingers, like Dad drumming his desk waiting for an email to come. Mum had her window open still and I could smell the rain: mud and grass crushed together.

'Are you sure this is the right way?' said Dad.

'There's no other way to go,' said Mum, waving the print-out. 'It says straight out of Belmont, left at the fork, straight to Uffle-Gent Lighthouse.'

Yes, you heard that right. Uffle-Gent. The only other lighthouse in that area was called Muckle Flugga, so it really could have been worse.

The land started rising, and our car huffed its way up, up, up. And when we reached the top, Mum wound her window down lower and stuck her head out and whooped.

'Look, J! Dan!'

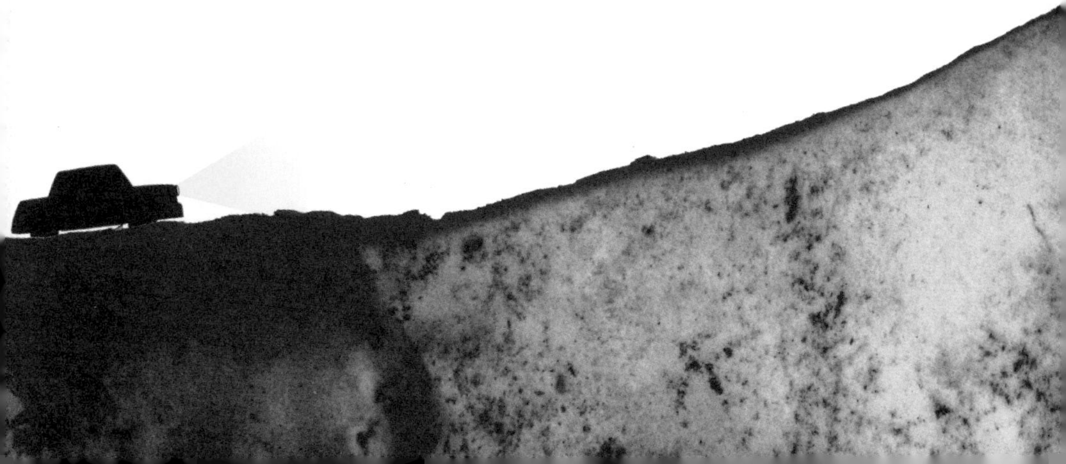

She said it like we might miss it, but it was impossible. At the top of the hill, the road finally flattened out into a scrubby piece of unpaved land, a sort of drive. And arrowing up from the overgrown cliff side, before which was spread a vast and rolling sea, was a round, white-and-black tower.

Uffle-Gent. Our lighthouse.

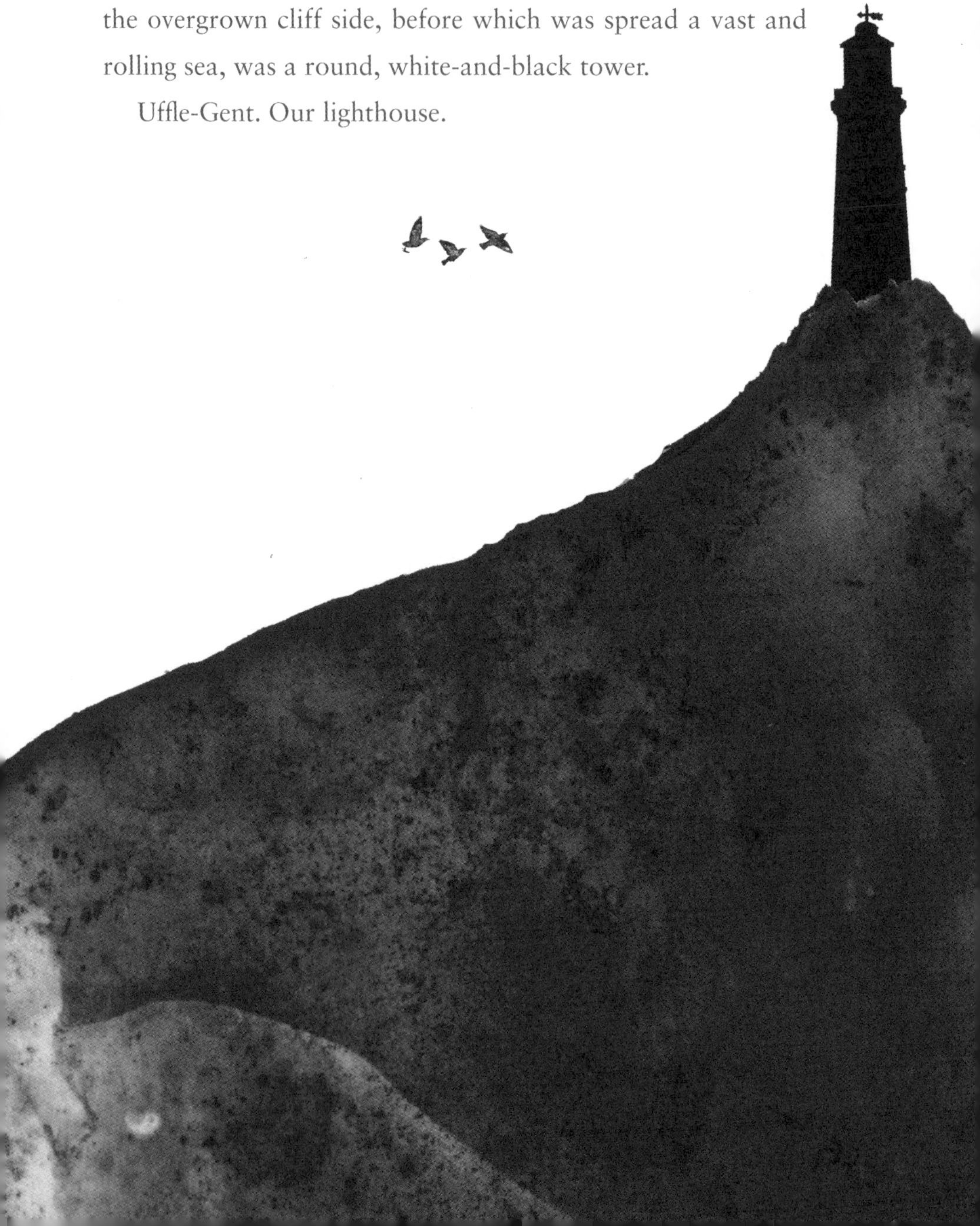

I could see why so many stories were set in lighthouses. It's a good place for adventures even before you go inside. There was a ladder stretching up the tower, the most direct way to the light. A railing ran along the top, protecting a walkway that wrapped around the light's cage. At the base were tangles of nettles and gorse that Dad had to root through to find the key. He swore a lot and Mum didn't even shout at him, she was so busy looking at the sea. Finally, he found it under an old tin bucket half-full of rainwater. He picked it up gingerly and wiped his fingers on his jeans. He can be a bit of a fusspot, my dad.

Inside was gloomy and cramped, and my heart sort of flip-flopped at the sight of it. You could walk across the whole bottom floor in ten strides, or six of Dad's, and the bathroom was right off the kitchen, the bath and toilet very close together.

The furniture had been left by the last lighthouse keeper, and it did not look happy about it. All the walls were round, and all the furniture was straight-lined so nothing fitted, and was placed at right angles like a shipwreck, jutting out and blocking doors. The walls were very thick, but still the damp chased up the sides in dark patches, and the whole place smelt like sea.

The stairway was curled right along the edges of the walls, like an inside helter-skelter. I let Noodle out of her crate and

she ran straight up them. We heard her meowing all the way to the top.

'This is going to be an adventure,' said Dad.

'A great one,' said Mum.

Dad opened his arms and gathered us in so I was squashed between them.

'Let me out!'

They laughed and kissed, so I made a *yuck* sound and followed Noodle up the stairs.

The walls were wet under my fingers and circling around made me dizzy. There were three levels besides the ground floor, all made of wood with big steel struts crisscrossing beneath. There was a double bed in the first one, together with a desk so there was hardly any space to stand.

I continued up. A single bed was on the next level, already made up with musty-looking daisy chain sheets, and a blue lamp on a wooden bedside table. My room. It wasn't anything like at home, with the walls painted like the sea and shells lined up on my shelves. My lip wobbled. It was only a summer, I told myself sternly. That's how long it used to take to sail to Canada from England. A long time, but not a lifetime. And then I'd be home with Shabs, Matty and Nell again. I went inside and flopped down on the bed. The sheets were damp.

Meowwww.

Noodle was calling me from above. When she gets like that you have to go and see what she wants or she won't shut up. The next level was directly below the light. I could see the cone of glass braced on metal struts hovering overhead, and imagined Dad would set his computer up here, doing embarrassing stretches as he automated the light.

After four days in the car my legs were jelly and I was breathless by the time I reached the top. Noodle was scratching at a red door with a rusted key in the lock. You couldn't hear the sea or the wind at all behind it. It must be nearly as thick as the wall.

'Mum!' I called down.

Her voice twisted faintly back up to me. 'Yes?'

'Can I go outside?'

I already had my hand on the key, but I could hear the hissing sounds of their discussion. Dad was obviously saying no.

'Yes,' she shouted after a minute.

'Be careful!' called Dad.

I turned the key, and pushed. The door grated with a sound like nails on a chalkboard, barely moving. I put my shoulder to the metal and leaned my whole weight against it.

It opened, and was caught and swung back suddenly on its hinges by the wind. I slowly forced my way out on to the metal platform, the weather like little slaps on my cheeks,

my
hair turned
to whipping snakes
lashing my face, making my
eyes sting and water.

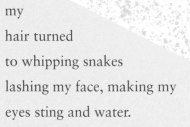

I wiped them on my sleeve, and the first thing I saw was not the sea, or the cliff, or the huge beacon, dim in its metal cage.

The first thing I saw, standing at the railing, was a boy.

THREE

He had obviously been looking out at the sea, and had clearly not been expecting company. He was a bit shorter than me, and had thick, black hair like Shabs. It was blowing around his ears, but I couldn't tell much more about him, because as I opened my mouth to say *hello*, or *oh*, or *what are you doing here?*, he swung himself over the railing and disappeared from sight.

I thought he'd jumped, or not been there at all, and my heart was slippery in my chest, sloshing around in panic. But when I threw myself at the railing and stared down, there he was, not splatted in the long grass below, or vanished like a ghost, but sliding down the rusty ladder on the edges of his trainers, his hands safe from the rough surface in gloves. It looked

like he was something from a film.

He landed in a superhero crouch, and then pulled a bike out from the overgrown grass and thorns. He leapt on and cycled really, really fast past our car and down the track we'd taken from the ferry. He didn't stop, or look back, and I watched him until his brown coat blurred in the green ground and was gone.

'Julia?'

Mum was standing behind me, her curly hair caught up in one hand to stop it whipping her in the face, her yellow mac billowing.

I don't know why I didn't tell her about the boy. Most likely it was because it didn't matter right then, because she reached out her hand to me, and led me back around to the sea-side of the lighthouse.

'That way is Orkney.' She pointed. 'That way is Greenland.' She pointed again. 'That way is Norway. And that way is the North Pole.'

'Which way's home?'

She grinned down at me, and prodded me in the chest. 'Right here. Wherever you are, our Julia.'

'Mu-um.'

But she was in one of her silly moods and knelt down behind me, spreading my arms and singing that song that goes all warbly, from that film where the boat sinks and nearly everyone dies.

And then Dad was behind her, and they were both singing, and Noodle was in the doorway, looking at us like we were mad. She had a point.

Unpacking didn't take long. Once our old walking boots and brand-new wellingtons – green for Dad, blue for Mum, yellow with daisies for me – were unpacked and lined up by the door, the tomato plants ranged on the high, narrow-lipped windowsill in the kitchen extension, it actually already started to feel like home. Mum put some music on her phone, and poured me a big glass of squash.

So long as I didn't think too much about home, I was almost enjoying myself. And there was the mystery of the boy to entertain me. I went outside while Mum and Dad fought over the litter Noodle had been quietly flicking all over the car. They couldn't find a vacuum cleaner in any of the narrow cupboards and Mum started scraping it out with her hands and Dad got funny about germs and *anyway* while they were arguing over micro-bacterial infection and how cat poo makes you blind, I went to the bottom of the ladder the boy had escaped down, and checked around the grass for clues as Noodle sat on the damp grass, watching me.

The ground was wet and squelchy, and I found a footprint from a trainer that was slightly smaller than mine. I pushed aside

a clump of purply flowers, and underneath was ...

'Treasure.' I held it up for Noodle to look at.

It was a red and gold piece of string, the two strands of colour wrapped around each other. I could see it had been tied in a knot, and obviously broken off next to it. The ends were frayed and unravelling, and maybe it wouldn't look like treasure to you, but I had a feeling about it, so I pocketed it before going back inside.

That evening it got dark really late because we are so much higher up the world and that means the sun is up for longer. Dad made twirly pasta with gloopy tomato sauce, and lots and lots of grated cheese on top.

We sat around the table, a small scrubbed thing worn smooth from lots of elbows, and I thought about our house in Hayle, which they'd let out to researchers from Plymouth University for the summer. It felt strange to think of someone else in our house, sitting at our table, using our knives and forks and Mum's shark-print napkins.

Noodle was crouched under the table too, eating her favourite food, albacore tuna in oil, which is a very fancy kind. I don't know what it tastes like because Dad only buys it for Noodle. I don't like tuna much since Mum left out one of her science magazines, and I read an article about how fishing with nets kills loads and

loads of other sea animals we don't even eat, like dolphins, and even though it's probably unfair to tuna to not mind as much about them getting caught in nets, I do.

Cats don't care about that sort of thing, though. Noodle would probably eat a dolphin if she could fit her mouth around one.

When we were finished, Mum and I washed up while Dad tried to tune the tiny, box-like telly on the kitchen counter. We didn't have one at home, so even this prehistoric model was a treat. There was no dishwasher here though, and no washing machine either.

'How will we wash our clothes?' I asked.

'There's a laundromat in town,' said Mum. 'But we can wash Dad's underpants in the sink for now?'

'Yuck!'

The sink was tiny and enamel, and we could only do one plate at a time. I dried them up as Mum passed them to me, and put them straight away as there wasn't room for a drying rack.

'They must have been very tidy, the people who lived here before,' I said.

'Person,' said Mum. 'The lighthouse keeper lived here alone.'

I thought of the single room with its neat sheets, and wondered if he'd hoped for visitors. 'Not even a cat?'

There was a clatter and Dad did a swear, immediately followed by, 'Sorry! 50p!' which is meant to mean he puts 50p in a swear

jar that I get to keep, but my parents stopped actually putting money in the jar when I made £32.50 last summer, and Mum said I was profiteering.

'Is that another 50p I heard, darling?' called Mum.

'No, *darling*,' replied Dad. 'But it would help if you could look for the remote.'

We played Ludo instead.

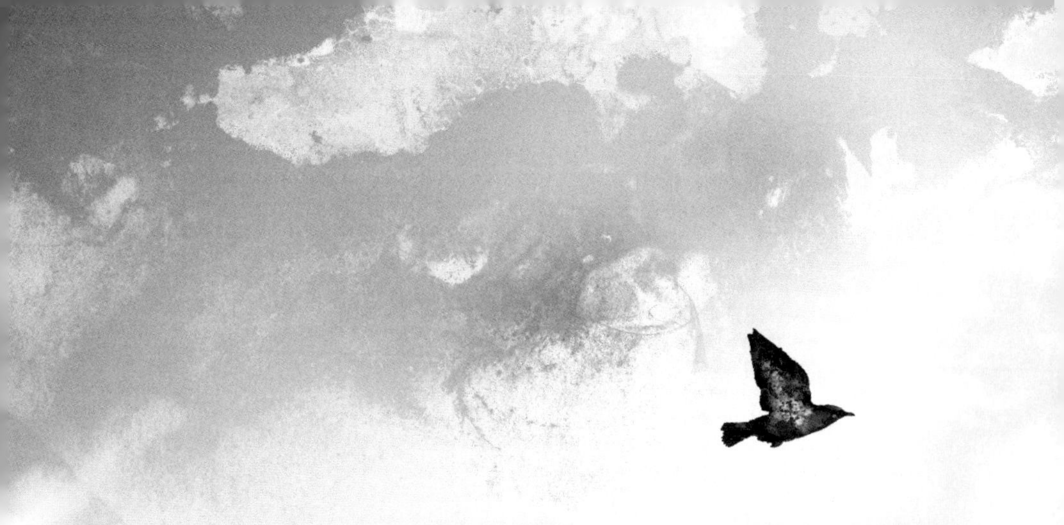

FOUR

One evening was all Mum needed to settle in. Perhaps it was because she loved being on the sea, which was always changing anyway and never the same water under you, that she managed to feel at home wherever she was. That is why she was what Dad called confident, and I called nuts. She just didn't care that much what other people thought.

So when she picked her yellow jumper and waterproof yellow trousers, along with her yellow mac to take me into town for the first time, she wouldn't have worried that she looked like a banana on the loose. But I was a little less excited about meeting our new neighbours accompanied by a human-sized fruit.

'Where first?' said Mum brightly, grinning over at me. 'Shops?

Or shops?'

'Shops.'

'Good plan, Batman,' said Mum, throwing the wheel left as we reached the end of the fork. I gritted my teeth and closed my eyes. She drove very fast.

Within minutes, we reached the town, strung out beside the sea. All the houses were built square and low, like our kitchen, painted white with grey slate roofs, and doors of yellow or red. They reminded me of seagulls, hunkered down along the stone quay.

Mum parked on the road outside a shop called GINLEY'S, which had fruit and vegetables outside, and fishing line and spades in the windows.

'Shall we look for a remote?' said Mum. 'And we can buy some apples at the same time!'

'We have apples,' I said, remembering the full fruit bowl in the middle of the too-small table.

'But *they* have apples. Let's get a remote and some apples at the same time because we can.'

Mum liked to seize the day. I loved that about her.

There weren't many people out, but those that were passing when we got out the car stopped talking and looked at us. It wasn't unfriendly, more curious, but it still made me go prickly under the collar of my coat. Mum gave them a cheery wave as we

walked into Ginley's, and they waved back. I pushed my hands into my pockets and watched my feet.

The shop had a bell that the door knocked when it opened, like Mrs Gould's Greengrocer in Hayle. It made me feel more at home, though Ginley's was nothing like Mrs Gould's. That was full of floral aprons and ceramic fish, nothing you could actually need. But Ginley's had superglue and rope, chocolate bars and mealworm bait. Useful things. I liked it.

'Hello,' said a cheery voice with a strong Scottish accent. You know how earlier I was saying there's all that room in words? Well, there are whole houses in accents. The man behind the counter had a white beard and very red skin on his nose and cheeks, sort of polished looking like well-loved boots. When he smiled at me, his blue eyes all but disappeared.

'You're new,' he said. 'The lighthouse?'

'My husband's working on it,' said Mum. 'But I'm Maura, and I'll be going out with the Norwegian ship.'

'*The Floe*?' He rubbed his thumb across his red forehead. 'Nice boat. After whales?'

'And other things,' she said, patting me on the shoulders. 'And this is Julia.'

'Nice to make your acquaintance, Julia. I'm Gin.'

He said it like the g in penguin, rather than Mum's favourite drink.

'I have a grandson about your age. Adrian. He's in bed but come back later and I'll introduce you. What can I help you with?'

Mum explained about the remote while I walked the line of sweets in jars. They had those jelly foods in miniature: hot dogs and burgers, even a whole breakfast with bacon and eggs and fried toast, but I knew better than to ask Mum to buy me one. She didn't like individually wrapped sweets, which meant we always bought the huge jars of them. It worked out better all around.

'Remote and apples obtained!' Mum stood behind me, grinning broadly as she balanced her purchases in her arms. 'Gin's told me where we can find the library, too.'

'See you soon, Maura, Julia,' said Gin, nodding his goodbye to us as Mum attempted to open the door with her elbow, dropping apples all over the floor.

'Don't tell Dad,' she said, scooping them into the tote I fetched her. 'He'll get up in arms about microbial bacteria.'

She blew on an apple and took a large bite, chewing and offering it to me. I shook my head. I'm somewhere in between Mum and Dad on things like germs. I wouldn't eat it off the floor like that, not without washing it. But Mum always seemed a bit invincible. Or at least, that she had better things to do than worry. She dumped the apples and remote into the car boot, and picked up another tote bag.

'Shall we head to the library? We should have brought your dad's underpants.'

I snorted. 'What?'

She took another bite of the apple and spoke with her mouth full. 'The laundromat is the library, too. Come on.'

We crossed the road and carried on towards the sea. We passed a fish and chip shop, and a newsagent's, before we arrived at the laundromat/library that meant we didn't have to wash Dad's pants in the sink.

I looked through the big glass window at the front. All the machines were churning round and round, and I couldn't see any books, or anyone inside except a bored-looking girl behind the counter.

She was older than me, maybe fifteen, and pretty. She had a very long, thick black braid over one shoulder, and a gold nose ring that glinted against her brown skin. She glanced up. I did my most grown-up nod at her and she raised a perfect eyebrow and nodded back. I felt, briefly, very cool.

'Here we are!' Mum pulled me inside. My feeling of cool evaporated as I tripped a little on my shoelaces. The air was humid, like a greenhouse, and I instantly began to sweat.

Mum bounded up to the girl. 'Hello! I'm Maura, and this is Julia, and we would like to avail ourselves of your library services.'

The girl's eyebrow arched again, but she smiled and jerked her head to the small room behind her. 'In there.'

'Ta ...'

'Neeta,' said the girl.

'Ta, Neeta!'

I tried not to trip on my laces again as we slid past the girl, and into a tiny room lined floor to ceiling with books. On the floor a green rug in the shape of a caterpillar was spread out like a lawn, and double doors at the back led on to a small courtyard, where a woman with Neeta's perfect eyebrows was sitting in a faded Winnie-the-Pooh T-shirt. She was reading a book that had a big man holding a small woman, who was fainting and pouting at the same time. She didn't notice us, so it must have been good.

The kids' section was the biggest, with the lower four shelves on the right side packed end to end. There werc all the usual series: *Murder Most Unladylike* and *How to Train Your Dragon*, *Horrid Henry* and *Sophie's Tom*. There were also loads of newer-looking books, their spines barely cracked. I slid one off the shelf.

'That's a good one.'

I jumped and turned.

'Here,' said the voice, and this time I noticed a gap in the far corner where the bookshelves didn't quite meet. There was a little rectangular space left between them and, peering around

the corner of one of the bookshelves, was a brown eye with very long lashes.

'It's you,' I said, certain, though I could only see a little of his face. 'From the lighthouse!'

'Shhh!' The boy jerked his head at me to come closer. I shimmied along on my knees. 'That's my mum.' He indicated the woman reading the book with the swooning lady. 'She doesn't know I go to the lighthouse. She says it's too dangerous.'

'It is if you jump off it like you did,' I said.

'Shhh!' he said again, looking nervously at his mum. She didn't look scary, with her large brown eyes and Winnie-the-Pooh T-shirt.

'You left this.' I pulled the gold-and-red thread out from my pocket.

'My rakhi!'

'What?'

'Rakhi. It's a bracelet my sister gave me.' He mumbled this, like he was embarrassed.

'That's nice of her. Was it your birthday?'

'No, just this thing we do. Sisters give their brothers a piece of string, brothers buy their sisters a present. It's not very fair, really.'

'It's a nice piece of string,' I said.

'Yeah, well, this one's broken now, so I have to put it in the

sea. Took long enough. It was so annoying wearing it to school.'

'Why?'

'Some of the boys –' he shrugged – 'they don't think boys should wear bracelets. But it's a rakhi, so ...'

He tailed off, like he was caught between embarrassment and pride. Looking at my walking banana of a mother, I felt like I understood.

'Can I come?'

He wriggled sideways out of the gap. He was shorter than me, as I'd remembered from the lighthouse, and thin, with very long fingers. His hair was curly and stuck out around his ears. 'Sure.'

'I'm Julia.'

'Kin.' He stuck his hands in his pockets. 'Ma?'

The woman in the courtyard *hmmm?*'d without looking up from her book.

'My rakhi broke. Can I go put it in the sea?'

She glanced up, her eyes flicking from him to the broken string to me. 'Straight there and back, *beta*.'

'Mum, don't call me that,' said the boy, shifting from foot to foot.

'Don't call me Mum,' said his mum, unconcernedly, turning a page.

'Yes, Ma.' He rolled his eyes, more to himself than me. 'You going to get that?'

I looked down at the book in my hand. I'd almost forgotten I was holding it. I opened it to the first page. I like books, obviously, because I like words, but only when things happen right from the first page. This one began with a plane taking off over a massive jungle, so I tucked it under my arm.

'Mum, I'm just going with Kin to the quay.'

'All right,' said Mum, scanning the shelves. 'Be careful.'

We emerged into the laundromat, and Neeta pulled a big ledger out from under the counter. 'You find something you like?'

I held out the book to her.

'We're just going to put this in the sea,' said Kin, holding up the rakhi.

'You still owe me a present,' said Neeta, taking the book. 'I'll write this up.'

We crossed the road to the stone quayside. The sea was choppy and blue, buoys bobbing gently up and down like birds. We leaned against the metal railings, and Kin threw the string in the water.

'Is that it?'

'I made a wish,' said Kin defensively. He sat on the railing, his legs swinging over the sea.

'Careful, *beta*!' His mum's voice echoed across the road, and

he stood up as though electrocuted, glaring over his shoulder. She and Mum were standing outside the laundromat. Neither was looking at us, but mums always have eyes in the back of their heads.

'I told her not to call me that.'

'Why does she?'

'It means son.'

I frowned. 'You are her son, though?'

'Yes, but it's ...' He chewed his lip. 'Never mind. It's not my name.'

'Kin is nice,' I offered, because he seemed upset.

'You think?' He didn't quite meet my eye. 'It's better than my real name.'

'You're not Kin?'

'You have to swear not to tell anyone.'

'Pinky swear,' I said, waggling my finger at him. He tapped his own pinky against it, looking confused, so I clarified, 'I promise not to tell.'

'It's ... Kinshuk.' He shuddered.

'I like it.'

'It means "flower".'

'I like flowers. Don't you?'

'I guess,' he said slowly. 'But the boys at school say—'

'They don't seem very much fun.'

'They're OK,' shrugged Kin. 'They're just a bit ...'

He tailed off and glanced back at the laundromat. Our mums were laughing now. My mum's snorts carried on the wind. 'I should get back.'

'Do you think your mum will let you come visit the lighthouse now we're living there?'

'I'll ask,' said Kin, looking hopeful.

'Come on, Julia,' called Mum, and we crossed back to them. 'Meet Vedi.'

The woman in the Winnie-the-Pooh T-shirt smiled. 'Here's your book, Julia. It's a good one, isn't it, *beta*?'

Kin nodded.

'Come back as much as you can,' Vedi continued. 'The council says we have to use it or lose it.'

'Of course,' said Mum. 'I'll be in with my husband's pants soon!'

I waved at Kin, and he waved back. Inside my chest a little bloom opened. Maybe we could make friends, if only for the summer.

Mum pulled me into her side. 'Shall we get chips?'

FIVE

'How are you liking Unst?' said Mum, her mouth full, legs dangling over the side of the quay.

'It's nice,' I said, picking out a particularly crispy chip from the bottom of the paper cone.

'Nice is a nothing word,' said Mum. 'What do you think of it?'

I thought, chewing and then swallowing deliberately so as to set a good example for my mother. 'It's friendly. It's grey. It's quiet.'

'The gulls aren't,' said Mum, eyeing them suspiciously. But they were small, speckle-backed, not the huge yellow-beaked ones we get in Cornwall that swoop down and steal ice creams,

whole battered fillets of fish, and once, Mrs Gould's chihuahua. 'Good words. I would add salty.'

'That's because of the chips.'

'It's because of the sea.'

'But the town isn't salty.'

'Go lick that wall,' said Mum, gesturing at the house behind us. 'Bet you the swear jar it's salty.'

I looked out to the sea, blowing on a steaming chip to cool it. 'How long will it take? To find the Greenland shark.'

'Not long,' said Mum confidently. 'The sightings are recent, and southerly. I wouldn't be surprised if I find one on my first outing.'

'Really?'

'Don't get all Dad about it,' said Mum, jabbing me in the ribs, and I rubbed the spot, feeling bad for questioning her. 'I only have two months, remember, so it'll have to be quick. And the boat I'm going out with tracked one last year.'

'Is this to do with your seaweed stuff again?'

'No,' said Mum. 'This is about Grandma.'

'Grandma Penny?'

'No, my mum. Grandma Julia.'

I blinked. 'What's she got to do with a shark?'

Mum snorted, wiping salt on her jacket. 'Dad would say a lot. But you know she had dementia? Her brain went wrong, and she

started forgetting things.'

I nodded, mouth full of hot chips. 'Nell's grandma has it, too. She wore slippers to our end-of-year concert.'

'Well, Grandma Julia had it young. Early-onset, they call it.' Her knuckles were white: she was gripping her yellow jacket very tightly. 'She was too young. It shouldn't have happened. If there had been a way to slow it down, we'd have had her longer. It was like a fire, the dementia. It swallowed her up, too fast.'

Her voice was tight, and I brushed my knuckles against hers. She cleared her throat, and smiled at me. But I could tell she was trying not to cry. 'But Greenland sharks, they're slow. They move like glaciers. That's why they live so long.'

I knew Mum was making sense to herself. Her brain did these leaps, connecting dots I never knew were there. She was clever like that.

'So?'

'So …' Mum's voice was strengthening now, her eyes clear. 'They seem to be moving so slowly they can actually slow time down. And some researchers believe that we can find out what causes this, and use it to slow down time for humans, too.'

It sounded like something made up, like something from a film. But Mum often told me facts that sounded like fiction, facts I wrote down in my yellow book. Some of my favourite ones are:

1. *The longest mountain range on Earth is underwater. It's called the Mid-Ocean Ridge (you'd have thought they'd come up with something more exciting), it's 65,000 kilometres long, and it's less explored than the surface of Mars.*

2. *The Pacific Ocean is wider than the Moon, and has over 25,000 islands in it.*

3. *There are more stars in space than grains of sand on every beach in the whole wide world.*

4. *There are more atoms in a glass of water than there are glasses of water in all the oceans on Earth.*

5. *Turtles breathe through their bums.*

She also told me the first shark existed before the first tree existed, so I already knew sharks had previous on the strange facts list. But centuries-old, time-slowing sharks? That was a whole other kind of weird.

'Maybe,' she said, in a small voice. 'It'll work. And other families won't have to lose their loved ones so soon.'

I snuggled into her side. My friends back home thought it was strange how much I loved my mum, how proud I was of her, but you can see why, can't you?

Mum nuzzled me on the head. 'Sorry. I didn't know it would come out like that. Words, eh? I just hope the funding comes through.'

'Dad could lend you some,' I said, remembering him jigging around the kitchen in Cornwall about how much the lighthouse people were paying him.

'Ha! He doesn't have fifteen million pounds, does he?'

I nearly fell off the quay. 'That's *mad*.'

'Immoral,' corrected Mum. 'But that's what research like this costs. Anyway, we're a long way off a lab. Got to find the sharks first, find a way of tracking them. Then we can work on ways to extract the cells we need.'

'You're ... you're not going to kill them, are you?'

Mum looked at me, shocked. 'No more than I would kill you, or a hundreds-year-old oak tree.'

I know that sounds a little strange, that she'd equate me with a tree, but really it's a compliment coming from someone like Mum, who really, really loves trees.

'That's partly why it's complicated,' continued Mum. 'But the ideas are sound.' She inspected the chip paper, checking to see if it was too greasy to recycle. She nodded approvingly at it

and put it in her pocket.

'Can I come?' I asked.

'Where?'

'On the boat? I want to help you find the shark.'

'Your dad wouldn't like it.'

'So?' Mum never usually cared what Dad thought.

She shrugged. 'Maybe. Let me get to know them all a bit. Now come on, my jewel, let's get a sparkle on.' Which is her horrifying way of saying 'get a wiggle on', which is Dad's horrifying way of saying 'let's go'. Parents were as embarrassing in Shetland as they were anywhere else.

Scraaape.

I woke up, teeth trilling like I'd chewed on foil. It was a sound like metal too – like a blade scratching a surface. I checked my starfish watch. 2:30 a.m.

Scraaape.

Perhaps I was imagining it.

Scraaape.

'Nope,' I said aloud. 'Not imagining it.'

Noodle emerged from the covers and leapt lightly down on to the floor, her tail fluffed up like a skunk's. She slunk low, and moved silently out of the door.

I took hold of my torch and followed, my thoughts galloping. The bedside light's little glow sprawled on to the opposite wall, sending my shadow monstrous, stairs curving up up and down down into dark.

Scraaape.

I knew I should fetch Mum. What if it was a thief? My heart thudded fearfully.

Noodle mewled from above, and I jumped, the hair on my arms standing up. I shivered, my bare feet cold on the wooden steps. A smaller scratching sound came, and I knew she was trying to get out of the door. I crept up after her, every muscle taut, ready to run.

Scraaaape.

The noise was louder here. Whatever it was really was on the other side. Noodle wiggled her bum, ready to pounce. Seeing her tiny, tigerish form ready to defend me made me feel braver. I placed my hand on the doorknob, and raised the torch high. It was rubber gripped, but heavy. I'd dropped it on my foot once and it'd hurt.

Before I could think better of it, I opened the door and charged, Noodle at my heels like a furred cavalry.

Outside, the night was crisp black, hundreds of stars misting the sky, the moon a half slice of silver-white. And there, silhouetted in my raised torch's glow, was—

'Kin?'

My momentum carried me forwards, right into him. As we collided my torch slipped from my grasp and skittered down over the railings to land with a muffled thump in the grass below.

'Ow.' He rubbed his forehead, and I noticed he was holding a rope in his other hand. 'Careful!'

'Careful?' I half-laughed, relief battering my ribs. 'What are you doing here?'

'What I do every clear night,' he said. Noodle was sitting by the open door, eyeing Kin warily, like she did to anyone new. Kin eyed her warily back. 'Is that yours?'

'She is. Well, Dad says we're hers more than she's ours, but …' Kin was looking at me with the glazed expression of someone who was Not One Of Our Own, which is what Dad calls anyone who isn't absolutely nuts about cats. 'But anyway,' I continued, switching tack. 'What're you doing?'

'Trying not to bash this around too much.'

He brought the object the rest of the way up and hoisted it with great care over the railing. I didn't think there was much point after the racket he'd made scraping it along the lighthouse, but I didn't say so, too intrigued by what it was.

'A telescope?'

He nodded proudly.

'Can I?'

I reached out. It was as high as Kin, and heavy too, I could tell just from looking. It had three thin metal legs that formed a tripod, and an eye rest cushioned by buttery red leather. The telescope itself was polished brass like our door handles in Cornwall. He bent over the eyehole, and began adjusting the dials that lined the telescope's length. Noodle retreated back indoors, but I stayed, watching him.

'There,' he said, ducking back up with a shy smile.

'Look.'

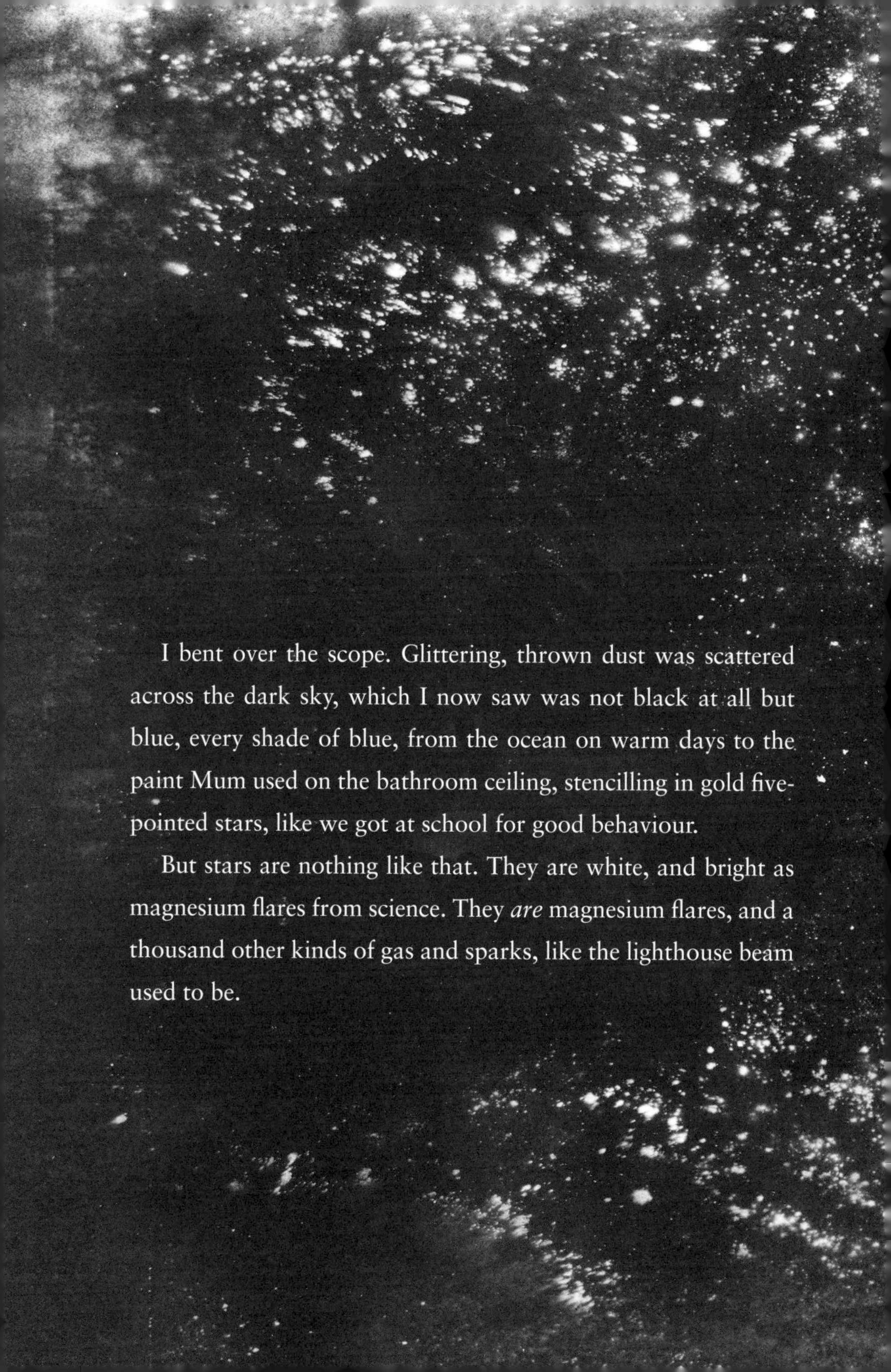

I bent over the scope. Glittering, thrown dust was scattered across the dark sky, which I now saw was not black at all but blue, every shade of blue, from the ocean on warm days to the paint Mum used on the bathroom ceiling, stencilling in gold five-pointed stars, like we got at school for good behaviour.

But stars are nothing like that. They are white, and bright as magnesium flares from science. They *are* magnesium flares, and a thousand other kinds of gas and sparks, like the lighthouse beam used to be.

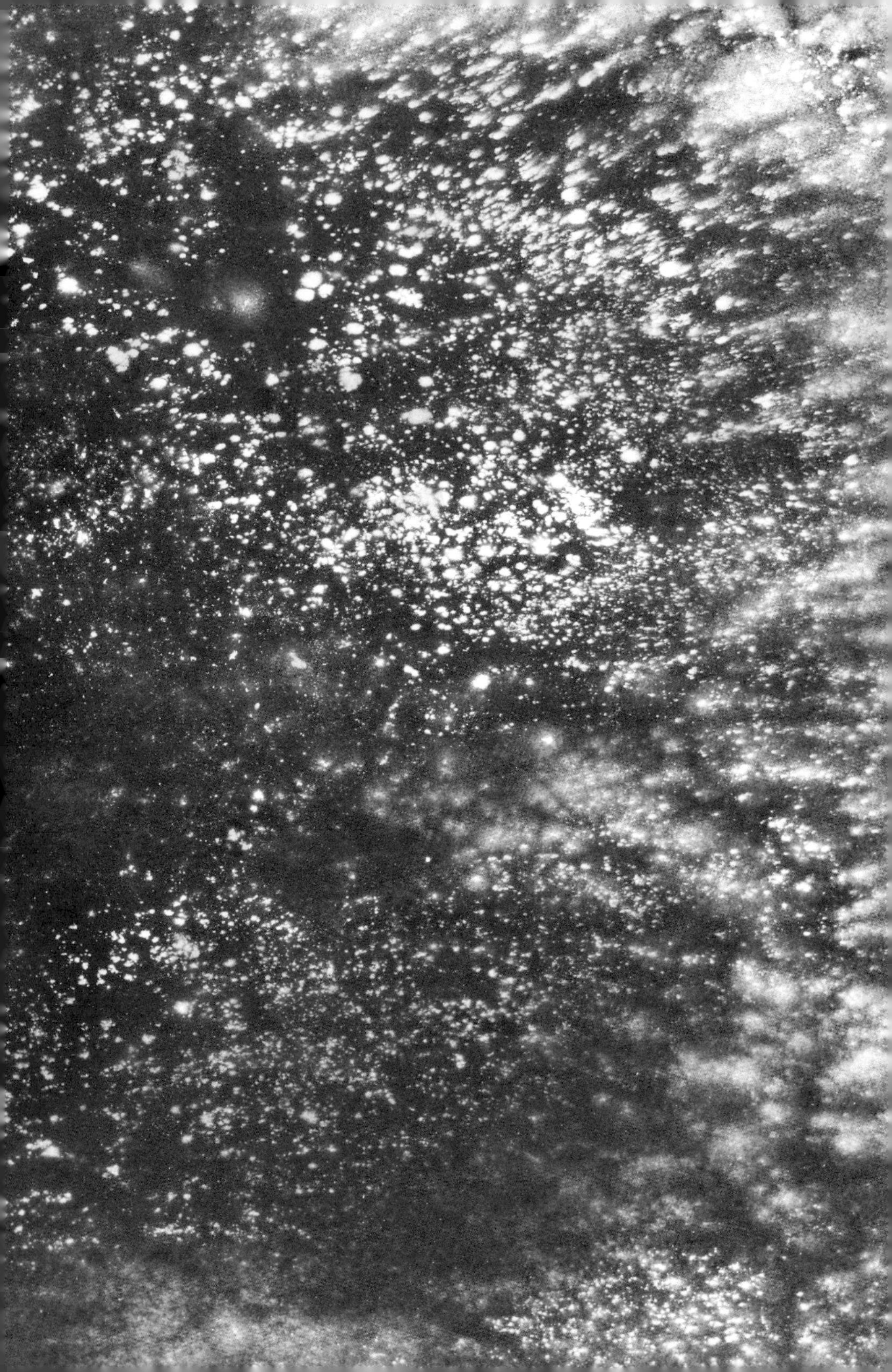

'These stars,' said Kin. 'They've been there millions of years. Millions. My bapi—' He stopped. 'My dad. He says they're older than anything we'll ever know, ever touch. And some of them are dead already. But their light keeps going because they're so far away it takes them for ever to reach us.'

'Dead?' I squinted at them. I had never seen something that looked more alive. I had the same feeling in my brain, the same stretching one I felt when Mum told me a fact I wanted to write in my yellow book. But that was for sea facts only. I had to keep focused if I was going to be a marine biologist like Mum.

'Mmm. Dad says their light will keep coming until long after we die.'

'That's ... nice?' The truth was it made me feel a little sad.

'Forget it,' he mumbled, and made as though to collapse the telescope.

'Wait,' I said, holding out my hand. 'I do see what you mean.'

'You do?' He wasn't looking directly at me, but somewhere off beyond my right ear.

'Yeah.'

'I thought you might. With your mum being a scientist and all.'

'She studies the sea, not the sky,' I said. 'But that's just as interesting. More interesting,' I added loyally.

Kin wrinkled his nose. 'More than that?' He gestured at the

enormity of the night around us.

'Yes, but *that*,' I shot back, pointing at the sea that was murmuring against the rocks below us. 'That's where the real secrets are. We know more about stars than starfish.'

I could tell he didn't believe me. But I didn't mind. Mum said the most important part of being a scientist is to listen and to communicate, because you never knew when someone else's ideas could make you change your own.

SIX

Kin told me to meet him in the laundromat.

'It's just me and Neeta today.'

'Are you working there?'

He shook his head. 'There's nowhere else to hang out since the council had to close the library.'

I wondered why he didn't want to meet at the beach. There were some sea caves nearby I wanted to explore. But seeing as he'd invited me, I thought it'd be rude not to go, and Mum said it was fine as long as I was back for dinner.

I pocketed a bacon sandwich, collected my bike from the stinking boat shed and pushed off down the road. The cycle got a lot easier once I was off our potholed stretch, and into the

tarmacked strait to town. It was no busier than the day before. Kin said a lot of the local kids went to the bigger islands or the mainland for summer. But his family always stayed, because 'the laundromat was important to the local infrastructure'. He'd looked proud when he said this, the way I must when I talk about Mum.

Gin's shop was open, and he was outside stacking some shelves with bait, a bored-looking boy beside him, holding a crate full of cans. Probably Adrian, his grandson. I waved at Gin's back, and the boy glowered at me. It made me wobble, and I had to put my hand back on the handlebars very fast.

Neeta was behind the counter like yesterday, and Kin was sitting on it, swinging his legs. Dismounting, I locked my bike to a lamppost and waved through the glass. He hopped down and stood in the open doorway.

'You came,' he said, sounding a bit surprised. 'It's a bit loud.'

He wasn't wrong. The machines rumbled and churned like miniature cyclones, nearly all of them going except one with an 'out of order' sign stuck to it. Neeta looked up from her phone and did her grown-up nod at me. 'Hey.'

I nodded back, and squeaked, 'Hi.' She really was very pretty.

'Can you guys watch it here for a bit?' She stepped out from behind the counter and stretched. 'I'm just going to Laura's.'

'Sure,' said Kin, climbing back on to the counter. Neeta

left, her thick braid swinging, and I watched her go with open awe.

'She's so pretty.'

Kin wrinkled his nose. 'The boys at school say so. It's gross.'

I plonked our laundry bag down on the bench and hopped on to the counter beside him. Kin kicked his heels. 'I didn't think you'd come.'

'Why?'

He shrugged, but I could tell he did care really because he wasn't looking at me. 'I thought you'd think it was weird, hanging out here.'

It wasn't the time to mention that I did, a bit.

'Where are your parents?'

'Mainland,' he said. 'Need new parts for that.' He pointed at the broken-down machine.

'And they let you and your sister run the shop?'

'And the library. They used to let me watch it on my own, sometimes,' he said proudly. 'Then …' He sighed.

'What?' I asked. I couldn't imagine Kin trashing the place.

'Just some boys at school. They sometimes come in here.'

'To ask Neeta out?'

'Ew, no!' He scrunched his lip up under his nose. 'Just, they aren't nice to me.'

I nodded, to show I understood. I was bullied for a bit last year

by some girls in the year above. They'd poke my belly and call me a whale, and Flubber, even though it's blubber that whales have. But telling them this just made it worse.

'Have you told your mum?' I asked, because that's what I did. She went to school the next day and they didn't bully me for the rest of the year, and then went to Year 7 somewhere else.

'No way,' said Kin. 'But Neeta noticed. She wouldn't leave me here unless I had someone with me. Not that I mind being alone.'

I watched him swinging his legs and I felt – not sad exactly, but I could imagine him here, alone. I didn't have a sister or a brother, unless you counted Noodle, which we do but most people don't, so I was used to being on my own. I didn't mind, and maybe it was like that for Kin, too. But I felt like his words weren't telling the whole story. That he'd been more than alone. That he'd been lonely.

'Are you OK?' He'd looked up suddenly, and seen me watching him.

'Yeah, why?'

'You look like this.' He did a funny face, like Noodle when she needs a poo.

'That's just my face.'

'Oh, sorry. Want some?' He pulled out a Twirl from his pocket. I took some and brought out the bacon sandwich, squashed from my cycle. When I held it out, he shook his head.

'I'm veggie.'

'My mum is too, mostly.'

'Mostly?'

'She does really like bacon. And sausage rolls.'

'Right. Pigs then?'

I nodded. 'She's sad about it, because pigs are really intelligent.'

'So why doesn't she not eat them?'

'I guess she likes the taste too much.'

We ate in silence, watching the washers going round and round. 'Are you going to come with the telescope tonight?' I asked at last.

He swallowed and shook his head. 'Storm coming.'

I chewed the inside of my cheek, trying not to think of Mum going out to sea the next day.

'Day after tomorrow, maybe,' he continued. 'If it clears up. I'm glad you like it.'

'The telescope?'

'And the stars stuff. Neeta thinks it's lame.'

'That's because she's your sister,' I said wisely. But Kin wasn't listening suddenly, looking at the window. It was like watching Noodle when she saw another cat. But instead of puffing himself up like she did, Kin seemed to shrink.

I followed his gaze. The boy I had seen helping Gin was standing outside the laundromat, grinning. But it wasn't a nice

grin. When I looked up his smile widened, and he pressed his red face to the window, breathing on the glass. I could feel Kin trembling.

'Is that Gin's grandson?'

But Kin didn't answer. It was like he was under a spell as the boy dragged his finger through the misted-up glass, his floppy blond hair making his face go in shadow. Then he waved, and sauntered out of sight.

Kin wilted next to me, breathing out in a great *whoosh*.

'Was that Adrian?'

'Yeah. The boys at school I told you about. He's their leader, sort of.'

I jumped off the counter, and inspected the drawing. It was a four-petalled flower. Kin came to my shoulder. 'I have to wash that off.'

'Why'd he do that?'

'My name,' said Kin miserably. 'He thinks it's funny it means flower.'

'That's stupid,' I said.

Kin grunted, and went behind the counter, coming back with a spray bottle and cloth. 'We're lucky Richard wasn't with him. He might have come in.'

'He wouldn't have done anything,' I said.

'He might have said something,' said Kin. 'Something horrid.'

'Like what?'

But Kin didn't answer. He went outside, checking left and right, and spritzed the marks away. His lip was wobbling when he came back in to sit on the counter again, and I tried to think of something to distract him.

'So what do you do in summer?'

'What do you mean?'

'For fun,' I said.

Kin shrugged, gesturing around. 'I usually read or something.'

'Do you go swimming, or—'

Kin shook his head. 'I can't swim.'

I sat up straight. 'You live on an island.'

'So?' Kin was sitting rigidly again, not looking at me. 'You sound like the boys at school. They tried to throw me in, once.'

'That's not nice,' I said firmly. 'But swimming is.'

'Vikings couldn't swim,' said Kin, jutting out his chin. 'They thought it was bad luck to learn, because it meant preparing to sink.'

I shifted on the counter. It was cutting into the backs of my legs. I didn't like that. Mum swam brilliantly, like a seal or an otter. But that didn't mean she was going to sink. I laughed away my worry.

'You're not a Viking.'

'I could be,' said Kin, his voice a little too loud even with the

machines going. He looked suddenly upset again. 'Why is that so strange?'

'I didn't mean—'

'Everything all right?' Neeta was in the doorway.

'Yeah,' said Kin, moving away from me. 'Julia was just going.'

Hurt jabbed at my chest. I didn't understand. 'Kin—'

But he was already pushing open the door to the library. 'Bye.'

It slammed shut behind him, and I looked at Neeta, who shrugged. Face flushing, I slipped past her and back to my bike. As I clipped on my helmet and started to cycle away, I heard a hoot. Looking over my shoulder, I saw Adrian standing with a group of boys. Their laughter chased me away down the street.

SEVEN

'What's up with you?' Mum was eyeing me suspiciously.

'Nothing.'

'No, something.' She always did that. Seemed to see right through me. 'Did you and Kin have a fight?'

'Leave her alone, Maura,' said Dad. He had a jumble of wires in front of him that the postman had delivered. He was starting work tomorrow, and had already developed a worry line between his eyebrows. Mum had her first day on the boat too, but where Dad seemed tense and quiet, Mum was like a coiled spring, ready to go. 'Are you taking Noodle tomorrow?'

I knew he'd asked to distract her, but still I had to bite down hard on the inside of my cheek to ask why I wasn't allowed to go.

I filled a glass of water from the tap. The water here was cloudy but it tasted all right.

'Of course.' She reached down and scratched Noodle under the chin. 'My little mascot. And tonight you'll be meeting Captain Bjorn Johansson.' She said the name in a low, gruff voice. 'He's coming for dinner.'

Dad stopped rooting through the wires. 'What?'

'I thought it was only polite,' said Mum, returning to her sea maps. 'You don't want your wife off with Bjorn Johansson –' the booming voice again, '– without meeting him surely?'

Dad sighed. He didn't like it when Mum was impulsive, and didn't tell him the plan. 'I think Bjorn Johansson is the one who should be worried.'

'Cupboard risotto tonight please, chef.'

Dad's cupboard risotto is whatever rice we have, cooked in a stock cube and any leftover wine in the house, with tinned peas and anything else from the cupboards. It takes a while for it to come close to tasting good, so I helped Dad clear away his wires so he could start cooking.

He led me up to his office beneath the light. I stared up at it, imagined it lit up yellow and hot.

'Just there, J.' I put down my armful where he had indicated. 'Cool, isn't it?'

He was pointing at the light. Dad is with electricity like Mum

is with the sea.

I smiled, hesitating before speaking. 'Dad.'

He was rummaging in his desk drawer. 'Julia.'

'Did you tell Mum I couldn't go with her?'

'What?'

'On the boat. Because if she wants me to, I want to go.'

'She didn't say anything to me, J.'

I chewed my already sore cheek. 'Oh.'

Dad was leaning on his desk, looking at me carefully. 'Are you all right, J? You do seem a bit upset.'

I wanted to tell him about Adrian, and what Kin had said about Vikings not swimming, and how I felt like I'd done something wrong, and I didn't know how to put it right. But then we'd have to have A Conversation and I didn't really want to.

'Noodle goes on the boat.'

'Noodle's Noodle,' shrugged Dad, like he was making a valid point. 'But we'll have fun, won't we? You can help me with the light.' I looked at the wires. Fun was not the word I was thinking of. 'And you have your friend. Kevin, is it?'

'Kin.' His name stuck in my throat.

'Well, he can come for lunch one day.'

I knew Dad wanted to suss him out before letting me hang around with him, but there was no need. Kin didn't seem to want to be friends any more. 'Maybe.'

Mum's voice came from the spiral staircase. 'Shall I start chopping?'

'Quick,' grimaced Dad, pushing himself off his desk. 'Before she butchers herself.'

The small kitchen quickly filled with the smell of garlic and wine. Noodle slunk upstairs when Mum added too much chilli powder, and by the time there was a knock at the open door we were all red-faced and spluttering.

Mum threw open her arms like she was greeting an old friend. 'Captain Bjorn! Welcome! Don't come in, you'll suffocate.'

The man outside was tall and thin. His eyes were pale blue and crinkly, his skin very reddy-brown with sunburn at the wrists when he held out his hand to shake Mum's. She hugged him instead, and pushed me forward.

'This is Julia, and that, coughing into the risotto, is Dan.'

Dad waved in welcome, eyes watering.

'Very nice to meet you, Julia.' His accent was thick and made his words clipped, with odd pauses. It was a nice voice.

'Will you help us carry the table out?' said Mum. 'It's not currently habitable in there.'

'Might as well make the most of the nice day,' said Captain Bjorn. 'The weather will turn tonight.'

Manoeuvering the table through the narrow door gave me a new appreciation for whoever had put it in there. It was only when Captain Bjorn screwed off one of the legs that we managed it, and found a patch of even ground, which happened to be directly below the ladder. I scooped up my torch before anyone noticed it, but Mum frowned at the trodden-down scrub, which suddenly looked very obviously a desire path.

'Looks like we have visitors sometimes.'

'Possibly otters,' said Captain Bjorn. 'They are busy here.'

Dad plonked the cupboard risotto down at the centre of the table, and we settled to eat.

Mum, as usual, started the conversation. 'What time do we start?'

'Early,' said Captain Bjorn. 'As long on the sea as possible. There'll be another storm coming westerly mid-afternoon.'

'And we'll lay our markers?'

'Yes.'

'And then,' said Mum, her mouth full. 'Maybe sightings?'

Captain Bjorn shrugged, but it wasn't dismissive. 'Maybe next week, maybe next month. Maybe never. They favour the depths.'

'That's why you have sonar.'

'Of course. I've never seen one though.'

'Your crew has?'

'But not me.'

'But I will.' She grinned at me, saying it definitely, and I believed her. When Mum was certain about something, she was right.

'Maybe,' said Captain Bjorn, and I saw Dad look from the captain's face to Mum's, with something like worry in his eyes. 'This research, which university is funding it?'

'None at the moment,' said Mum cheerily, heaping seconds into his bowl. 'Seed money only. But I've got the wheels moving.'

Captain Bjorn chewed for a lot longer than the cupboard risotto needed chewing. 'Is this why you've only chartered us for two weeks?'

'Two weeks?' I asked. 'Two months, I thought.'

'Yes.' Mum wafted her hand, like it wasn't an important detail. 'I'm paying as we go. It'll work out. The money will come. The science is sound.' She said these sentences like a mantra, a prayer.

'And what's the science?' he asked. 'If you don't mind me asking.'

Mum had her mouth full again, so I answered for her.

'The shark can slow time. Mum's going to use it to slow down time for people, too.'

'Something like that,' said Mum.

Captain Bjorn raised a pale eyebrow. 'These sharks, they are not easy to find. It may not be possible.'

I glared into my cupboard risotto. Who was he, to tell Mum what was possible or not?

'I'm not easy to hide from,' said Mum, and there was something in the air there. Something taut, like they both had hold of an invisible rope and were pulling it between them.

'They swim many metres down.'

'Over two thousand,' shrugged Mum. 'But they come to the surface.'

'Sometimes.'

'Exactly.'

Captain Bjorn toppled first, shrugging. 'All right.'

'It will be,' said Mum, unable to resist having the last word.

I felt my own hand clench as hers flexed on the table, and Dad laid his own over it. I shifted in my chair, searching for something to say to puncture the swelling tension.

'Captain Bjorn, can you swim?'

'Of course.'

That was something, at least.

After dinner, Mum and Dad had a little fight. I didn't stick around to listen, but I think it was about money. It usually was. I knew they'd borrowed a lot for our house in Cornwall so the bank owned it twice, or something. I forced myself to stay awake, using my facts book to work out that two thousand metres is the height of twenty Big Bens stacked on top of each other.

That's how deep the sharks like to swim. Twenty Big Bens. On top of each other. Under the sea. I felt another needling prickle of worry in my chest that Captain Bjorn might be right, but I forced the thought away. Mum believed, and that's all I needed to know.

Finally, I heard them go to bed, and Mum started snoring. She took pills to help her sleep, but still I crept very quietly upstairs, lifting my slippered feet carefully.

I was already learning the lighthouse, where to step so the stair didn't creak, the slick patches where my slippers had no grip, and it was already becoming less extraordinary to me.

It was the way of things to become ordinary after a while, and that was why I liked what Mum did so much. Instead of things becoming more ordinary the more she looked at them, they became more interesting. Sharks, whales, even algae.

I knew Kin wasn't going to be there. Even if we hadn't fallen out, the clouds he'd mentioned from the storm Captain Bjorn promised were arriving, misting the stars in grey froth. The sea was quiet, and so dark I couldn't see it. It was like there was a pit below me, reaching all the way to the centre of the earth, further even than my imagination could reach.

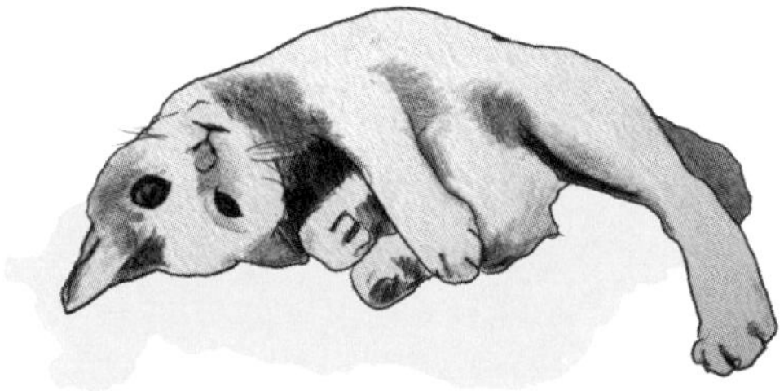

EIGHT

Mum came back from sea fizzing. Noodle seemed proud of herself too, curled up on Dad's lap so he could brush out the knots in her fur where wind and salt had matted it.

'It's *wild*,' said Mum, looking wild herself. She grabbed my hands and spun me around. 'The waves were high as this, more than that, and the colour!'

She let go and my hip bumped the table sharply. I plonked myself down, wanting, suddenly and stupidly, to cry. Mum didn't notice, chattering on. 'So different from Cornwall, a sort of crispness to it. And we saw *Phocoena phocoena*, dozens of *Phocidae*—' she broke off, looking at me expectantly.

'Harbour porpoises, seals,' I recited dully.

'Hey, what's up with you?'

I shrugged, one of those shrugs that really means, *Oh, I don't know, Mum, maybe it's that you've dragged me up here away from my friends to the middle of nowhere and you won't even let me go on the boat with you.* Adding to my mood was the fact I'd had a very boring day helping Dad untangle the wires and lay them into rainbow stripes on the floor. All I could think about as I sorted them was how much more fun I could be having with Mum at sea, or even with Kin in the laundromat. But neither Mum nor Kin wanted me.

'What's up with her?'

Dad shrugged too, and I wondered if his meant something more as well.

'You're about as communicative as Bjorn.' Mum sighed. 'I'll need another layer tomorrow. The storm brought a cold front, but at least it'll be clear.'

'Did you see any Greenland sharks?' I asked, and Mum's energy seemed to wilt a little.

'No, but that's to be expected. They're tricky to spot at the best of times.' I didn't remind her that's not what she said yesterday. 'We weren't far enough north. We're mapping at the moment, to track their movements. We'll find one, I'm sure. It's only the first day.' She seemed to be talking to herself more than us. 'And this means I can write to the university again, and tell

them we've started. They'll have to give us the funding now we're actually out there. I'll need a new camera at least, to document everything.'

Dad's forehead creased. 'I thought you'd basically secured the money already.'

Mum waved her hands, wafting his comment away. 'This sort of research, it's not been done before. There's no precedent. We'll need to train people.'

Dad nodded slowly. 'How long is this going to take?'

'As long as it takes.'

'Julia has school, and I'll be done in two months—'

'And I might be done then, too. Or in three. This is a once-in-a-lifetime opportunity, Dan, and—'

'Maura.' Dad flicked his eyes to me, like I was still little and wouldn't notice they were already fighting.

'I might go read,' I said, and before they could stop me I picked up my library book and climbed the snail shell staircase, Noodle running ahead of me. I threw myself on to the bed, trying not to listen to Mum and Dad hissing at each other below me, and reached under my pillow, pulling out my yellow notebook.

Noodle curled on to my lower back as I turned over a new page and split it into three columns. I wrote the date and the number of hours Mum had been at sea in the first two, and then harbour porpoises and seals in the third. Chewing my pencil, I

considered the page and then, feeling a little traitorous, drew a fourth, very skinny column and put an X in it. Tomorrow it would be a tick. I had to believe it as hard as Mum, or else I'd be letting her down as badly as Dad.

I turned a new page. I wanted to write down what Kin had told me about the stars, and about Vikings. But we weren't friends any more, and they weren't strictly sea creature facts, which is what my yellow book is for. I sighed and put it away. You have to have some rules, like gravity. Otherwise you could float right off the edge of the world.

When Mum and Dad finally went to bed, I picked up my rescued torch and pulled on a jumper. Noodle followed until she realised I was going up, not down to feed her. She mewed pitifully, but I ignored her. Nerves fluttered in my belly, though there was no reason for it. It was my lighthouse. I lived here, even if it was only for a summer. I could go outside if I wanted.

But Kin wasn't there. The narrow passage around the blank beam was empty. I walked around it once to make sure, then slumped down beside the door, telling myself I didn't care. In two months I'd be home in Hayle, and I wouldn't even remember Kin, or the lighthouse. But – and this felt like a bad thought, a thought that made me feel a bit sad – my friends from home didn't care

about the things I cared about.

Remember the whale, who went around the world on the wrong frequency? Sometimes, when they were talking about YouTubers or making up dance routines, I felt like that whale. Like they could see me, but not hear me. And Kin – I think he was the same, from what he'd said about the boys at school. It sounds stupid I know, but I thought I'd found someone on my frequency. And then I ruined it, and I didn't even understand how.

The next morning a parcel arrived for Mum while we were having breakfast. When the knock came it wasn't the usual postman, but a man in a smart red and yellow uniform.

'Brilliant,' beamed Mum, as she signed for the package, her mouth still full of scrambled eggs. 'Worth every penny!'

'What is?' asked Dad, his worry line back between his eyes.

'The guaranteed delivery,' said Mum, cheerily waving the delivery man off and brandishing the package at us before pushing aside Dad's cereal bowl and sending soggy cornflakes sloshing. 'I needed this to arrive before I left.'

She attempted to get through the packaging, hacking unsuccessfully with a butter knife until Dad handed her the kitchen scissors. His worry line was deep as the Mariana Trench (the deepest place in the world so not literally, obviously) as she

lifted a neat white box with a photo of a black camera on it.

'Ta-da!' She held it out to me. 'Look, Julia! All the best wildlife photographers use these.'

'But you're not a wildlife photographer,' said Dad.

'No, but I do need to photograph wildlife,' said Mum breezily, as I opened the box and pulled the camera from its casing. It had three lenses and was black and very shiny.

'Did you get your grant then?' I said excitedly, remembering how she'd said a camera would be first on her list when she did.

'Honestly, Julia,' said Mum, snatching the camera from me a little too roughly. 'You sound like your dad. This is an investment, see? I have to go charge it before I leave. Excuse me.'

She dashed out of the kitchen, and I blinked very fast to hide that I was about to cry. I hadn't meant to burst her excitement bubble.

'It's OK, Julia,' said Dad, but the way he said it sounded like the opposite.

After she'd charged her new camera, Mum left for an overnight voyage, which meant I wouldn't be able to focus on anything all day, and meant Dad cradling the radio they used to communicate like a baby to his chest. That night I waited until I heard his door close, and snuck back up to the platform.

The hope was smaller this time, but still it stung a little when Kin wasn't there. In Dad's sternest voice, I told myself I didn't

need him. I had Noodle, and Dad, and a mum who was doing important, life-saving research. I could cope for two months in a strange place with no friends.

It was very cold on the platform, the sky even brighter than the first night. Kin would love it. I shook my head to loosen the thoughts of him. Really, it was good he wasn't here. I could get a decent night's sleep, and maybe Mum would let me go on the boat next time—

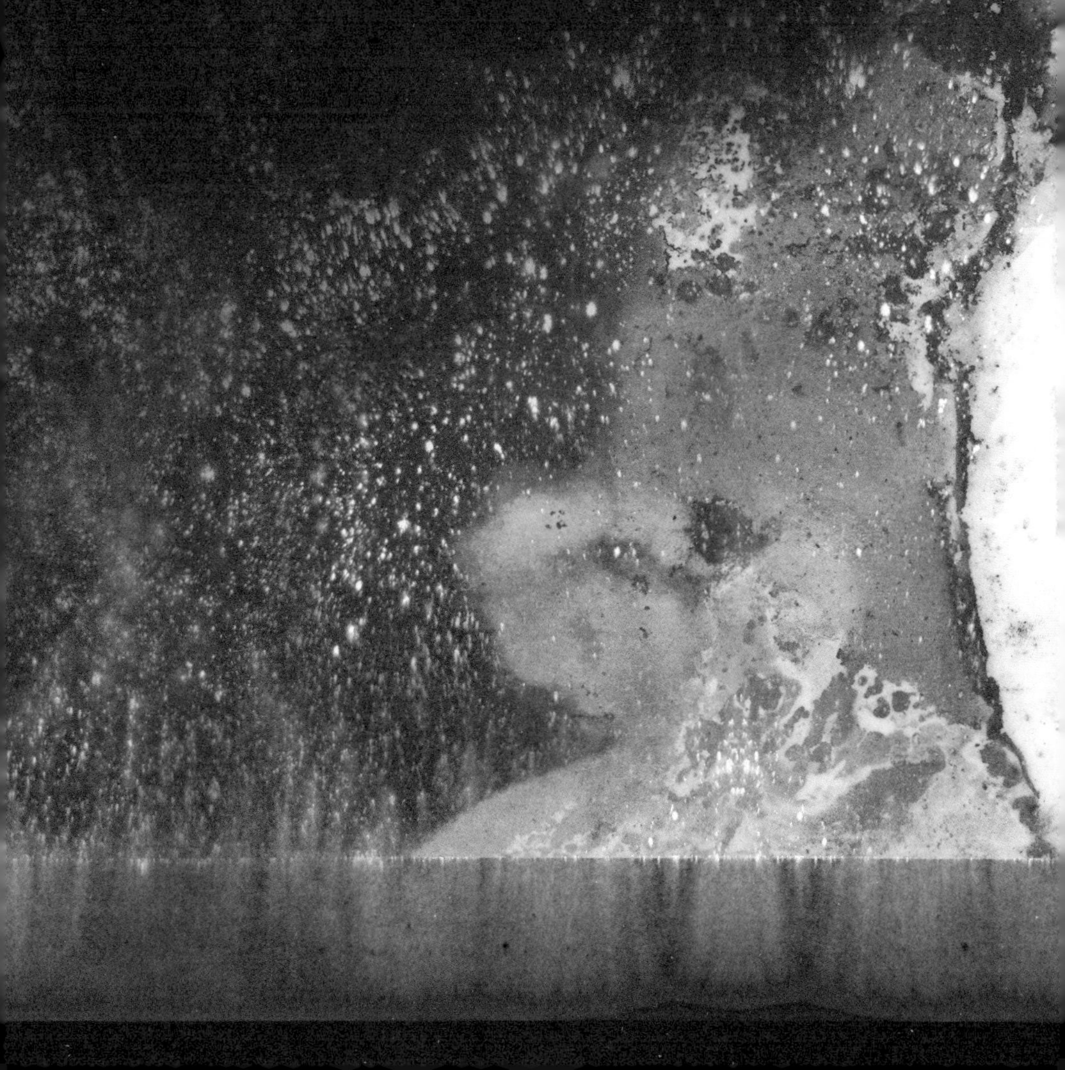

'Hi.'

Kin's head was hovering on the other side of the railing.

'Hi,' I said back casually.

'I'm coming up,' he said. 'Catch.'

He threw a rope to me, impressively accurately. It was rough and strong in my hands. The telescope rope.

I watched him wordlessly as he leaned over the railing and started drawing it up, heaving it over the metal and adjusting the tripod.

He looked through the lens, moving the telescope slightly until he found what he wanted, tightening the screw to hold the telescope in place. My heart was drumming hard, and just as I was about to give in and say *sorry* or *I'm glad to see you* or *did you know Greenland sharks smell of pee*, he turned.

'Come on then.'

Careful not to grin, I stood, and went to look through the lens. The buttery leather was soft against my cheek, and the slice of sky I could see was so beautiful I sighed before I could stop myself. He had focused it on the Pole Star.

'See it?' asked Kin. 'Dhruva Tara?'

'Bless you.'

He narrowed his eyes. Again I had the feeling of saying something wrong, and zipped my lips up tight. 'It's the Dhruva Tara. That's what my dad calls it.'

He was looking at me very intently, his face illuminated in the starlight. It seemed like this was a test, a test I was desperate to pass.

'I like it. What's it mean?'

'Dhruva was a king. Tara means star.'

Carefully, I nodded. 'My mum calls it the Pole Star.'

Something shifted in his face, like clouds parting. He grinned. 'Yes. They're both names for it. The Vikings called it the lodestar. Other people call it Polaris.'

'What do you call it?'

'Depends if I'm feeling more like my dad or a Viking.'

I nodded, understanding. 'Tonight?'

'Both.' He scuffed his foot on the metal platform. 'Julia—'

I knew he was about to say sorry, but I didn't need to hear it. 'Me too,' I said.

Still addressing his feet, he said, 'Adrian and the others, they said this island was for Vikings, and that I couldn't be one, because my parents are from India, and I have different names for things. But things have lots of names. Even me.'

'Like stars,' I said. 'I wasn't saying you couldn't be a Viking.'

'I know,' he mumbled. 'I just got ...'

He tailed off, but I already knew what he was talking about, the way feelings get bunched up under your ribcage and tear out all spiky.

'That's why I was here, the day you arrived,' he went on. 'I did used to go to the beach, but they hang out there. They tease me about the swimming.'

'Have they been to the laundromat again?'

He nodded miserably. 'And when I went cycling the other day, Adrian came right at me. I fell off trying to avoid him.'

He held up his hand, a scrape mark clearly visible on his palm. Anger spilt hot as tea inside me. 'Didn't you tell your mum?'

'No way! And you can't either. Promise?'

I promised, but his face was crumpled like a piece of old tissue. He looked up at the stars. 'I wish I could see these all the time. I wish it was always dark, and clear.'

I looked back through the telescope. A thought arrived bright as Polaris.

'Kin,' I said, straightening. 'My mum has a spare camera. A really good one that she doesn't take out with her on the boat because it's not waterproof. We could take some photos of the stars.'

He was already nodding. 'Now? We won't have a night this clear again for ages.'

I crept back inside, keeping to the edges until I reached Mum's desk. I found the old camera in the top left drawer, and brought it back up to Kin. 'Here.'

I turned it on. The memory card was full so I deleted some photos of a field with some sort of swarm over it, and aligned the lens to the telescope. Keeping very still, I pressed the shutter. The first photos were blurry and I had to keep deleting and retaking them.

'Let me try,' said Kin. His came out better, and we flicked through, him telling me the different names for each bright speck.

My teeth started to chatter. The clear night meant it was so cold I could see my breath, misting the air like the stardust. Kin was shivering, too.

'You should go,' I said. 'We'll dress warmer next time.'

'Next time?' He smiled. 'You sure?'

'Of course,' I said. 'And if you don't want to go to the beach or hang around the laundromat, you can come here. My mum's out on the boat all the time and my dad is just sorting out wires.'

He looked up at me, uncertain. 'You really don't mind?'

I nudged him with my elbow. 'I want you to.'

He smiled then, a proper smile that stretched his cheeks wide. 'All right.'

I watched him climb down, and lowered the telescope after him. Before I went back inside, I flicked through the photos again, whispering the names of the constellations he'd taught me. *Cassiopeia. Jasi. Sarpa, Ursa Major.* Just because they couldn't go in my yellow notebook didn't mean I wanted to forget them.

I was just about to turn the handle when the door was flung open with a grinding sound. Dad stood in the doorway, hands on hips, the radio blinking at his hip.

'Julia Ada Farrier. Just what do you think you are doing?'

NINE

Dad bundled me straight into a hot bath, muttering about pneumonia and how I was just like my mother.

'Anything on the radio?' I asked, my teeth chattering.

'Nothing,' said Dad, a little too brightly. 'But she said that would be the case. They're further north than yesterday. So don't you worry.' He rattled on before I could tell him I wasn't worried. 'So are you and Kin friends again?'

'How did you know we weren't?'

'I might be your dad, but I still notice things.' He smiled. 'Next time you go adventuring, wear a jumper.'

'We weren't adventuring. We were stargazing.'

'Wear. A. Jumper.' He picked up the camera from where I had laid it on the sink. 'And be careful with this, J. You can use my

camera if you like.'

'I *was* careful.'

'I know,' he said soothingly.

'She has that new one now anyway.'

'Yes,' said Dad. 'Though I'm going to talk to her about sending it back. I looked up the model and ...' He sighed. 'Anyway. It's extravagant. But this one,' he brandished the camera, 'is special. So we're going to leave it to Mum, OK?'

'OK.'

He left me to wash, both the radio and the camera now cradled to his chest. Noodle came to sit on the edge of the bath, straight-backed like it was the prow of a boat.

'Are you sad Mum left you behind too?' I asked her, and she blinked mournfully at me. The water further north was too rough to take her, which meant really Mum shouldn't be going either. But I comforted myself with the fact Captain Bjorn seemed sensible.

I thought about what he'd said, about never seeing a Greenland shark himself. How Mum might not find one at all. The shadow that had moved under Mum's face when he said it, like a fin cutting just under the surface of water. It had been exactly like Kin's expression when he'd seen Adrian at the laundromat window.

I shuddered, the water suddenly feeling as cold as outside.

Noodle batted at the bubbles, but I couldn't relax, and I got out. I changed into clean pyjamas, and Dad came down from his office to tuck me in, layering an extra blanket on top of my duvet.

'How's the light thing going?' I yawned.

He chuckled. 'You really are like your mum. You know the Latin names for sea creatures and yet you still call my work "the light thing".' I smiled proudly as he rubbed his eyes with the heels of his hands. 'Not easy, not like I hoped. But I'll make it work.' He stroked back my hair. 'Go to sleep, J.'

It was easier said than done. The wind picked up, and soon it was howling, making the lighthouse creak and pop, like trodden-on floorboards, whipping the smell of grass and salt through the gaps of my door. The sea was the worst, though, so loud, roaring like a monster. I half-expected it to seep through the walls. I took hold of my yellow notebook for comfort. The rough seas had reached us,

and I hoped Mum

was

holding

on

tight.

The bed was a boat, and the sheets turned to foam under my fingers. The whole room was rocking, and above me the roof was gone, replaced with lightning lashing the low, thick clouds, long tongues of fire furling and unfurling, tracing veins of burning silver – but silent. It raged and raged, without a sound.

And there was something in the water.

It was deep,
moving slowly
through the black sea.
The water rose above the rolling shape,
huge and swallowing as the sky.
I couldn't move,
couldn't see it.
It was quiet, all so quiet
I felt caught behind glass.
I couldn't turn my head,
but I knew it was rising,
knew it was opening
a mouth
wide as
the world—

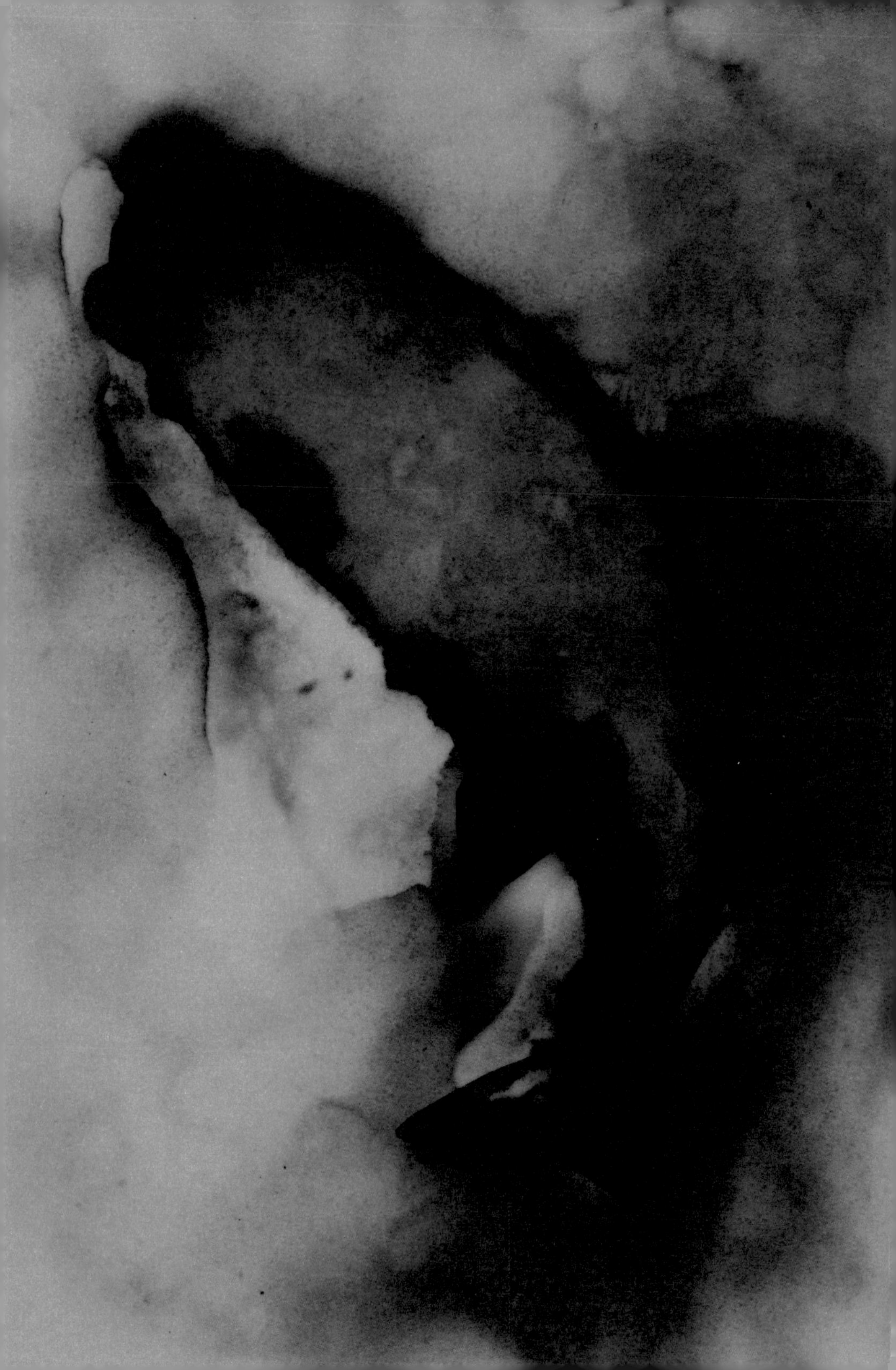

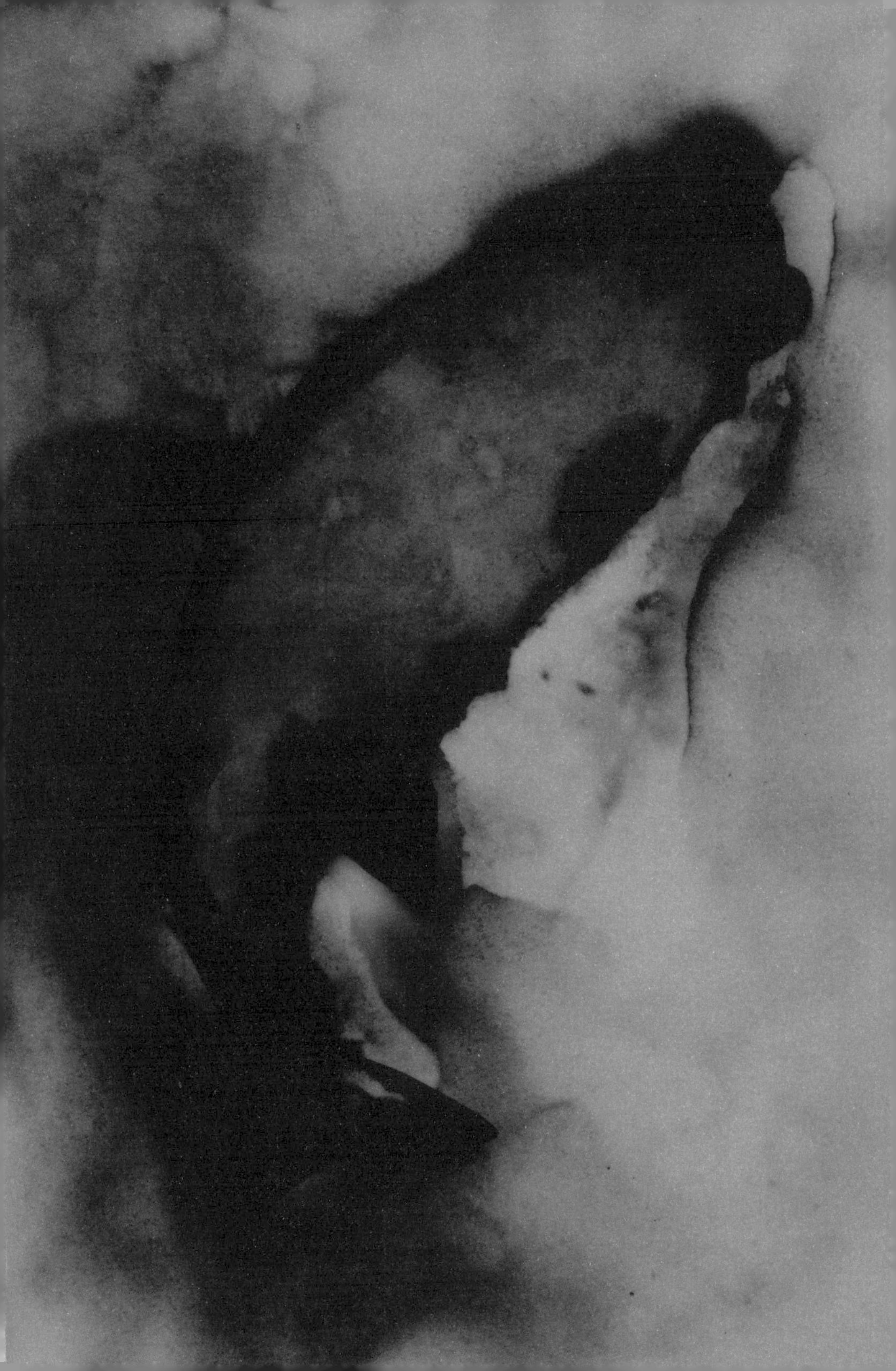

Wailing woke me. I lay still, heart beating too fast from my nightmare, until I recognised it as the screeching of the kettle, boiling on the stove. I squinted at my watch. 3:23 a.m. I sighed, and rolled over. Dad had clearly not been able to sleep after all.

Then I realised he was talking, a low rumble. But it was not Noodle's answering squeak that came next, but Mum's voice, quiet and fast. Relief spread warm through my body, and I swung my legs out of bed. She would come in to kiss me like she always did, but I wanted to hear how it had gone.

I started down the stairs when there was a thump, a bang as though something had been slammed on the table. I stopped short and sat down on the stairs, breathing quietly.

'Complete waste of time,' came Mum's voice, floating in and out of listening level. I crept down another step. 'I said he was being too careful—'

'No such thing as too careful,' said Dad soothingly. 'He knows what he's doing.'

'Or he's on the make,' said Mum. 'He knows we don't have the budget at the moment, and the grant application won't be processed for days.'

'He has to make a living—'

'Whose side are you on?'

'You're not being fair, Maura—'

A bang again, and I realised Mum was hitting her hand on the table. Noodle shot up the stairs, coming to a halt next to me, rubbing against my knee.

'No, *you're* not being fair,' Mum sounded even angrier. 'You know what this means to me. If I could just get someone to believe in me—'

'I believe in you. Julia does. Your mum did.'

There was a gasp, and soft sobs that scared me almost as much as the ferocity had. Mum was crying. The noise made a lump swell in my throat. I felt like I'd heard her cry like that before, but

I couldn't remember when.

'Shhhh,' said Dad gently. 'It's all right. You mustn't get like this, Maura. You know what happened before.'

'I won't. I'm not – I'm sorry. I just want this to work, Dan. I need this to work.'

'And I know you'll do everything you can. But your health is more important. Are you taking your pills?'

'I know that.' The impatience was back in Mum's voice, and she ignored Dad's question. 'I don't want to talk about it any more if you're going to patronise me.'

There was a scrape as Mum pushed her chair back. I scuttled around the curve of the staircase, leaping into bed just as I heard her footsteps on the stair outside.

But though I heard her pause outside my room, she didn't come in.

She pulled the door to, softly, and I lay in the dark, listening as she went back down, the floorboards of their bedroom creaking as she got into bed. The kettle was still screaming. It levelled off into a low whistle as Dad lifted it off the hob. I pulled out my yellow notebook and put another cross into the fourth column.

TEN

Our new life found its rhythm. Kin came to visit most days, and we'd talk about books and stars and the sea. I'd try to get him to talk about Adrian, but he refused. I understood, sort of. When I was bullied it made me feel sticky and gross, like a slug, and it took me ages to tell anyone.

Dad would clatter about the light, squeezing past us on the balcony with wires, swearing and shouting 'Swear jar!' by turns, and Mum was hardly ever home.

She stayed away for nights at a time while her two weeks with Captain Bjorn ticked down. I didn't hear any more arguments, even about the expensive camera, but maybe it was only they had them more quietly.

Kin and the stars were almost enough of a distraction from

Mum's leaving, and I was getting good at remembering the star names. He was teaching me about quadrants, and how the same star sometimes had a hundred different myths. In return, I was telling him about my mum's research, which sounded as far-fetched to him as his stories did to me.

'A shark, older than trees?' He shook his head. 'And she's going to stop people dying with it?'

'Not exactly,' I said. 'She's trying to slow down aging. My grandma was sick, and she died before they could find a cure.'

'I'm sorry,' said Kin. 'It's nice your mum is doing something for her. Have they found one yet?'

I shook my head. It seemed to be going better since the first failed overnight expedition. They were away for days at a time, covering vast distances, stretching all the way into the Arctic Circle and beyond.

'It's so beautiful, J,' she'd sigh. 'I'll take you someday.'

I'd bite my tongue, holding in my question of why she could not take me this moment, now, the very next day. But though Mum came home with photos on her new camera of orcas and humpback whales, seals and porpoises, sea ice and every kind of seabird, there was hardly any mention of the shark.

The truth was that when Mum was at the lighthouse, she wasn't exactly easy to be around. One morning she got back so late it was daytime, and Dad and I went to the big supermarket

on Mainland, Shetland to get a tub of her favourite sausage rolls. We made a bow for it out of old newspaper, setting it on the table so it would be the first thing she saw when she got in. We even set the table with knives and forks, so it was like a proper party.

But when the key turned in the lock, Mum barely seemed to notice us, let alone the sausage rolls. Her eyes had huge dark smudges under them like storm clouds, and there was an unsettling energy around her too, like the approaching crackle of lightning. It reminded me of how Noodle gets sometimes, chasing shadows and things that aren't there, but it's a lot less cute when it's your mum. Her round face was thinner, more straight-lined, like the furniture in the curved rooms of the lighthouse. Like she wasn't fitting her skin.

'Hey little J, missed me?' She hugged me, and she smelt of the sea. I nodded into her coat, the rubber making small squeaking noises, and tried to ignore how I could feel the bones in her back, when usually she was lovely and soft.

I didn't need to ask if she'd found the shark – I could feel from her hug she wasn't happy. She hugged Dad too, but instead of sitting at the table with us she picked up the giant tub of sausage rolls from the table, seeming not to notice the bow as it peeled off, and went upstairs, muttering about work.

'Never mind, J,' said Dad bracingly. 'Pasta?' But I suddenly didn't feel hungry.

That evening wasn't much better. She emerged for dinner so late it was almost fully dark outside, talking about sightings on Norwegian fisherman forums, and grant applications, and not at all about me or Dad.

Her brain was obviously still at sea, searching for the shark, and when she did eventually ask me questions, her eyes were sort of glassy and far away. I knew she was brilliant, and that her brain was very clever, but she wasn't good at focusing on more than one thing at once.

We had a few nights like this, and every few days an envelope would arrive, A4 and thin, with Mum's name on it: Dr Maura Farrier.

The first time, Mum had ripped it open at the kitchen table.

'It's here, Dan, look!' But she fell silent, and read the brief contents with her lips pressed tight together. She scrunched up the piece of paper, and threw it on the wood burner where it crumpled up to ash.

'No?' said Dad tentatively.

Mum shook her head. 'Plenty more fish in the sea.'

And even I laughed, because she hadn't made one of her stupid jokes in a long time, and I'd missed them, even though they were terrible. When more envelopes came, though, they were no thicker than the last. After the third one, Mum didn't even open them in front of us.

A fortnight after we arrived in Unst, I was writing in my notebook when Mum came through the door with an armful of flowers, a bottle of wine under the other.

'Where's your dad?' she said, planting a kiss on the top of my head. Without waiting for a response, she leaned up the stairs and shouted. 'Dan! Dad! The girls require your presence!'

Noodle came running downstairs at the sound of her voice, and Mum scooped her up and plonked her on to the table.

'What's going on?' I snatched up my notebook as Mum scattered the flowers over it and Noodle. She always refused extra packaging, even when it wasn't practical.

She rattled about in the kitchen drawer, finding a corkscrew. 'We are celebrating!'

'Celebrating what?' Dad was standing on the bottom step, eyeing Mum warily. She pulled the cork out with a flourish, even though it was only just gone lunchtime.

'Progress!' She slopped three glugs of wine into three glasses.

'The grant?' Dad stepped forward, relief plain on his face, but Mum waved his question away.

'Much better.' She put the glasses down in front of us, and Dad surreptitiously poured mine into his glass as Noodle sniffed it and, realising it wasn't something she wanted to drink,

jumped off the table.

'The shark?' I clapped my hands. 'You found the shark!'

'Soon,' she said, raising her glass in a toast and looking around at us both triumphantly. 'I bought a boat!'

She drank a big gulp of wine, her swallowing the only sound in the silence.

'A boat?' I repeated, saying it slowly to give my brain time to catch up.

'Maura,' said Dad faintly. 'What do you mean?'

'What I said, silly!' Mum poured more wine into her glass, and I saw her hands were shaking. I moved my notebook out of the way to stop it getting splashed, watching her nervously. 'Captain Bjorn said he couldn't wait any longer for the grant to come through, and so I thought, why not get my own boat?'

'Because,' said Dad, 'we can't afford it.'

But Mum ignored this, chattering on with a strange brightness in her too-wide eyes. I clamped my hands under my armpits, hugging myself and breathing slowly, like that might calm her down, too.

'I can sail just as well as him,' she said, 'and it'll work out cheaper in the long run. Gin had his old fishing boat just rotting away, and I have the transmitters from Falmouth, and the radar, and it won't take a week for me to get everything ready. I'll need your help, of course, and Julia can do some of the mending, if

you want to, J? Kin can help, too.' She looked at me expectantly.

Dad sat down heavily, and reached for Mum's hand. 'I'm not sure—'

She snatched it away. 'I'm going to email the uni now, and tell them the new plan.' She smiled brightly at us both, and disappeared upstairs. I looked to Dad, expecting a reassuring remark or a rueful grin, two of his usual reactions to Mum's plans, but his face was creased with worry. I squeezed my arms tighter.

'Give us a minute, J,' he said, and, without looking at me, he followed Mum up the stairs. I didn't want to listen to another argument. Loosing my hands, I snatched up my yellow notebook and slid it into my pocket.

'I'm going to see Kin,' I called, and without waiting for an answer I went to the shed for my bike.

My thoughts cycled hard as my legs. The brightness of Mum's eyes, the worry in Dad's voice, and in my chest the increasing feeling of nervousness whenever we talked about the shark. At the beginning, that hadn't been there at all. In the beginning, I had been as excited as Mum. But her excitement had an edge to it now, like desperation.

It was strange, but somehow familiar, like I'd seen her like this before. The memories were fuzzy like someone had rubbed Vaseline on my brain. Under all this was the worst thought: the

traitorous thought. That maybe Dad was right about the boat being a bad idea. Which meant Mum was wrong.

My legs and lungs were burning by the time I reached town, and from the heat in my face I knew I was red as the tomatoes growing on the windowsill. So when I rounded the bend to town, and saw Adrian and two other boys cycling towards me, I kept my head very low down and wished to be invisible, like I had been to Dad at the table. It didn't work.

'It's Flower's girlfriend!' Adrian swerved in front of my bike, and I had to brake very hard.

'She's twice his size,' snorted one of his friends.

'Isn't your mum a whale scientist?' said the other, a tall boy with curly hair. 'Is that why she had you?'

I glared at him, pulling my jeans up higher where they had slipped down as I rode. 'She's a marine biologist.'

Adrian yawned widely, showing gappy teeth. 'Don't care.'

I put my foot on the pedal, but he didn't move.

'Excuse me,' I said in my best Mum voice, the one she uses when someone pushes in front of her in a queue and she wants to sound polite while actually threatening their life. 'Let me through.'

Adrian got off his bike and wheeled forwards a couple of paces. My heart was beating so hard I was sure he'd hear it. Surely he wouldn't hit me? Not here, on the main street, in the

middle of the day? But instead he just walked around me, his wheel almost touching mine.

'Later, whale,' he sneered.

I pushed off, being very careful not to look back.

I found Kin in the library room at the laundromat, and his parents let us into their little courtyard at the back and gave us milk and digestives. I was still shaking from my encounter with Adrian and his cronies.

'We have to do something about them. They can't just go around being like that.'

Kin shrugged, his face going closed off like it had when Adrian had come to the laundromat. 'You have to just ignore them.'

'Bit hard when they're standing in my way. Maybe we should tell Gin, he's his granddad right?' Kin didn't answer. He obviously wanted me to stop talking about it. I sighed, then snapped my fingers. Mentioning Gin made me realise the reason I'd come to see Kin in the first place.

'Gin's boat?' Kin's eyebrows lifted like two black caterpillars when I relayed Mum's plan. 'It's really old.'

'She's good at fixing boats,' I said. 'And she said you can help.'

Kin looked unsure. 'I'm not sure I'd be any good.'

'You've never tried,' I said. 'It's a useful Viking skill.'

His face lit up at that. 'Yeah, suppose. What will I have to do?'

They say you can't smell anything in dreams, but that night the stink of the shark filled my nostrils. I tried to open my eyes but they were frosted like glass beneath ice, and every breath was full of water. The shark was beneath my bed, growing large as the room, large as the lighthouse, rising from unfathomable depths until it ripped the whole island from its roots.

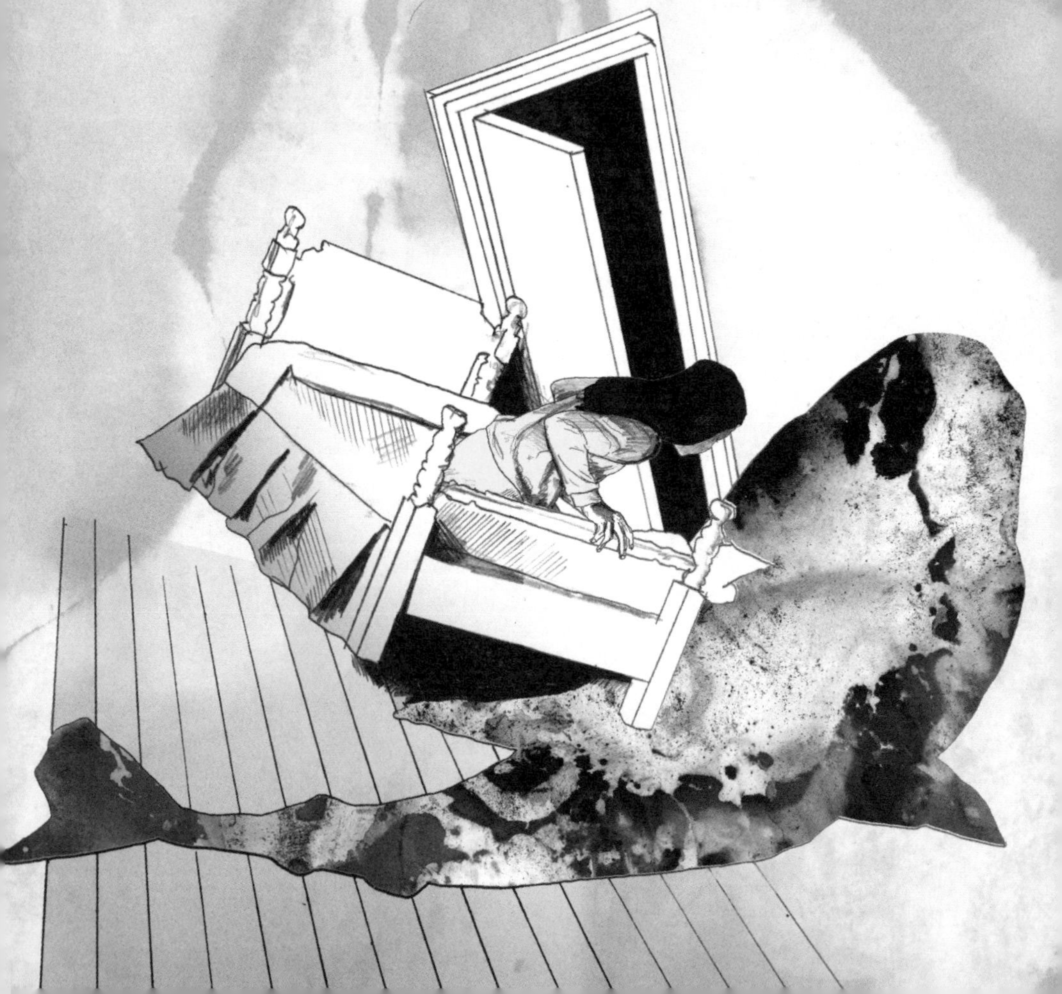

The bed was a boat,
the shark a tide,
and it pulled me so far out to sea
I was only a speck, a spot, a mote,
a dying star in an unending sky.

ELEVEN

Things at the lighthouse felt sticky and strange, like the air before a thunderstorm. Mum was lightning, sizzling with her unnatural energy, and Dad was the thunder, grumbling and rumbling and trying to talk her out of the boat. I don't know where Noodle and I fitted in – I didn't feel like we did. All they talked about, snapped about, shouted about, was the boat, which was really about money. But Dad couldn't stop the boat coming.

Gin towed it to the little cove below the lighthouse in his old 4x4.

'You've got quite a project on your hands.' He smiled. I was about to return it when I saw who was beside him. A sullen-faced, floppy-haired figure. Adrian. I shrank back in horror as he hopped out to help Dad unlatch the boat from the van.

Mum clapped her hands together.

'You'll see. It'll be the finest vessel Unst ever knew.'

Gin chuckled, and Adrian laughed too, but it wasn't a nice laugh. I knew he wouldn't say anything with grown ups there, but still I couldn't relax until Gin drove off, waving as they bumped away down the potholed road. We turned to look at the boat.

I could tell Dad was trying to put on a brave face for me, but I could also tell that he was worried. I was a little, too. Actually, I was a lot. Gin hadn't used it in years, and it was obvious why. It looked like a wreck, washed up on our shingle beach. The hull needed patching, and the stuffing on the benches in the small cabin was leaking out. The whole thing smelt of fish, and there was barely room for all the equipment Mum needed.

'It'll be snug,' said Mum merrily, 'but it's far more nippy than *The Floe*. I'll chase down that shark in no time.'

Kin came to help, and Mum put us in charge of tarring the hull. It made our hands black, and smelt of melting roads, and took days to fully fade off our skin. Dad went through the electrics. I got the feeling he was glad not to work on the lighthouse for a while. From the puffing and swearing that came from his office every day, and the fact that the lighthouse beam was still unlit, I wasn't sure it was going that well. He spent all week installing the software Mum needed, and drove to Mainland to buy new lifejackets, flares and distress beacons.

Before he left, Mum told him Gin was coming to check our work on the hull while he was at the shops, but he never showed

up. When Dad came back and asked how it went, Mum said 'Fine!' in that dazzlebright voice, and I chewed my tongue.

She rattled around the house, cooking big bean stews and planting chillies, replanting her tomato noodle pots and eating a lot of sausage rolls. She seemed distracted and absolutely focused all at the same time, and I wondered whether this was what Ms Braimer meant when she said Mozart was a genius, but he was terrible at normal life.

Maybe her days and dreams were all full of the shark and its possibilities, like mine. But she couldn't be afraid of it like I was, or she wouldn't dare go out in an old boat to look for it.

Finally, a week after the rusting boat had arrived, it was ready for its maiden voyage.

'Looks good,' said Dad, sounding impressed despite himself, and I agreed. Mum had painted it white and grey, like a seagull, and in great, looping, yellow letters she'd handwritten its name on the side, uneven and tailing off at a slant at the end where she'd got bored:

My heart swooped. Seeing my name like that, beside the shark's, made all Mum's moods worth it. I mattered, just as much as her research.

Dad towed it into the water, and we all cheered as no leaks came through. Kin and I high-fived.

'Excellent tarring,' I said, bowing.

'And to you, good sir,' he said, bowing back.

Mum snorted. 'Very good indeed. We can invite Gin and his grandson out on it!'

Kin visibly flinched, but Mum rattled on. 'Let's have a photo. I'll get the camera.'

She went galloping inside, and Dad bent to pick up Noodle, an essential component of any photo our family takes.

'Well done us,' he said, grinning at us both. 'Maybe she'll be able to sell this on for a tidy profit in a few weeks.'

My tummy went all swoopy then. I hadn't thought about how little time Mum had left to find the shark. Or how little time I had left with Kin. I didn't look at him, but he moved a bit closer, so maybe he was thinking the same thing.

A cry came from the lighthouse. Dad frowned but before he could move we saw Mum whirling down the slope, her oversize cardigan slipping down around her shoulders, her eyes wide.

'Did you do this?' she said, waving something at Dad. It was the camera, the spare one I'd taken star photos on.

'Mum?' She wheeled around, and tried to pull her cardigan back up. Kin took a step back.

'Julia, Kin, I think you should go inside for a minute.' She turned back to Dad. 'Did you borrow this?'

'No, Mum, I—' I swallowed. 'I borrowed it. I kept it out of the rain ...'

She pressed the button, and it whirred into life. The guilt retreated a little. It wasn't broken.

'Did you do this?' Her voice was calm, but shook a little at the edges. She was flicking through the pictures of the constellations.

'Yes—' I started.

'Did you delete some?'

'No, I—' I stopped, remembering the field, the swarm. 'Maybe. It was full, the card. I checked they weren't of anything important.'

'Weren't anything important,' said Mum dully, and it was scarier than if she'd shouted. She turned to Dad helplessly. 'Gretna Green, Dan. She deleted the photos I took at the murmuration, that last time.'

It didn't mean anything to me, but it obviously did to Dad. 'Maura, it's OK. You probably have them backed up somewhere.'

But she was already shaking her head. 'I lost the lead, remember? I was getting a new one posted. I never got round to it, with the funding stuff.'

'Julia didn't know,' said Dad. 'It's OK, J. Isn't it, Mum?'

Mum's back was to me, and she was taking big, heaving breaths, like she was crying.

'Maura?' prompted Dad.

'Not now, Dan.' Her voice broke. I knew it was my fault. My eyes smarted too, the lighthouse blurring behind her, the damp warping and spreading until it was all I could see. It was like the shark was bleeding through it, making everything shimmer and come loose.

'Why don't we ...' said Dad, looking apologetically at Kin. 'Kin, why don't we take a photo another time?'

I didn't want Kin to go, but I couldn't ask him to stay, not with Mum so clearly upset. A hot prickle of embarrassment scuttled across my cheeks and I ducked my head, feeling Kin look at me.

'It's fine,' he said uncertainly. 'I guess I'll go?'

The question in his voice was directed at me, but I didn't want to look up in case he saw the tears now dripping off my chin.

'I'll see you soon, Julia.' I felt Kin's hand, warm and dry, squeeze mine briefly, and heard the crunch of Dad and Kin's shoes as they walked together up the slope to Kin's bike. When I was sure Kin was out of sight I looked up at Mum. She was hunched over the camera with her back to me, breathing deeply.

'Mum?'

She flinched, and I felt like I had when I fell off a climbing frame two years ago, all the air punched out of me.

Dad came back and pulled me into his warm side. 'Mum, Julia needs a hug.'

She turned, then. The camera was clutched to her chest, and her eyes were glassy as she looked at us. She looked like something from a sad film, the light seeming to settle grey and heavy over her shoulders, her skin mottled as the shark's.

'Mum?' Dad prompted. 'Maura?'

Mum stepped forward and hugged me, but it felt spiky and strange, when normally Mum's hugs were like jumping into a warm bed. I couldn't hug her back, not properly.

'There,' said Dad bracingly. 'All better. Shall we take that photo, then?'

'Photo?' Mum let go of me, and was looking at the camera again. She seemed to have forgotten all about *Julia & the Shark*, bobbing in the shallows behind us.

TWELVE

Mum went upstairs, and while Dad boiled the kettle I sat at the table with my insides churning like a washing machine in Kin's laundromat. Dad chattered cheerfully, and I could tell he was hoping I would forget what had just happened and be happy, but I couldn't.

'Dad,' I said finally, when he stopped to draw breath. 'What's Gretna Green?'

His shoulders tensed a little, but his voice was still light as he plopped the tea bag into the mug.

'Just somewhere important to your mum.' I waited. Dad sighed. 'A murmuration happens there.'

'A murmuration.' I turned the word over. It was familiar but I couldn't remember why.

'Birds,' said Dad. 'When they all fly in to roost. Thousands of them. A hundred thousand, sometimes.'

If I'd asked Mum, it'd have been a far more vivid description. But words are Mum's thing – trust Dad to have focused on the numbers.

'She scattered her mum's ashes there,' he continued. 'At the murmuration the year she was pregnant with you.' I must have looked stricken, because Dad hurried on. 'Don't worry. She's just tired. You know she's a monster when she's tired. This boat stuff has taken it out of all of us.'

'But ...' I bit my lip. I didn't know how to put what I wanted to say, and for the first time I wished I could think like Dad, put down my thoughts into a sum, express myself with an equation that he could easily understand.

'It's OK, Julia,' said Dad softly. He was looking at me with very kind eyes, and it made me want to cry. 'What is it?'

'I think I remember ...'

Dad waited. I spoke to my lap, my fingers twisting white. I knew I had to say it like he would, binary and straight.

'She's been like this before.'

Dad's listening became loud, you know how that happens when someone is really concentrating and you can feel the white noise of their attention.

I screwed up my eyes, the better to see the memory. Mum in the

garden in Cornwall, scrunched up like a piece of old paper below the ash tree. Her shoulders shaking, the sound of her weeping. I shuddered, and looked up at Dad. His face was open and kind.

'I remember when I was little. She was walking around all strange and then she was crying in the garden.'

Dad's touch landed lightly on my head, like he was trying to stop my racing thoughts. 'You have such a clever brain, Julia. You were tiny when that happened.'

'So it did happen?'

'Yes.' Dad's voice was nearly a whisper. 'When you were three. And another time, when she was pregnant. But it's nothing to do with you, Julia. It's the shark.'

I hadn't thought it was until he said it. But the shark hadn't been there when she was pregnant, or when I was three. I had been. Now my heart began to beat very hard.

'She was fine then, and she'll be fine now,' said Dad, seemingly taking my silence as a good sign, because he took his hand off my head. It felt like it was going to spin off my neck and float away. Dad strained the tea bag, placing it on the side so Mum could use the grounds for her tomatoes, and sloshed some milk into her favourite blue mug. 'You want to take this up?'

Feeling oddly nervous, I circled the steps, the washing machine in my belly kicking up to its final crazed cycle. Their bedroom door was closed, Noodle sitting hopefully outside. Scratching

her neck, I pressed my ear to the door, but if Mum was crying, I couldn't hear it. I knocked. There was no answer, and for a minute I thought about putting the tea down for Noodle and leaving. But that was stupid. It was only Mum.

I pushed open the door, Noodle snaking in behind me. The room was dim and airless, and a shape shifted on the messy bed. For a moment it looked like a deep sea, a fin breaking the waves – but then it was only Mum's hand as she reached out to me. 'Come here, J.'

Setting the tea down on the bedside table, I climbed in beside her. She was barely warm though the blankets were pulled right up to her chin, and her breath smelt sour. Still I snuggled in close, trying to get comfy next to the new, unfamiliar angles of her body. Noodle climbed on top of us both, stretching out like a sausage.

I tried to relax, to enjoy being with her. But her voice was too sad, her body too thin. She felt like a different person. She didn't even smell like Mum – she smelt of indoors. But soon, I reminded myself, she'd be out on the boat, and she'd go back to normal. She'd be fine, like Dad said she'd been before. She had to be.

We listened to Noodle purring. There was something that was nibbling at me, like those parasites who attach themselves to the Greenland shark's eyeball until it goes blind, and in the dark I felt all right to ask it.

'Mum? Why did you lie to Dad?'

Mum stiffened slightly, and Noodle let out a warning mew. 'When?'

'About the hull, about getting Gin to come and check it?'

'Oh that.' She relaxed again, yawning though it was only the afternoon. 'Because Gin couldn't come for a while, and I wanted to get going. It was fine anyway, wasn't it?'

'You don't know that yet,' I pointed out. The boat had only just gone in the water.

'I do know,' she said, and it was so nice to hear her definite again I let it go.

'Why did you react like that, when I mentioned Gin's grandson?' She'd done that thing again, the leap from one thought to another without showing her working.

'Like what?'

'You want to talk about it?'

I shook my head, but she pushed on anyway. 'My best friend got bullied at school. She had big ears, and one of the older boys used to lift her up by them.'

'It's not that,' I said, horrified. Kin had normal-sized ears, anyway. 'Was she OK?'

'Oh yes,' snorted Mum. 'The thing about bullies is they pick on people who they think are weaker. So we worked out *his* weakness. He was scared of spiders, and I collected any dead ones I found for a week, and then put them down his shirt.'

She mimed flailing about and screaming. Noodle jumped huffily off the bed and soon we were both laughing. Mum stopped first, and sighed. I could feel the atmosphere in the room shift again, becoming low and gloomy.

'It's going to be all right,' said Mum, more to herself than to me. 'I'm going to find the shark. I just need people to believe in me.'

There was a horrible, plummeting sensation in my tummy. I hadn't believed in her lately. My yellow notebook, with its lines of crosses and coordinates, was proof. I'd become like Dad, looking at the numbers. I needed to be more like Mum. I used my words.

'I believe in you.'

Mum laughed, but it was a hard sound, like a fist hitting wood. 'Do you have fifteen million pounds, J?' Mum shifted impatiently. 'Scooch over. You're squashing me.'

Her eyes were starting to flutter closed, and I slid out of bed and pulled the door to. But more than anything, it felt like Mum was shutting the door on me.

For once I was above water.
For once I wasn't afraid.
The sky stretched huge over me,
and at its height was a small flock of birds.

They dived and twisted and lifted, and as they wove through the clear sky, more joined them, and more and more.

They were like a cloud now, a gathering storm. And then there were so many the sky started to crack at its edges, a blue balloon swarmed by birds.

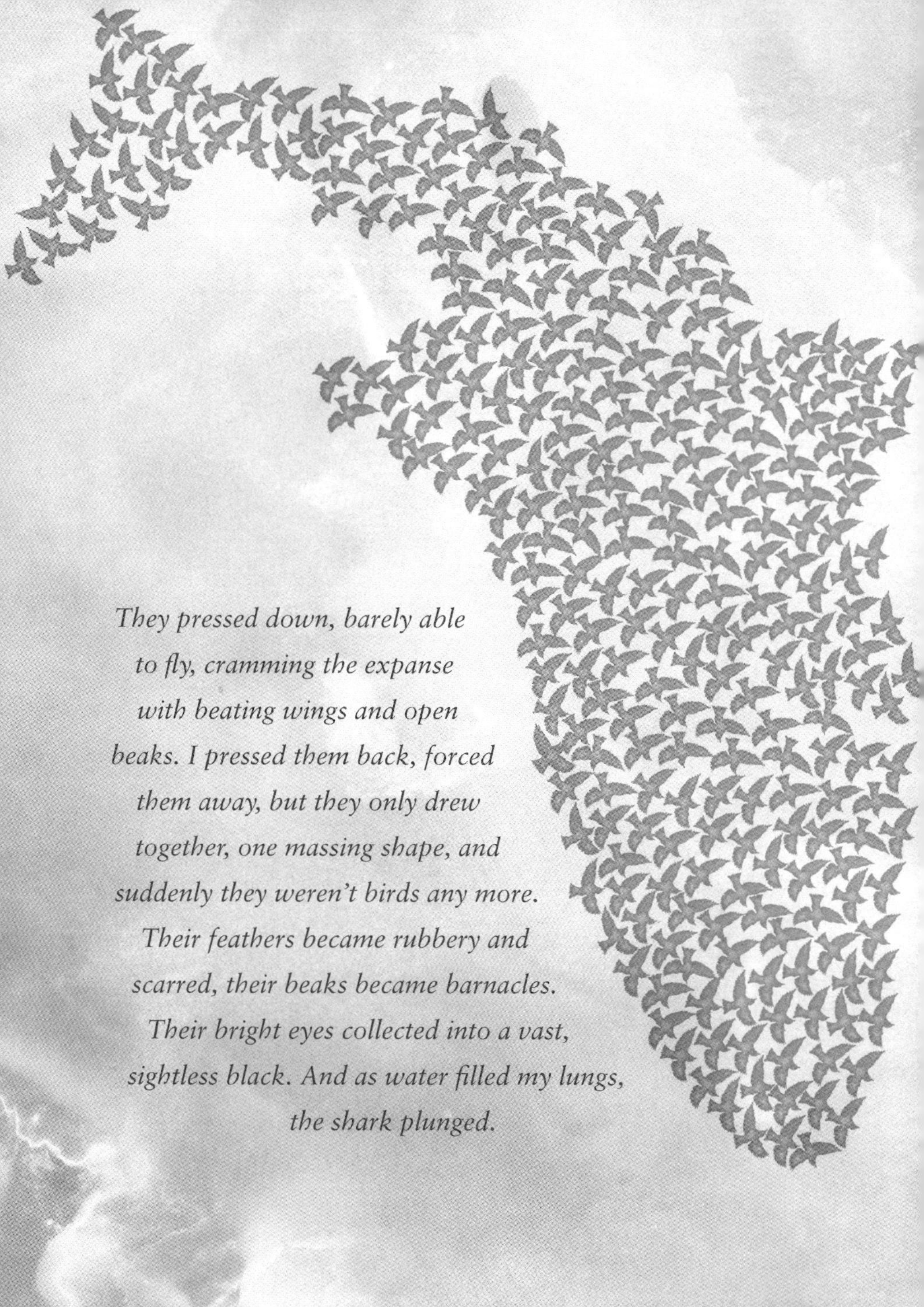

They pressed down, barely able to fly, cramming the expanse with beating wings and open beaks. I pressed them back, forced them away, but they only drew together, one massing shape, and suddenly they weren't birds any more. Their feathers became rubbery and scarred, their beaks became barnacles. Their bright eyes collected into a vast, sightless black. And as water filled my lungs, the shark plunged.

THIRTEEN

It was just the four of us on the maiden voyage of *Julia & the Shark*. Noodle liked the boat instantly, leaping into the prow and leaning into the wind like a figurehead, which I took as a good sign. Another good sign was that when Mum let me turn the key in the ignition, the engine started on the first try.

'High-five, J!' she said.

She was trying, I could feel it. But that was part of the problem. Her smile seemed thin and fragile, like a tracing paper mask with the real frown showing through.

I sat down on the repaired leather seat, and Dad put his arm around me. I wondered if he noticed Mum's mask, too. His grip tightened when Mum started to steer the boat out of the bay,

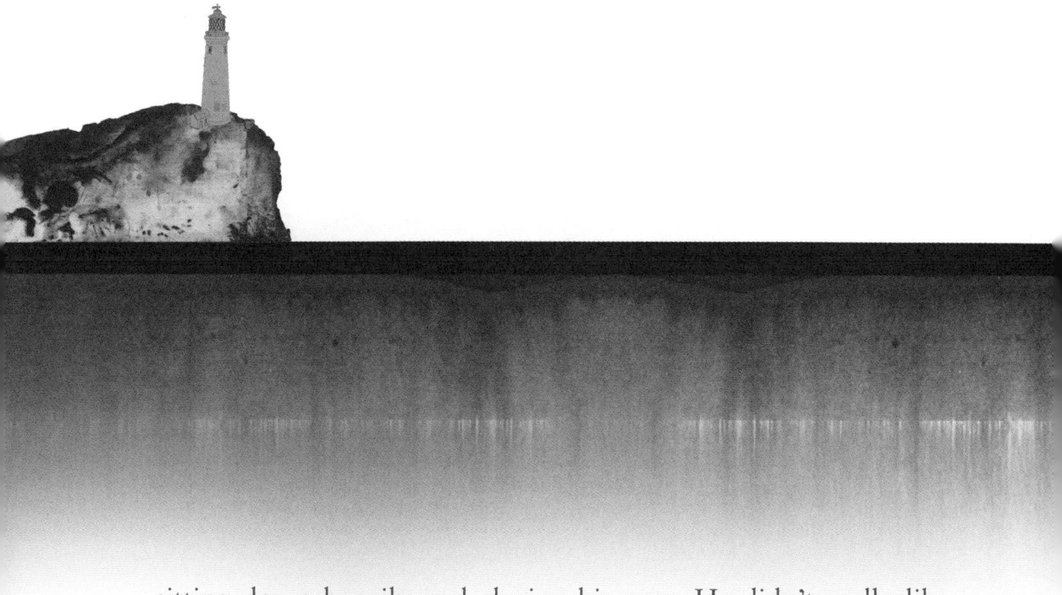

sitting down heavily and closing his eyes. He didn't really like boats, which was a grave error when marrying Mum.

The lighthouse was soon a speck. The boat was fast, and even Mum slowed it a little, spray misting down over us, and soon my jumper was covered in a layer of neat droplets. I huddled deeper into Dad, and once we were on open sea, he seemed to relax a bit. The water was calm, with no wind making waves, and he moved to sit in the stern with Noodle on his lap.

Mum stopped the engine and brought over her nautical map to show me. It's laminated and massive. Fully open it would fill the whole of the lighthouse's kitchen, so it was folded into squares, covered in Mum's messy black writing. There were crosses dappled all over, and with a jab of guilt I remembered my notebook, all the marks I'd made highlighting Mum's daily failures.

'So here's where the shark was sighted last, by a fishing boat.' She pointed to a place closer to Shetland than I'd expected. 'And it only moves about half a mile an hour. So this is the radius I'll be exploring.' She showed me the area – two square's worth. Even though it looked small on the map, I knew a parcel of sea that big was not going to be easy to cover. Not when there was just one of her, and one of the shark.

'I can help,' I said. 'Come with you?'

'I don't think so,' said Mum. 'It'll be a squeeze with all my equipment.' I tried to seem like it didn't hurt, but Mum wasn't even looking at me anyway.

I was as much worried as disappointed. The sea seemed very big out here. In Cornwall you could always see land, and I knew that in every direction there was either Ireland, or England or Wales. But here there was nothing, our lighthouse a speck on

Unst, which was in turn a speck on the horizon behind us, so small and faint I felt like I could rub it from sight with my thumb. And Norway was somewhere over there, to the east, and Iceland to the west, and they felt like much wilder, far-off places than Mum was used to.

And somewhere in the depths was the shark, moving slower than time, growing more ancient and as steadily as a tree.

It was like the voyage of *Julia & the Shark* was a good omen, because the next day Dad finished his programming. He and Mum drank a whole bottle of wine each to celebrate, and we went outside to watch the lighthouse lighting itself automatically as soon as darkness fell. It stopped Kin and I stargazing from there, but sometimes he'd come to sit with me anyway, watching the beam sweep the sea, searching for something.

Some nights, Mum was out there too, and Dad woke with big rings like bruises under his eyes, and I barely slept. I distracted myself with the stars. There was a meteor shower due, and Kin and I had plans to go to the cliff nearby to watch, now that the light was working.

Though Dad was finished, there was no talk of us leaving early. I noticed Dad making phone calls to the bank back in Cornwall, and we had cupboard risotto most nights. Part of me insisted I

didn't care, that anything was worth Mum finding the shark, but another quieter and larger part wished she would stop, and come back to me from the sea.

The night of the meteor shower, I got permission to meet Kin alone on the cliff because I said Neeta was going to be there too, but of course she wasn't. We cycled the ridge of the coast, the ground rising and the sky over us getting darker all the time as we left the lit lighthouse behind.

Kin had the telescope strapped to his back, and the bike light Dad made me use glinted off the metalwork. As we approached the spot Kin had shown me on the map, I smelt something. Smoke. Kin came to an abrupt halt, and I swerved to avoid hitting him.

'What?'

His eyes were huge under his helmet, and he was looking straight ahead. 'Adrian,' he mouthed.

I followed his gaze, and saw a small fire on the clifftop. Around it were three dark figures. I recognised the floppy hair straight away.

'We should go back,' muttered Kin, making to turn his bike.

'No way,' I said. 'We've been looking forward to this all week. We can just go further on.'

But Kin was shaking his head, and I was about to give up and

follow him when a shout came from the fire.

'Flower! Whale!' I saw their silhouettes grow taller as the three of them stood and started towards us.

'Go!' said Kin in a panic, but he was unbalanced because of his telescope, sliding sideways off the seat and his trouser legs catching in the gears.

I checked over my shoulder, thinking too late to turn off my bike light. The boys closed in as I helped Kin untangle himself.

'What have we here?' Adrian was smiling, his arms crossed, horribly lit by my bike light and flanked by his two friends. They looked like something from a horror movie. 'Richard, Olly, look what we've found.'

'Technically, we found you,' I said.

'Technically,' mimicked Adrian, and Richard and Olly laughed. 'All right nerd, calm down.'

'I am calm.'

'So you are a nerd then?'

'Fine by me,' I said. Kin was tugging on my sleeve, but I stood my ground. Mum had told me bullies reacted to weakness, so I would be strong. 'I have a brain, at least.'

Richard snorted, and Adrian elbowed him in the ribs. 'Do whales even have brains?'

'Of course,' I said, feeling bolder. 'Way bigger than yours. Are you stupid or something?'

Olly snorted too this time, and Adrian rounded on him. 'Cut it out.'

'Julia, let's go,' muttered Kin.

'What's that, Flower?' Adrian was now advancing on Kin, pointing at the telescope. 'Give it here.'

Kin backed away, his bike between his legs. 'It's my dad's.'

'He won't mind me having it. Give it here.'

Adrian lunged for it, and Kin backed away, going sprawling. I heard an ominous *crunch* as he landed on the ground.

'Whoops,' said Adrian in mock horror, as I hurried to help Kin up.

'If you broke it,' I hissed furiously, glaring at the boy. I felt hatred running through me, pure and hot and powerful.

'I'll explain to his dad, shall I?' Adrian sounded bored. 'Oh, but can he even understand English?'

This time it was me holding Kin back, and I had a lot more luck, being bigger than him.

'I'm going to tell your granddad what you said,' I said. 'He won't like it.'

'See if I care,' said Adrian. 'How's your mum's boat, by the way? Has it sunk yet?'

Terror and rage sloshed in my stomach. I let go of Kin and stepped towards Adrian, my fingernails biting into my palms. 'Don't say that.'

'She's a weirdo, like you,' said Adrian, grinning.

'So is your mum a loser like you?'

Adrian stopped smiling. 'What did you say?'

'Where is she, even?'

Kin tugged my sleeve. 'Julia—'

'Why isn't she around?'

'Shut up.' Adrian's voice was low and threatening, but there was something else in it. Something shaking. A weakness, just like Mum said. I needled at it.

'Did she decide she didn't like you, and run away?'

'Take that back!' Adrian shouted.

'To be fair it must be disappointing.' I felt powerful, staring at him on the cliff in the dark, his face very pale, his eyelid fluttering. I pulled the thread further out. 'To have such a loser for a son.'

Adrian unravelled.

I don't remember him hitting me. All I remember is being on the damp grass, the wind gone from my lungs, hands pulling Adrian away from me.

'You take it back!' he shouted, and there was a definite catch in his voice. As I lay gasping I saw his eyes were bright with tears.

'Leave it, Adrian.' Richard and Olly pulled him away. 'Let's go.'

They ran off, pulling Adrian with them, back towards the fire.

Kin dropped to his knees beside me. 'Are you all right?'

I sat up slowly, experimentally rubbing my belly. 'Yes. He just caught me by surprise.'

'Not as much as you caught him.' Kin's eyes were owl-huge. 'How did you know?'

'Know what?'

'That stuff about his mum? It wasn't …' He hesitated. 'It wasn't nice, Julia.'

'He wasn't being nice,' I said, amazed he seemed to be telling me off. 'He asked if Mum's boat had sunk!'

'But it hasn't,' said Kin. 'And Adrian's mum *did* leave him. And his dad. A couple of years ago, in Year Four.'

'I didn't know.'

'Still,' said Kin. He was looking at me like I was a stranger. 'His dad wasn't a nice man. He used to talk to my dad the way Adrian talks to me, but way worse. He left too, last year. Went to work on an oil rig. That's why Adrian lives with Gin.'

I struggled to my feet, remembering Adrian's face, the tears on his cheeks. I'd found his weakness, and now I felt slightly sick. Kin was inspecting the telescope.

'Is it all right?'

He shook his head, miserably. 'I need to get it to Bapi.'

I dusted off my jeans. 'I'll come and explain.'

'No,' said Kin, a bit too loud. 'You've done enough damage.'

He cycled away, fading fast into the dark. His words seemed

to echo in the night around me. Biting my lip to keep it from wobbling, I clambered back on to my bike, the thready light picking out the path back to the lighthouse.

As I got closer, I realised it was getting darker around me, not brighter. The light was out again, the outline of the lighthouse illuminated only by the stars. I put my bike back in the shed and went inside. Dad's voice drifted down swearily, Mum soothing him, and only Noodle came to greet me. I picked her up and started climbing the stairs. As I passed Dad's office, Mum poked her head out.

'Sorry about the language,' she said. 'We might have to give your dad a free pass on the swear jar. The light's stopped working.'

'Yes, I think she might have noticed that,' muttered Dad. I could see him up a ladder at the centre of the room, red and green wires trailing like veins down his arms.

Mum rolled her eyes. 'How was the meteor shower?'

'Kin couldn't make it,' I lied. 'I was just about to go and look.'

'Lovely!' said Mum brightly, too distracted to even tell I was lying. 'I'll come up in a bit. Take the crab net. We can try to catch some.'

It was a silly joke, something I used to do as a child, trying to net stars in rock pools. But I fetched the net anyway, went to the platform and waited.

Noodle got bored and leapt out of my arms, slinking back inside. I waited a bit longer, and the sky started to spark. Bright points of light began to streak across the sky, one or two at first,

and then one or two a minute. I picked up the crab net, waving it over the railing, imagining a hot white piece of starlight landing in it. It would burn right through.

Suddenly, a flare of light came from behind me. I heard a small cheer as the beam began its slow blink. I looked out at the sea, so vast, the stars so far away, and my arms reaching out my tiny crab net.

'Stupid,' I muttered, dropping the net. I wrapped my arms around my knees, wishing Kin was there to tell me what I was seeing, wishing I could stop thinking of Adrian's stupid, tear-streaked face, wishing I could stop the hot cauldron of guilt churning in my stomach.

As the stars seemed to fall from the sky,

and Mum still didn't come,

I'd never felt more alone.

The walls were moving. They bulged, and pulsed, mould chasing itself up the walls until it was dark, dark as the ocean. The shark stirred, enormous, slow, unstoppable. The floorboards creaked as it shunted against them, pressing its bulk until they splintered and the whole bed rose, the lighthouse ripped from its roots, as the shark surfaced and carried us all out to sea.

FOURTEEN

Things got worse the next day. When I came down for breakfast in the morning, Mum and Dad were sitting at the kitchen table, looking at me sternly.

'Sit down, Julia,' said Mum. 'Gin's just called. Adrian came home in tears last night. He said you teased him about his mother leaving.'

Dad's forehead creased. 'Julia, how could you?'

'I didn't know. I didn't!' I said, as Dad raised his eyebrows in disbelief. 'I just guessed, because he lives with Gin.'

'Why would you do that?' Dad asked.

'He was bullying Kin. He's horrid.'

'You should have told a grown up.'

'I did, sort of. Mum told me what to do.'

'What?' Mum looked confused.

'You told me about your friend, and finding a bully's weakness, and I thought—'

Dad made a furious sound, like an enraged bull. 'All right, Julia. Go upstairs. I want you to write a letter to this boy, to apologise.'

'But—'

'No buts. One of us has to teach you right from wrong—'

'Excuse me—' started Mum, but Dad continued talking to me.

'Go. I want to read it before you send it.'

In a silly song we sing at school assemblies, it said that rainbows always follow rain. But that day, that week, it felt like the rain never stopped. Not only did I have to write that letter to Adrian, but Dad said I was grounded. Not that I had anywhere to go, with Kin so angry.

The worst part was Mum. One day, Dad had to go to Mainland to get a new screwdriver, and she had to stay and look after me even though the day was still and calm, perfect for the boat.

'I'm running out of time,' she said. I could hear her foot tapping the kitchen tiles, while I hid up the staircase with my book as an alibi, listening. 'Can't you take her?'

'I think she'd rather have a day with her mum,' said Dad. 'Why don't you take her out on the boat?'

'I told you,' snapped Mum. 'There's no room. She'll get in the way.'

My stomach plunged through the step below me. I knew I was irritating Mum recently, but I didn't know how much until that moment.

'Not to look for that bleeding shark,' hissed Dad. 'To spend *time* with her, Maura.'

'But I don't *have* time!' Mum's voice burst from the kitchen, and I had already heard enough. I climbed to the beam, heaving my heavy heart with me.

Dad drove off a short while later, and Mum didn't even come looking for me until lunch. I watched the sea, and re-read my book that I dreaded having to return to the laundromat, and saw the postman come and go before she called up the spiral staircase.

Mopily, I flopped down on to a kitchen chair, while Mum cut thick slices off the loaf of bread Dad had baked that morning, sending steam into the kitchen. It was too hot, the wood burner piled up high and roaring, but Mum didn't seem to notice, even when her glasses steamed up.

Searching for something to say, my eyes landed on an A4 envelope on the table. It was addressed to Mum, and had a

university logo stamped into one corner. It couldn't be good news, or Mum would have told me, would have come dancing up the stairs, a big smile on her face. Instead, I could see her face was red and raw-looking under its tan, her lips pulled thin as the envelope.

'Mum ...' I started, but I didn't know what to say. She didn't hear me anyway, busy opening a can of tomato soup and pouring it into the pan. As she waited for it to heat, she stood looking out of the window, which was too fogged for her to see anything.

I pretended to read my book, about Greek gods arriving into modern life to help a boy with his sick mum, but really I was watching her. She was as inscrutable as the window, the shadows under her eyes the same colour as the mould on the wall behind her. It seemed to bulge in the too-hot kitchen, blossoming before my eyes, ballooning like Adrian's neck, like something was breathing in the walls.

Mum poured the soup into two bowls, and buttered my bread for me.

'We can go in the boat tomorrow,' she said suddenly. 'Maybe we can find those famous otters.'

'What? I mean, yes,' I said, confused but seizing on the idea. 'I'd like that.'

She rambled on about otters, about how their fur is so thick their skin never gets wet, how they use tools like rocks to open

shells, and I pretended to be noting them in my notebook, but all the while I was watching her. Her eyes seemed to get further and further away, as though she was being carried on the tide of her own voice, out to sea.

When we were finished, Mum washed up, taking the empty tomato soup can and rinsing it in the sink, staring out of the window again. I watched her as she soaped it, red running down the enamel.

'Mum,' I said, scrambling over to her. 'Your finger.'

She looked down, dazed. Her finger was bleeding where she'd cut it on the can.

'Yuck,' she said, swaying. 'Sorry, Julia.'

'You don't need to say sorry, Mum. Do you need a plaster?'

'I'll get it.' She tottered again, walking up the stairs heavily, like she was a hundred years old. I waited for her to come down again, but she didn't. I went up, and found her in her and Dad's bedroom, still in her clothes and asleep, curled like a question mark on their sheets.

Dad got home just after six. He was whistling tunelessly, carrying a tote bag of shopping, and smiled broadly when I opened the door for him.

'Perfect timing, J-cat. Did you go out on the boat?'

'No, but Mum said we can look for otters tomorrow. Dad—'

'Brilliant!' He put the kettle on the hob. 'I'll come with you. I love otters. When I was young—'

'Dad.'

'What's wrong?' He looked around the kitchen, at the washed-up bowls and the envelope in the centre of the table. He sighed heavily, and set down the tote bag. 'That's that then.' He smiled at me sadly. 'Is she all right?'

'I don't think so. She's in bed.'

'It's OK, J. She tried, and that's what matters. It's a shame, but maybe now she can do something else.'

'She doesn't want to,' I said. 'She wants to find the shark.'

He began unpacking the shopping. 'I think she needs a rest now, don't you?'

'I guess. But she never stays in bed all day. Is she really sick?' I could tell Dad wasn't saying something, and I pushed on. 'Is it what Grandma had?'

Dad stopped unpacking. 'What makes you say that?'

'Mum said Grandma was in bed all the time before ... before she ...'

Dad took my hand. 'Your grandma had dementia.'

'Yes, but before that, was she like Mum?'

'It's all right. Mum's just very tired.'

'She's never like this,' I insisted.

Dad hesitated, and ran his thumb along his jaw, the way he does when he's searching for words. I could tell he wished it was something he could explain in numbers. 'Mum is brilliant, yes? Her brain is brilliant. It's also complicated, and sometimes, things go wrong. Sometimes she feels happy, but it's almost too happy. Like that day with the boat, remember?' I nodded, recalling the flowers, the wine, Mum's too-bright smile. 'So then the opposite happens. She gets sad.'

'Is that why she's in bed?'

'I think so,' said Dad. 'This research has really got to her, the rejection, I mean. She's worked too hard, and her brain's got tired.'

I nodded, taking it all in. It made sense, in a strange way, of why Mum sometimes bounced around like Tigger, and other times she was mopey like Eeyore. 'But she'll be all right?'

'Of course,' said Dad bracingly. 'These things just take time. When we're home she can take it easier. You don't have to worry about anything, Julia.'

But he was wrong.

I had to worry about everything.

The shark was back.

It carried the
lighthouse out to
sea, further each time,
to a place of ice floes,
the world locked together
by cold. Its skin was rough as
bark, my whole room papered
with it, and it was living rock,
a fossil with crystals shining deep
inside its eyes. Sightless, it turned for the
fathomless deep.
I knew Mum was beside me,
still as stone, but I couldn't
reach her, couldn't see her
and even though I called, she
didn't answer before the
shark
slid under
the ice,
carrying us
all deeper under.

FIFTEEN

'Julia.' Dad shook me gently. 'Sorry, Julia. It's all right.'

'What?' I sat up blearily, and Dad turned my bedside light on. I squinted at him. My clock said ten past midnight, but he was fully dressed with a coat and gloves, his boots laced and trailing mud across the floor. 'Have you been outside?'

'I need you to get up,' he said, and though his voice was calm the room crackled with tension. 'Everything's all right, but I need you to get dressed. I'm going to drop you at Mr Ginley's house. I tried to get him to come here, but his grandson's at home.'

'Adrian? I can't go there.'

'It's all right,' he repeated. 'He's not angry at you.'

The more he said everything was all right, the more I realised something was very wrong. 'Why?'

'I need to take your mum somewhere. She'll be OK, but it can't wait until morning.'

I looked down at his boots, the laces untied. 'Where have you been?'

'Come on.'

I was too confused to ask the right questions. I got up dumbly, and dressed in a mismatch of clothes, picking up my notebook and following him downstairs. Noodle was meowing and rubbing at our ankles.

'Can I take her?'

'We'll be back soon,' he said. 'Mr Ginley's grandson is allergic.'

Of course he is, I thought bitterly, bending to rub Noodle's ears.

'I've filled her bowl. Please, Julia,' said Dad. 'There's no time.'

It was really serious, then. There was always time to stroke Noodle and check she was settled before we went anywhere, even for a night. I looked at the coat hook. Mum's coat was still hanging there.

'Dad,' I said, properly frightened now. 'Where's Mum?'

'Somewhere safe,' said Dad. 'Please, Julia, I have to get back.'

'Get back where?'

But he was already striding off down the drive to the car, and I hesitated only a moment longer before snatching Mum's mac from the hook and tripping after him, pulling the door shut behind me.

Mr Ginley lived above his shop. The apartment was warm and filled with shells on every surface like my bedroom at home, and smelt of tobacco and kippers, which was a lot nicer than it sounds. Adrian wasn't up when I arrived, which I was glad about, seeing as I looked like I'd dressed in the dark, which of course I had.

'Thanks for doing this, Mr Ginley,' said Dad. 'It'll only be for tonight. I'll pick her up in the morning.'

'Not at all,' said Gin in his rumbling, kind voice. 'My Mary had her share of troubles. I understand. She'll be all right with me.'

Dad hugged me, and ran back out into the rain. With a jolt, I realised he'd left the car running. He never did this, ever, because of the environment. He and Mum would even go up to people on the school run in Cornwall and tell them to turn off their engines because of the emissions. It really was an emergency, bigger than climate change.

Gin had made up a bed on the sofa, with a little plug-in nightlight that projected dolphins on the walls. 'That's Adrian's favourite.' He winked. 'He won't be happy if he knows I've nicked it.'

I stored this information to share with Kin, then remembered

we weren't friends at the moment. I felt a bit sick, knowing Adrian was nearby. 'Is he ...'

'Asleep. And you mustn't worry about all that business at the cliff. I try to keep an eye on him, but with his parents gone ...' he trailed off. 'I hope he'll come round. Not like his father.'

'What's happening?' I asked tentatively. 'Is my mum all right?'

'She's in the best place. Here, I made you a Horlicks. I'm just in my study,' he said, pointing at an open door. I couldn't see a bed in the tiny room, only an armchair with a blanket draped over it. 'Adrian's got my bedroom. So if you need me, just knock.'

He closed the door softly, and I lay down on the sofa. It was broad and quite saggy. I watched the dolphins leaping across the walls. Though I was sure I would never be able to sleep, my body dragged me down, and soon I felt the world melt away.

Groggily, I opened my eyes. Daylight was seeping in through the curtains, and Adrian was sitting at the kitchen table across the room from me, eyeing me suspiciously.

I sat up and tried to comb my hair flat.

'Morning,' said Gin merrily, stirring a pot. 'Porridge? I have salt in mine but Addie here likes strawberry jam.'

I sat as far away from Adrian as possible, which wasn't very far considering the table was smaller even than the one at the

lighthouse. Gin placed a bowl in front of me.

'Thank you.' I blew on the steaming porridge. 'Has my dad called?'

'He'll be round about ten. Sorry about the early start, I've got to open the shop soon and wanted to see you fed.'

I nodded. I was desperate to ask about Mum, but I didn't want to in front of Adrian.

'Jam? Homemade,' twinkled Gin.

I took it tentatively, and spooned in a glob.

'You stir it in.' Adrian was watching me. He seemed to be trying to be nice. I stirred, and tasted. 'Good?'

I nodded. I had to admit, it was great.

'Right,' said Gin, checking his watch. 'I need to open up. I think Addie has a few things to say. I'll be downstairs if you need anything.'

He closed the door, and we heard his footsteps disappearing down the stairs. Adrian's eyes were determinedly fixed on his empty bowl.

'Sorry,' he said. I blinked at him, astonished.

'What?'

'Sorry,' he said, a little louder. 'I am. I'm going to see Kin today too, to apologise. I've been an idiot.'

I was too shocked to speak.

'It's not an excuse,' he carried on, talking to his spoon. 'But I

was jealous, I guess.'

'Of Kin?'

'And you.' He shrugged. 'Your parents. They really care about you.'

A lump filled my throat. I wasn't sure, in that moment, if it was true.

'Anyway,' said Adrian briskly. 'I'm sorry, and I mean it. And sorry about your mum.'

'What about her?'

'About hospital.'

My heart throbbed painfully. 'What?'

He hesitated. 'She's at the hospital. On Mainland.'

I felt my mouth fall open. 'The hospital? Why?'

Adrian looked aghast, paler than ever. 'I thought you knew,' he said. 'I heard my granddad on the phone with your pa. She took some pills—'

'Pills?' It made no sense. 'What do you mean?'

'I …' Adrian searched for the words in his bowl. 'Nothing.'

'Tell me,' I said, desperation making my voice too loud, and he jumped.

'Julia—'

'Tell me!' I pushed my chair back from the table, and it caught on the rug, clattering to the floor. I stumbled towards Adrian, desperate for him to explain, and he leapt up, placing his own

chair between us like a shield. I knew I was scaring him, but I didn't care.

'That's all I know, I swear!' said Adrian, cringing. 'She took pills. You know. Lots of them.'

A roaring sound started to fill my ears. I felt salt stinging my eyes, and my voice retreated to a whisper small as the sea caught in a shell. 'She … she tried to …'

I couldn't voice it. Couldn't even think it. Not Mum. Not my mum, loud and lovely and brilliant. But she hadn't been lately, had she? Even her face had changed as she lost weight, even her smell. My hands started to shake, and I clenched them tightly.

'I don't know any more, honest I don't. She had to go to hospital.'

'I have to go.' My voice was drowned out by the roaring sound in my ears, like waves smashing a beach, my vision blotchy and blurred as sharkskin.

'No,' said Adrian. 'You should stay here. I'll get my granddad—'

'I want to go now.' Salt was in my throat now too, like the sea was spilling out from inside me, filling me. The walls began to warp, like I was stuck in one of my dreams. The shark was here. The shark had found me.

'Sit down, Julia.' Adrian's hand was gentle on my shoulder, but I pushed him away roughly.

'I want to go,' I snarled, and Adrian raised his hands in surrender.

'You can take my bike,' he said. 'It's outside. If Granddad sees you—'

'He won't.' Mum's mac was lying slack on the sofa, crumpled and empty. I shuddered as I put it on. Mum's spare lighthouse key was in the pocket, attached to the key for the boat, and I gripped it tight enough to hurt.

'Are you sure you don't want to stay? I could get Kin ...'

But would Kin even come? He'd made it clear he hated me for what I'd said to Adrian, and everything was unravelling like the loose thread I'd pulled on the clifftop. But it was my life that was coming apart. I'd said Adrian's mum had left because of him, and now my mum – she had ... she had tried to ...

Was it me? Dad's voice came back, that day in the kitchen. *It was nothing to do with you, Julia.* But grown ups lied, and what if Dad was lying now? The walls shuddered, the floorboards rolling as though I stood on a boat. The thought was too horrid to bear. There must be another explanation. My heart thudded. *The shark. The shark. The shark.*

'I really think you should stay,' said Adrian nervously. He seemed scared to touch me. 'You don't look well.'

I shook my head, and breathed deeply to try to calm my heart, but it wouldn't stop hammering against my throat. I had to get

out of this tiny room, away from Adrian. I wanted Mum, or Dad, but Noodle would have to do. Pulling the coat tight around me, I opened the creaky door and flew down the narrow staircase.

It spat me out in the far corner of the shop. The high, cluttered shelves shielded me from the counter where Gin was busy with a customer, and it was easy enough to slip past him. Adrian's bike was unlocked outside, as he'd said. Across the road, the door to the laundromat was closed, the windows fogged up. I longed to see Kin, for everything to be OK between us. When had everything gone so rotten? Heart swooping, I started to pedal.

SIXTEEN

I knew Mum and Dad wouldn't be there, but still my heart sank when I turned the spare key in the rusty lock and pushed my way into the empty kitchen. Noodle wrapped herself around my ankles, mewling, and I paused long enough to fill her bowl with fresh food and water, careful to avoid looking at the mould on the walls. My hands were still shaking, my body still unsteady as I took the stairs two at a time.

I stopped outside their bedroom. I hadn't been inside since I'd left Mum curled on the sheets, and I hesitated, but Noodle had finished her meal. She came upstairs and nosed in through the gap, jumping on to the desk and rolling for a belly scratch. I went in after her, holding back tears as I looked around for clues,

something to show what had happened to Mum, why she had done what she did.

'What do I do?' I murmured to Noodle, my voice breaking. She mewed and I walked over to the desk. It was papered in rejection letters, but something broke the monotonous black and white. A photo.

Mum was younger, in a blue floral dress, her hair loose, her arms cupping her swollen belly. Cupping me.

She was turning away from the camera, and her face was slightly blurred, but there was no mistaking her expression. She looked hollow-eyed with sadness, like she had the last few days, and I remembered Dad saying she had been miserable after her mum died, while she was pregnant with me. But she looked more than miserable. She looked sunken in, shrunk.

I shuddered, and buried the photo in the bottom of a drawer. As I turned it face down, I saw something scrawled on the back in green ink.

Never Again

All the breath rushed out of me. Here it was, the proof I didn't want to find … did she mean having a baby?

Did she mean me?

Knock knock knock.

I ran down the stairs, scrabbling for the door. It would be Dad, maybe even Mum—

'Captain Bjorn?'

His hand was raised to knock again, and he lowered it.

'Julia,' he said in his gentle voice. 'Is your mother here?'

I remembered her talking about him not believing in her research, and glowered at him. 'She's not.'

'Ah. Will she be back soon?'

'No.'

'That is rotten luck,' he said, sighing. 'Rotten luck. Is there any way of contacting her?'

'No.' I narrowed my eyes. 'Why?'

'The shark,' he said, and my breath caught in my chest. 'One's been sighted, not too far from here. Just below the surface, they think cruising for prey, possibly. I would go myself but I'm about to sail for Oban.' He held out a piece of paper. 'I wrote down the coordinates. It'll have moved on by now, but not far. It moves slow—'

'Half a mile an hour,' I said shakily.

He nodded. 'Exactly. If she can leave in the next hour, she'll have a good chance of catching it tonight.'

I took the paper in trembling fingers. Captain Bjorn smiled at me, and made to leave, before turning back.

'Can you also tell her sorry?' He grinned ruefully. 'I was skeptical at first, of course, but … it's a shame the universities were not funding her. If I could have worked any longer for free,

I would have. But I have my crew, and it is not only my family who have to eat.'

My whole body was trembling. My ears were full of water, the floor unsteady. Captain Bjorn frowned. 'You are not here on your own?'

'No,' I lied. 'My dad's upstairs.'

'Perhaps I could speak to him?'

'He's working,' I said hurriedly. 'He can't be disturbed.'

'All right,' said Captain Bjorn. 'Well, I wish you luck, Miss Julia. I hope me and your mum will make friends again, and I can come back for dinner soon. That cupboard risotto was quite delicious.'

He smiled warmly and left. I shut the door and unfolded the paper he'd given me.

I suddenly understood why Dad thought numbers were so beautiful. Here it was, the shark Mum had searched for all these weeks. I stroked the paper, and rummaged in Mum's coat pocket, drawing out the keys to *Julia & the Shark*.

The roaring in my ears stopped. The floor ceased rocking. My heartbeat became more like a drum, like a battle thrum. I imagined the shark moving below me, slower than time. It had followed me on to land, and now I would chase it back to the sea. I would find it, for Mum. I would show her I believed in her when no one else did. I could make it all better, could make Mum proud, make her happy she had me. I knew what I had to do.

SEVENTEEN

Julia & the Shark sat high in the water, bobbing gently like a gull. I waded out to her, Noodle in my arms, and climbed on, hauling her anchor into the stern. Something like hope filled my chest as I drew out the coordinates Captain Bjorn had written down.

63°30'31.7"N 0°29'17.1"W

Clipping them on to the clipboard beside the huge folded map, I keyed them into the navigation system with great care. Every digit was important, and if I got just one wrong, I would end up miles off course.

The headboard blinked into life, and Noodle jumped on to

the padded bench, purring contentedly. For a moment I felt overwhelmed, all the lights blinking on and off, compass spinning, radar beeping, but then I took three deep breaths, just like Mum had taught me.

'Most of these don't matter,' she'd said. 'You just need to know this. That means go, that means stop. That means turn. That means help.'

I turned the wheel, aiming the boat out of the bay, and sailed into open sea. I didn't look back for ages, eyes fixed to the ever-vanishing horizon. After about an hour, the radio crackled to life.

'*Julia & the Shark*, this is the harbour master. Please confirm your destination, over.' I scrambled to pick it up, deepening my voice as I pressed the *transmit* button and spoke as I'd heard Mum do.

'Hello, Harbour master, this is *Julia & the Shark*.'

'What is your destination?'

I hesitated. 'Oban.'

'Please be advised, heavy sou'westerly with increased pressure zone coming. Advise you return to harbour.'

Knowing I was going nowhere near Oban, I dismissed the worry before it started.

'Negative,' I said, trying to sound like the submariners in Dad's favourite film. 'We are confident of our course.'

'Noted,' said the harbour master. 'Safe sailing.'

'Roger,' I said, wincing at the chuckle on the other end.

'It's Pete, actually,' said the voice. 'Keep the radio on.'

The boat moved fast on the flat water, cutting a frothy trail behind us that soon melted into nothing. When I finally glanced over my shoulder, land was gone. Only the sea for miles.

The summer days were long this far north, and I was only going further in that direction, towards the Arctic. Captain Bjorn had said Mum could reach the shark by evening, and so could I.

Our supplies were limited to a very brown, very soft banana and an equally soft orange I'd found in the fruit bowl, and a couple of tins of sardines in oil from the cupboard. Thanks to Mum and Dad not having a telly back home in Cornwall, I was used to being bored, and it's actually quite hard to feel bored when you're on your own with a cat in the middle of the sea.

My mind kept circling back to Mum, cutting through the surface of every other thought like a fin, and I wrestled it back down each time. If I could find the shark, and tell her so, then she would be all right. She would be happy again. She would be Mum again.

Even rescuers get hungry. The porridge had been a good idea, and my tummy didn't start to rumble until the clock on the boat's dashboard flicked over to three in the afternoon. Noodle started to meow around then too, her fur on end to keep her warm. It

was matted with salt and sticky to the touch.

We had been at sea for over six hours. Dad would have come to Gin's at ten, would have checked the lighthouse. Perhaps, I realised too late, I should have left a note. But there hadn't been enough time. There were still hours to go until I reached the shark. Guilt tangled in my mind, but I brushed it away. Dad would be fine. It was Mum I needed to worry about.

My stomach grumbled again, so I checked the wheel was fixed on course, and sat on the padded seat, pulling the supplies towards us. I knew I should only eat a little, save the rest for later and our return trip, but suddenly the banana was gone, and the orange, and Noodle had licked the sardine tin clean. She meowed for more, so I shared the second tin with her, running my finger around the inside.

'We probably shouldn't have done that,' I said to Noodle, but she only bent over and started licking her bum. I guess cats don't really care about rationing.

It was starting to get cold, though the sky was still light. I searched the cupboards under the seats, and found blankets for Noodle, the flares Dad had brought Mum when she bought the boat, and a whole tub of sausage rolls. I stored them gratefully, within reach of the wheel, and as I went to close the cupboard I spotted a blister pack of pills. It was empty, and my stomach flipped, remembering how Adrian had said *lots of them*. I kicked

the packet into the dark back of the cupboard, and slammed the door shut.

Noodle burrowed into the blanket, turning so only her pink nose showed from the musty fabric. I clamped my hand under my arm, letting the long sleeve of Mum's coat fall over the one on the wheel. I imagined I was her, as she used to be, brave and brilliant, and stopped trembling.

The hours dragged by, with only the sighting of seagulls and a couple of seals. I crossed my arms, and watched the blinking lights of the navigation system. The soft beeps of the radar were like a lullaby, the rocking waves soothing. I let my head tilt back, only for a moment.

The radio crackled, like tinfoil against my eardrums. I stumbled to my feet, tripping over the blanket, hearing Noodle mew.

'Noodle,' I said admonishingly. 'Why didn't you wake me?' Her eyes glowed back at me.

It was dark, properly night-time, but there were no stars, only a thick blanket of cloud. I wished I could see Dhruva Tara, Polaris, the Pole Star, the lodestar.

I checked the time – 23:39 – and our coordinates. *63°30'31.7"N 0°29'17.1"W*

'We're here,' I said, checking the map. 'We're here!'

I shouted it, and my voice went on and faded into nothing. I swallowed, looking around. Nothing and nothing and nothing. I could have been alone in the world. I could have been in space.

My teeth started to chatter. The boat swayed, and it no longer felt like a cradle. I spoke into the silence, to try to fill it.

'Time to turn on the radar,' I told Noodle. The radio crackled again, and I ignored it, focusing on twizzling the knobs, checking the depth gauge. 500 metres. I swallowed. That was very deep water.

The waves were a little rougher now, rolling the boat around like a skipping stone. Far off, there was a flash, and a moment later, a rumble of thunder. That storm the harbour master had promised. But it was far away, and I would miss it by miles.

'We're all right,' I said to Noodle. 'We're all right.'

She licked her paw, unconcerned, which calmed me a little, too.

The boat lights swung over the rolling waves. The boat was really rising and falling now, feet at a time, the hull slapping the water. I winced, wishing Mum had paid a professional to tar the

hull, and not relied on Kin and me. Still, it had served her all right. The boat was sound. Dad wouldn't have let her out in it if it wasn't. But then again, he thought Gin had checked it, when I knew he hadn't.

Another flash, and I was sure it wasn't my imagination that it was closer this time. I heard no thunder, but the wind was louder, rushing in at my ears and grasping at Mum's coat, whipping its toggles against my face.

'I'm just going to put you down here,' I said to Noodle, lifting her down to my feet, slotting her safely behind the pedals. She burrowed deeper under the blankets.

I tried to stop my hands shaking. *Julia & the Shark*'s light swept the sea, and the stars were still gone, swept up under the rug of clouds, thickening all the time over my head.

I shuddered. Sou'westerly, the harbour master had said. But maybe he'd made a mistake. Or maybe I hadn't heard him right, because the next flash of lightning was much, much closer, illuminating the endless, rolling sea, and not even the screaming wind could disguise the grumble of thunder, so loud I felt rather than heard it, rippling under the soles of my feet.

Suddenly the steadiness I'd felt since deciding to find the shark evaporated. What had I done? I'd brought Noodle out into the middle of the ocean, in search of a shark not even my mum could find.

Panic poured into the space where my certainty had been, hot and sharp. I should have stayed at Gin's. I should have waited for Dad and got my answers from him. A high sound grated my ears and I realised I was making a frightened squeak like a trapped fox, a horrible noise that frightened me more than the approaching storm. I closed my eyes. I couldn't lose control here. There was no way to wake up from this nightmare.

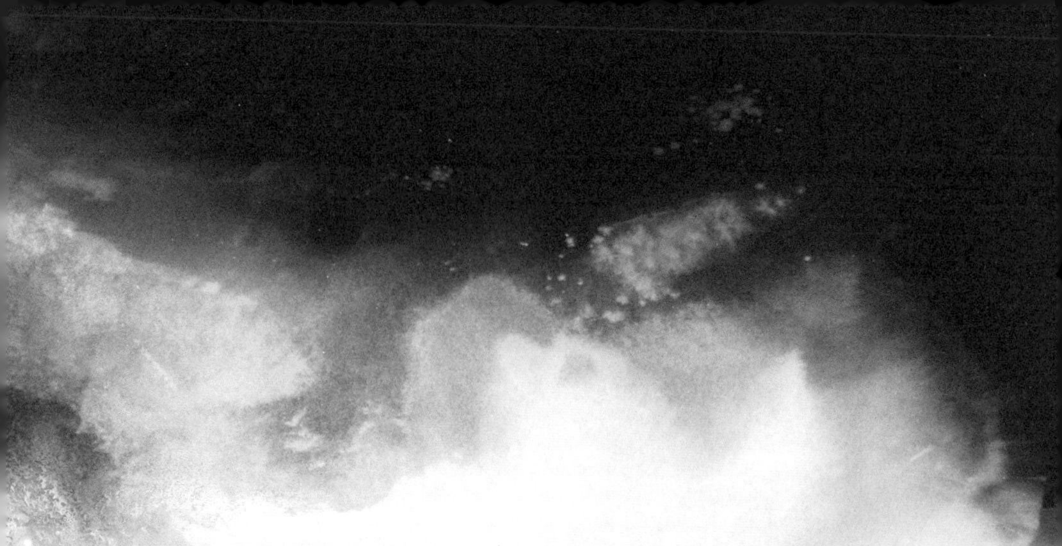

'We have to go,' I said aloud, to make it real. 'We have to go back.'

Another lightning flash, burning my eyes, and Noodle yowled almost as loud as the thunder.

'All right,' I said to her, kneeling down under the navigation board, pressing my body close to her. 'I'll take us home. It's all right.'

Groping for one of the flares, I sent it blazing into the sky.

The lightning whipped the sea, the waves climbed, and now the rain came. It didn't begin like usual, with a few drops giving warning. It was like someone emptied a mighty bucket over the boat. Instantly I felt water slosh around my ankles.

I lifted Noodle again, wedging her into the cupboard next to Mum's sausage rolls.

I used one of the empty tubs to bail out some of the water, my fingers instantly freezing, but it was pointless. I skidded on the slick floor and hit my head on the padded seat, my temple slapping against the hard plastic beneath. Dazed, I dropped the empty bucket, and it bobbed on the sloshing water. My feet were numb, my shoes soaked through, and my head felt hot. There was no point bailing. Our best hope was trying to outrun it.

Reaching for the wheel, I readied to spin it, when the radar beeped. I froze, the wind stinging my face, and watched the screen.

Something huge was moving. Something massive, only metres from the boat.

I hit the side, hands slick on the guardrail. The waves rocked me up and down, lifting me from my feet while I kept tight hold of the metal. I couldn't see anything. And then, in another flash of lightning, much too close, was a massive shape.

Just below the surface, a vast, pitted expanse.

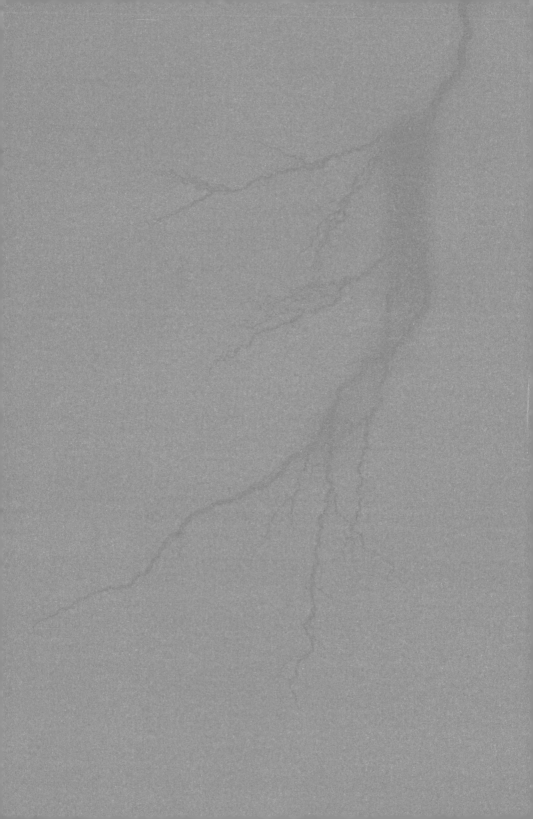

It felt like the storm dropped, just for a moment. I swung the boat light around and saw greenish skin, the surface scarred and rough as seawrack. It was impossible, and real, and the smell hit my nostrils so hard it was like a slap. Something sharp and rotten and alive, animal and ancient.

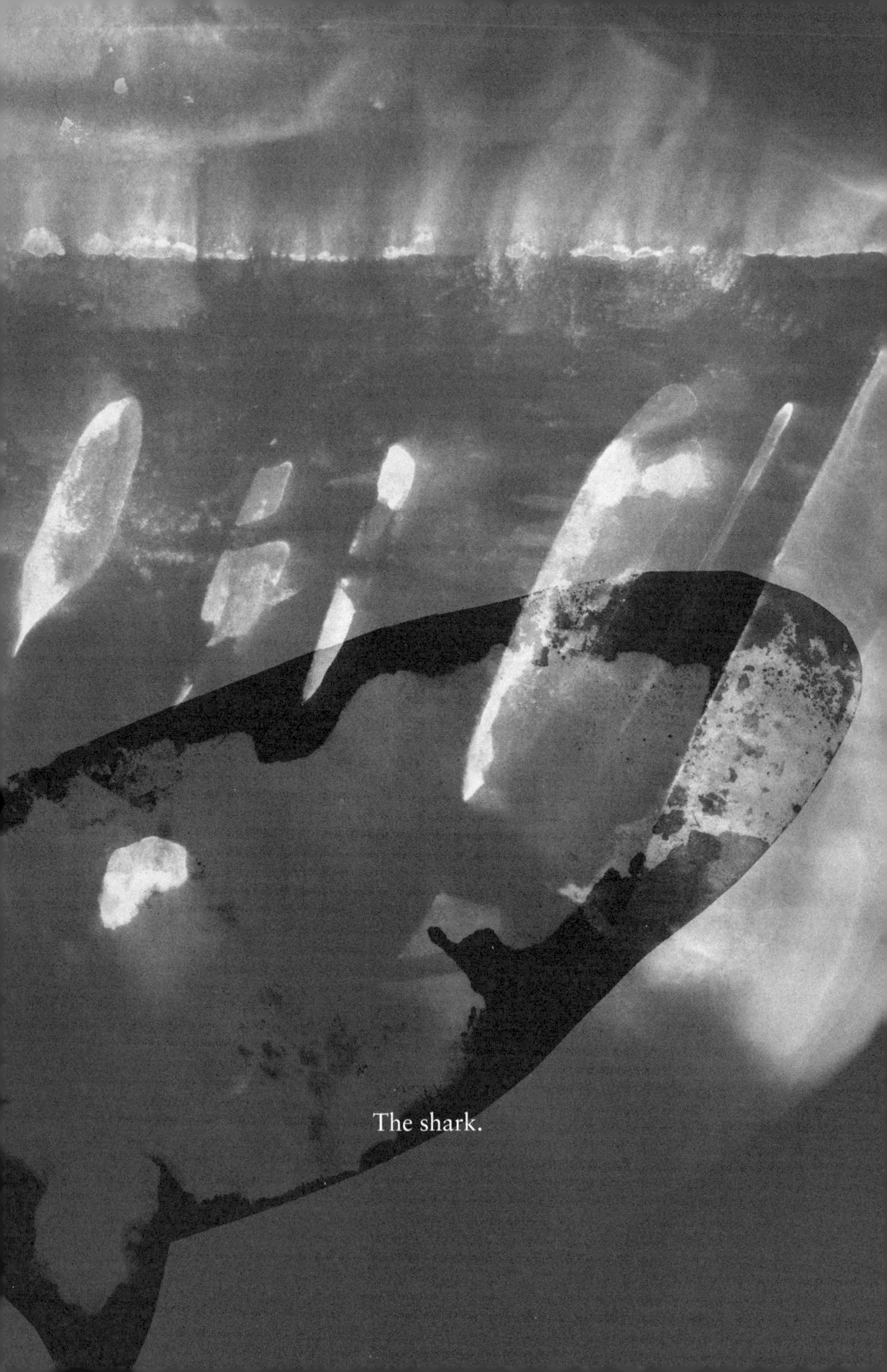

The shark.

My hands loosed the light and it swung crazily away, dragging a thick line across the surface and the shark did not seem to end, it seemed to go on until the whole sea was shark, green and torn by time. I could have sworn I saw an eye, black and glinting, thick with crystals, rolling away from the boat light.
And then, slowly, so slowly,
it began to dive.

‘No!’

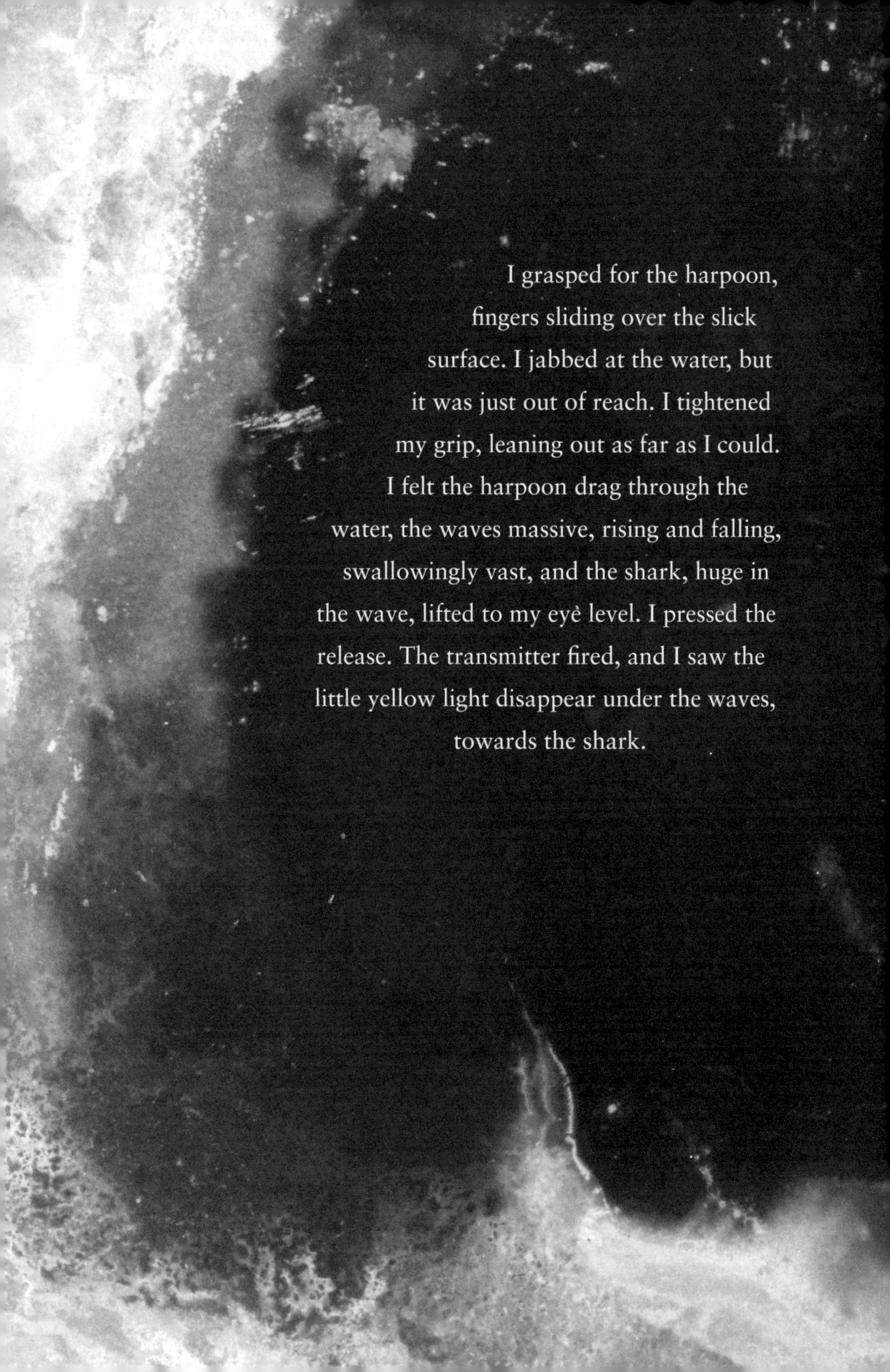

I grasped for the harpoon, fingers sliding over the slick surface. I jabbed at the water, but it was just out of reach. I tightened my grip, leaning out as far as I could. I felt the harpoon drag through the water, the waves massive, rising and falling, swallowingly vast, and the shark, huge in the wave, lifted to my eye level. I pressed the release. The transmitter fired, and I saw the little yellow light disappear under the waves, towards the shark.

The boat tipped, and just as my heart leapt, I felt my gravity shift. The world span away from me, and suddenly I wasn't on the boat any more. My hand no longer held the guardrail. My hand no longer held anything at all.

Something told me to take a breath, and I did, just as the water closed over me like an icy fist, and the waves knocked all the air from me.

I didn't feel anything.
The cold was too absolute, too consuming.
It was so cold, it was almost warm.
The pain in my temple vanished, and all was quiet,
the thunder a far-off purr.
I tried to kick, tried to move my arms,
but Mum's coat had slipped over my shoulders.
It was dragging me down.
It could only have been a moment,
but I felt like I was a whale, a tree, a shark, time
moving slower for me, as I felt the coat tighten,
holding me close as one of Mum's hugs.

It was easy to stop kicking,
much easier than forcing
my way to the surface.
The cold was a cloud,
as heavy as one, as wet and total,
and Mum's coat shrunk close
and sucked at me,
tugging
me
down.

Something nudged my legs.
They were so numb,
it felt like it was happening very far away.
A current, helping to pull me deeper?

Feebly, I opened my stinging eyes, seeing light like stars covering the whole world. It was so cold. My legs were nudged again, and this time I moved, a definite movement up, some instinct knowing which way was which even without air in my lungs to carry me to the surface.

It may have only been water, or the pumping of my blood fighting the freezing sea. But even as my mind started to stop, it found another answer.

It was something rough and alive, something travelling since Mozart played, seen rare enough to be myth.

It was something blind and beautiful and terrifying, nosing its way through the dark, through history, through our lighthouse and my dreams. It was the answer to Mum's darkness, the thing that had led her there, and could lead her out of it. And now, it was here to do the same for me.

And then there were lights in the water, real lights, and something slapped down on the surface.

A ring, a halo, dark against the lights sweeping over.

Mum's coat was heavy as a pocketful of stones,
the rubber stuck to my frozen skin.

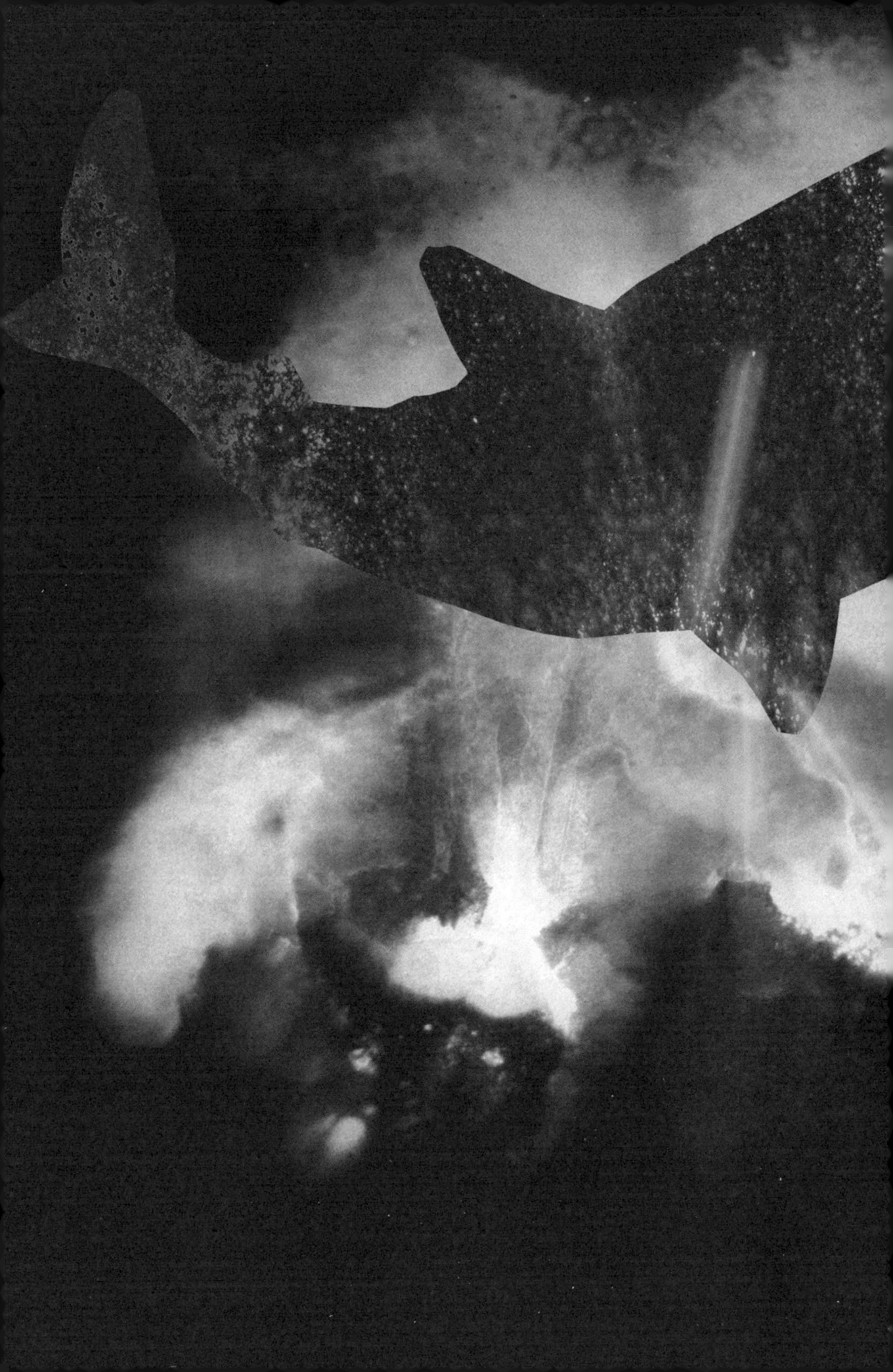

And though I did not want to,
though I wanted to hold on to the coat
like it was Mum, and haul it to the surface,
I let it slip over my shoulders.

I let it go.

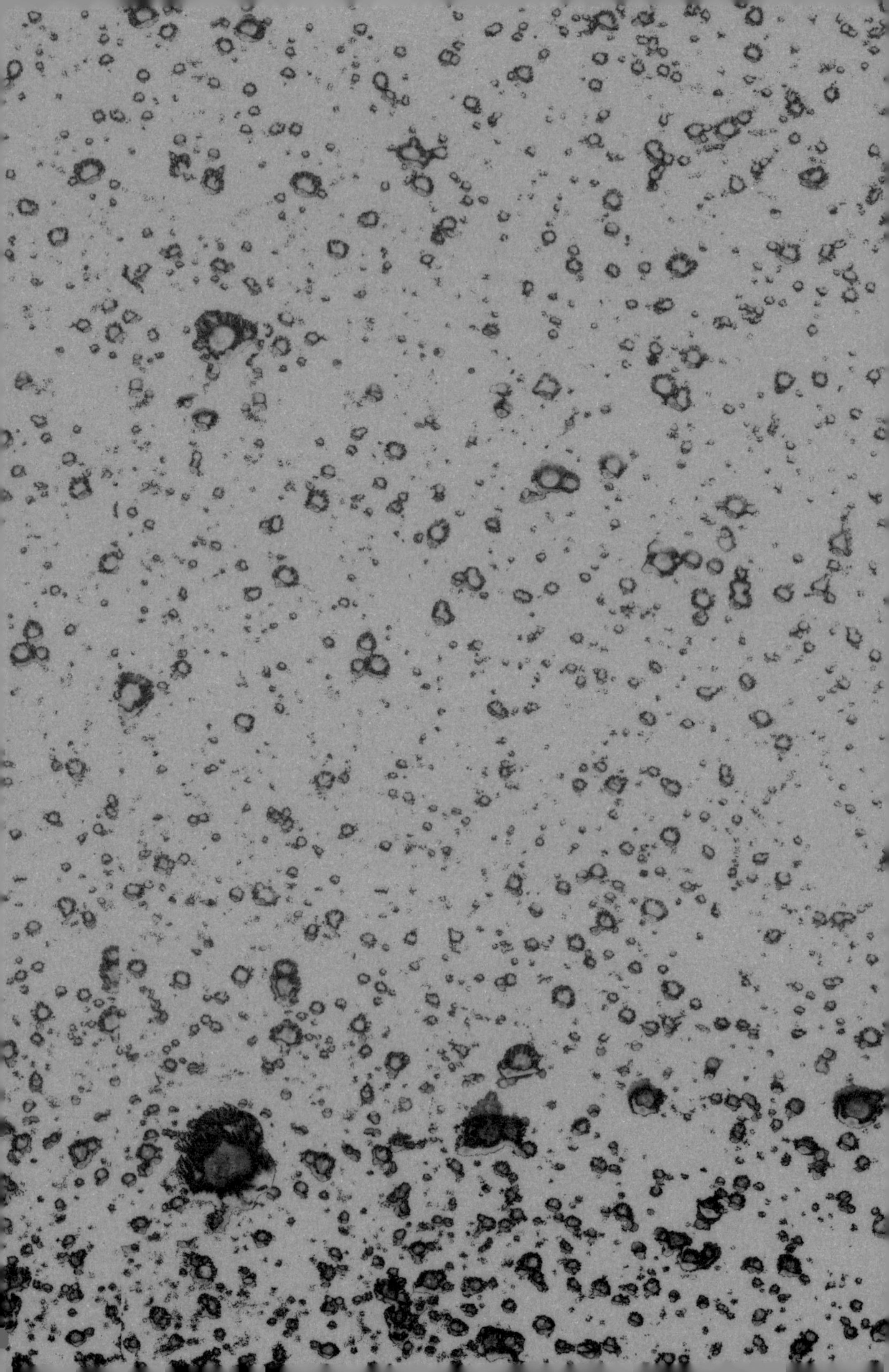

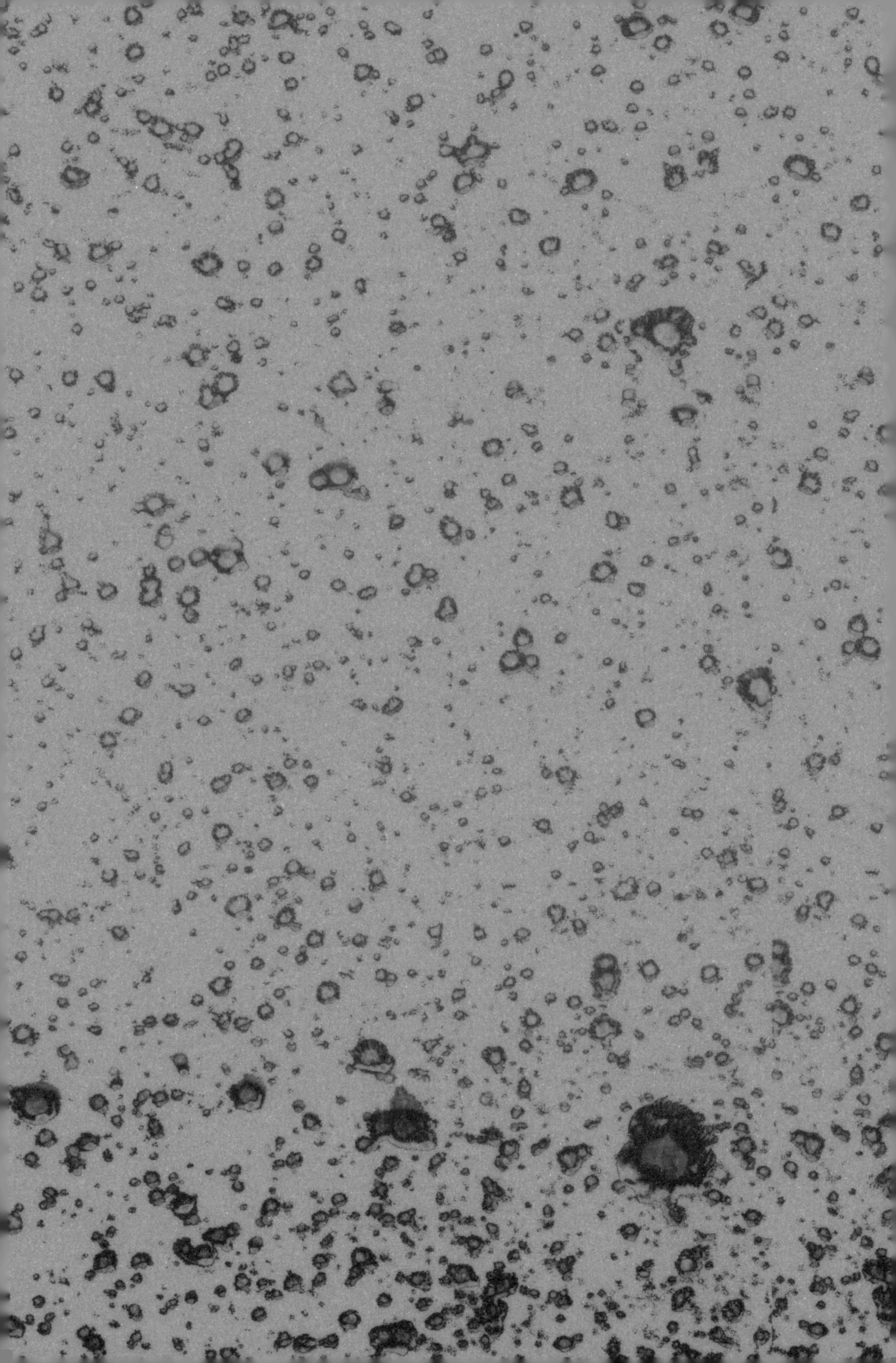

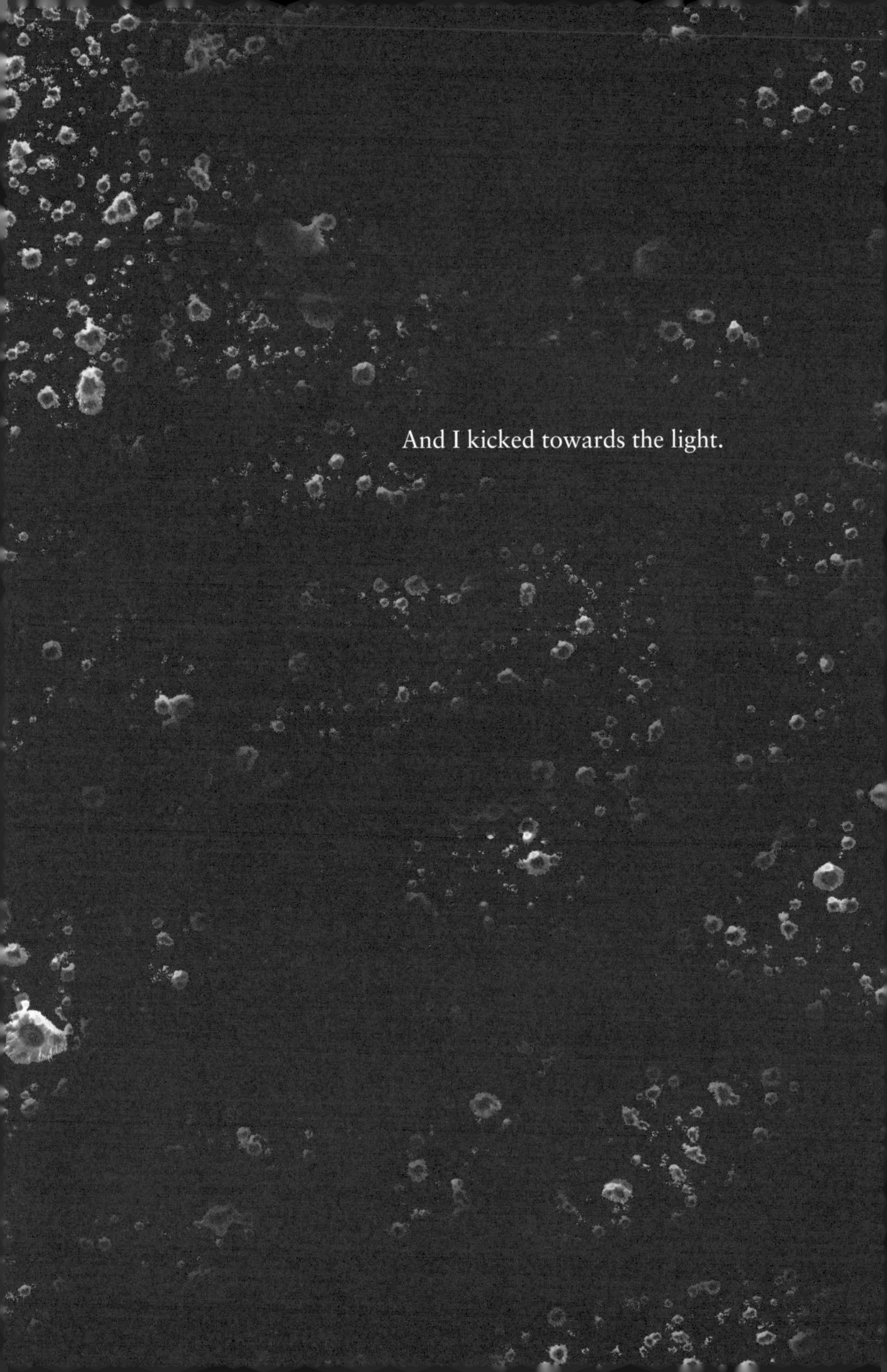

And I kicked towards the light.

EIGHTEEN

I can't tell you for sure that a shark older than trees saved my life. I can't tell you for sure that its enormous body moved beneath me in a freezing sea and pushed me to the surface, where Captain Bjorn and his boat were waiting.

But I can tell you that's what I believe, and doesn't that count for something?

Captain Bjorn reached us just in time. He'd encountered Adrian and Kin searching for me in town. Yes, you read that right. Adrian and Kin together, looking for me. Weird, right? Weirder than me being saved by a shark, I reckon.

They used Kin's telescope to search for me, and caught the

draglines, the froth coming from behind the boat. Captain Bjorn realised I was going after the shark alone, and he and his boat tailed me. He threw the life ring for me, and rescued Noodle from the boat.

I was unconscious and hypothermic, which means I was so cold from being in the sea I nearly died. I didn't, though, because Captain Bjorn knew just what to do. He tucked Noodle close to my heart, and she kept me warm while his crew rushed me to land. An air ambulance flew me to the hospital, the same one Mum got taken to. *Julia & the Shark* drifted almost to the Arctic, and Dad has had to pay a lot of money to get it retrieved.

He told me this once he had stopped crying long enough to speak. He and Mum were with me the whole time I was asleep. Mum had to get special permission because she is an inpatient at the psychiatric ward there. The ward is painted pale yellow, the colour of an egg yolk from sad hens, and smells of antiseptic. It smells worse than the shark, but it's the safest place for her at the moment.

She told me the name for what she has, for what Grandma Julia had. Bipolar disorder, but it has nothing to do with the north and south poles – I checked. It means, like Dad explained, she swings between being really happy, and really sad. The happiness is as dangerous as the sadness. That's why she believed she could find the shark without any funding, without any help.

The sadness is so bad it means she can't feel anything happy and everything is hard, like moving through mud. She had an episode – that's what it's called when she feels really hyper or really low – before, after Grandma Julia died, while she was pregnant with me. This is what the *Never Again* meant on the back of that photo, Dad said. She never wanted to feel like that again. It wasn't to do with me at all. I still have to tell myself that, over and over. It wasn't my fault.

The first time I saw Mum after I found the shark, I was very tired so went to sleep again very fast, but when I surfaced again she was still there. She was dressed in one of her big cardigans, and the only thing that showed she was a patient was the bracelet on her wrist: 93875400.

'I heard,' she said, 'you've had an adventure.'

'I suppose,' I said. 'I found the shark.'

She brushed my hair back from my face, and kissed the top of my head.

'I did, didn't I?' I tried to sit up, but Mum soothed me gently. 'I tagged it.'

'They couldn't track it,' said Dad gently.

'But I used the harpoon –' I looked at Mum desperately. 'I saw it! I ...'

I didn't want to tell her about the nudge at my legs, the way I felt like I was pushed towards the surface.

'I believe you,' said Mum.

'I found it,' I said again.

'I know,' said Mum. 'You were brilliant and clever and stupid. Julia, you could have … we might have …' She pulled me in closer. 'You mustn't do things like that.'

'Like what?'

'Dangerous things. Like going out on the boat on your own, especially in a storm.'

'You did.'

I felt her stiffen beside me, and Dad stared intently at her.

'Yes,' said Mum slowly. 'But I was sick. I am sick, J. My moods, they go up and down, up and down.'

'Like waves.'

'Exactly.'

I swallowed, a new worry springing up like a jack-in-the-box. 'Am I … will I be …'

'Like me?' Mum reached out and squeezed my hand. 'No, Julia. There's plenty of your dad in there, too.' I wrinkled my nose, and she laughed. 'No two brains are the same. But if you ever feel strange, you tell me. You mustn't worry about that, J. We'll make sure you're always safe.'

Before, I'd probably have been disappointed to not be exactly like Mum, but now I was glad Dad liked numbers and certainty and solidity. It meant the ground beneath my feet was stable,

even if I loved being at sea.

'What was it like?'

'When I was doing all that, with the boat and the storms?' I nodded, and Mum sighed. 'Honestly, I felt like I was invincible. Immortal. But it was silly, because I'm not. I needed to be more careful. And then, after the highest highs, I got low. I sank.' She took hold of my hand. 'But that's not going to happen again. I know the signs now, I'll be careful not to take on so much again. And they're going to give me medicine to help.'

'You'll get better,' I said firmly. 'You can do anything.'

'For you,' said Mum. 'I will.'

'And yourself, Maura,' said Dad. 'We need to keep you on an even keel.'

'Like *Julia & the Shark*.' I grinned. 'Where did it end up?'

'Reminds me,' muttered Dad. 'I need to check on it.'

He went outside with his mobile, because there's signal on Mainland, to call Captain Bjorn. Mum slid her hand into mine.

'We're going to donate it to Kin's family. They're going to use it as a library, moored in the harbour.'

'Don't you need it? Now we know the shark's around—'

'Julia,' she said, and her voice was thick. 'I'm not going to look for the shark any more.'

I gaped at her. 'But your research—'

'I love my work. I love you, too. And I love being well. And at

the moment, I need to choose. And I choose to get better.'

'Does this mean you're not a marine biologist any more?'

'Silly.' She poked me gently. 'I'll always be a marine biologist. Just like I'll always be your mum, or always love Dad and Noodle. There are so many uncertainties in the world, but those are the things I'm sure of.'

I threw myself forwards and hugged her. I believed her, just like she believed me. She would be better soon.

'I might need some time,' she said, speaking into my hair, 'in the hospital. When we get back to Cornwall.'

Even though I wanted her home, wanted her dancing around the kitchen and making stupid jokes in the mornings, I knew she wouldn't ask unless she had no choice.

I squeezed her hand. 'That's all right.'

I realised then what I'd really found by finding the shark.

Remember at the beginning of this story, how I said I lost my mum? Really, what I meant was I lost my idea of Mum. The idea she was perfect and invincible and always right. But as well as the shark, I found the real Mum, with her complications and tangles and tears, and I love her just as much as ever. More, maybe. I told you to watch out for words, they are tricksy.

I also said what I was trying to get to was Mum. But now, I think that was a mistake. I think by spending all this time worrying about her, and caring about the things she cared about,

I was losing myself. Mum and me aren't the same person, and that's all right.

Dad poked his head around the door.

'You have a visitor.'

I knew who it would be, even without asking.

Dad stood aside, and Kin shuffled past him. He was looking at me through his fringe, his lips a tight line. He looked as nervous as I felt, and knowing that, seeing him, broke my fear like an egg. I nodded my best Neeta nod, and his face lit up. I know it's a cliché when people say that, but it's true. Like the lighthouse, he actually *beamed*.

Mum left us, and it was like that night with Adrian never happened. He told me about their search for me, and I told him about the shark, and an hour gulped by in a moment. Just before he had to leave, he pulled out a notebook from his coat pocket. It was nothing like my yellow one, lost in the sea. It was navy blue, with a gold J pressed into the front.

'I thought you'd want a new one of these.'

I took hold of the notebook and opened it to a clean page. This wouldn't only be for sea creature facts. This would be for myths about stars and mountains and forests, and maybe a few numbers if Dad wanted. But first, Kin could tell me the names of the constellations.

I had found the impossible shark, but it hadn't been the answer

Mum was looking for. Only she could find those, inside herself, by herself. It wasn't up to me to fix anything, to fix her.

Now I was ready to find something of my own. Something mine. Something new.

NINETEEN

It's February, and the ground is cracking with frost. We've driven eight hours from Cornwall to reach Gretna Green, but that's nothing compared to Kin. His parents drove him here, and it took nearly a day and a half. Even though Unst is in the same country as Gretna Green, it's still a world away.

We had to time it perfectly, and we did. When we arrive, Kin and his parents are waiting in the car park. Even Neeta is here, and this time she actually smiles at me. I still do my cool nod back.

Dusk is gathering in the eaves of the trees above us, and Dad ensures I have my jumper and my coat on before he lets me run and hug Kin. He makes me wear extra layers all the time since I had hypothermia.

Once we've all said our hellos, Mum leads us away from the other people heading to the path, and follows a desire line through the trees, up a short hill where no one else is around. Dad grumbles about rule-breaking, but Mum only laughs. She's back to herself now, silly and giddy and working, but not so much we need to worry. I watch for the waves, the rough waters that carried her off last time, but she seems to have found her feet.

Kin's dad sets up his mended telescope, and we sit on the crest of the hill overlooking pylons, and wait. The sky is purple and deep-sea-blue, melting into the dark ground. We wait a long time, and Dad frets, but Mum shushes him, tells him to be patient.

Kin and I sit a little way off. He tells me the floating library is a great success. 'It's still called *Julia & the Shark*, but it's full of shelves now.'

We talk about school, and how Adrian's getting on, about everything and nothing, even though we speak most weekends since I moved back to Cornwall. It's not the same as seeing him. It was easy to slip back into hanging out with Shabs and Nell and Matty, but none of them understand me like Kin. We're two whales on our own wavelength.

'Here,' I say, and from my coat I take a piece of string. A rakhi, to show how we are more than just friends now, even though I'm back in Cornwall. To show we're family. I made it myself, tying blue and silver around each other, for the sea and the stars, which

brought us together. 'To say thanks for the notebook.'

I tie it on his bony wrist, and we grin stupidly.

'Look, J, Kin!' Mum is calling and pointing, her camera ready.

It starts as a smudge, a gathering in the distance. It could almost be a wisp of cloud, but it moves like water. I say 'it', but really, it's lots of things. Starlings, moving together, coming home to roost in the fields. A murmuration, just like Mum used to watch with Grandma Julia.

More and more gather, bunching and turning, like shoals of fish. Kin is watching through his dad's telescope, but I want to see it all, the whole picture, the birds darting and weaving as though patching invisible holes in the sky.

It's like they're being conducted,
have practised this a thousand times,
and I know I'm gasping aloud and that Neeta can hear
but I don't care. Cold is biting my ears,
and the rushing, tweeting sound of the starlings is enormous,
like walking through a windswept forest in full leaf,
or plunging
into a freezing ocean.

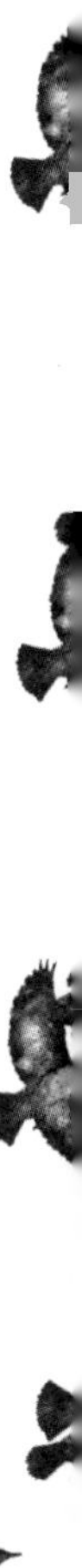

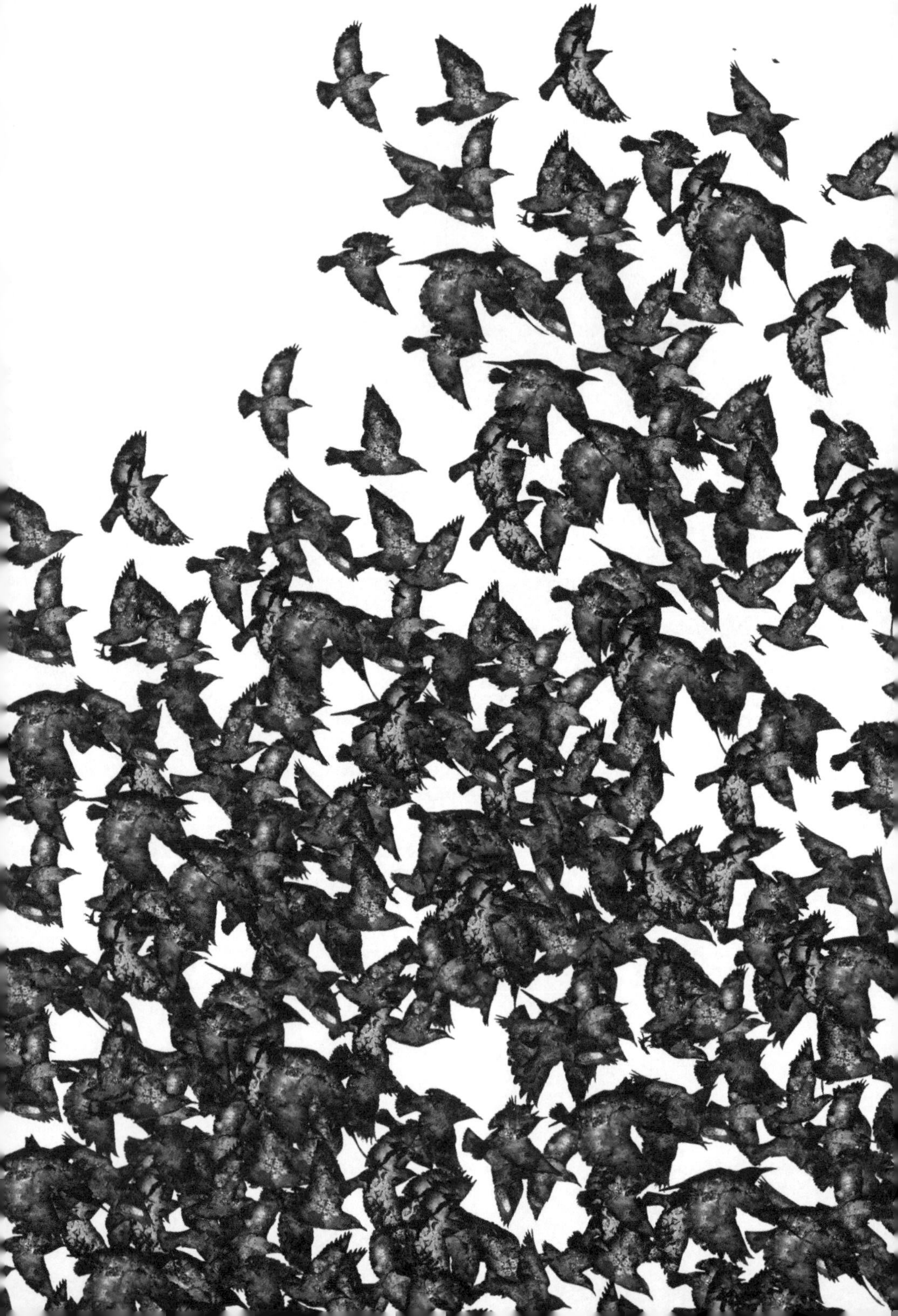

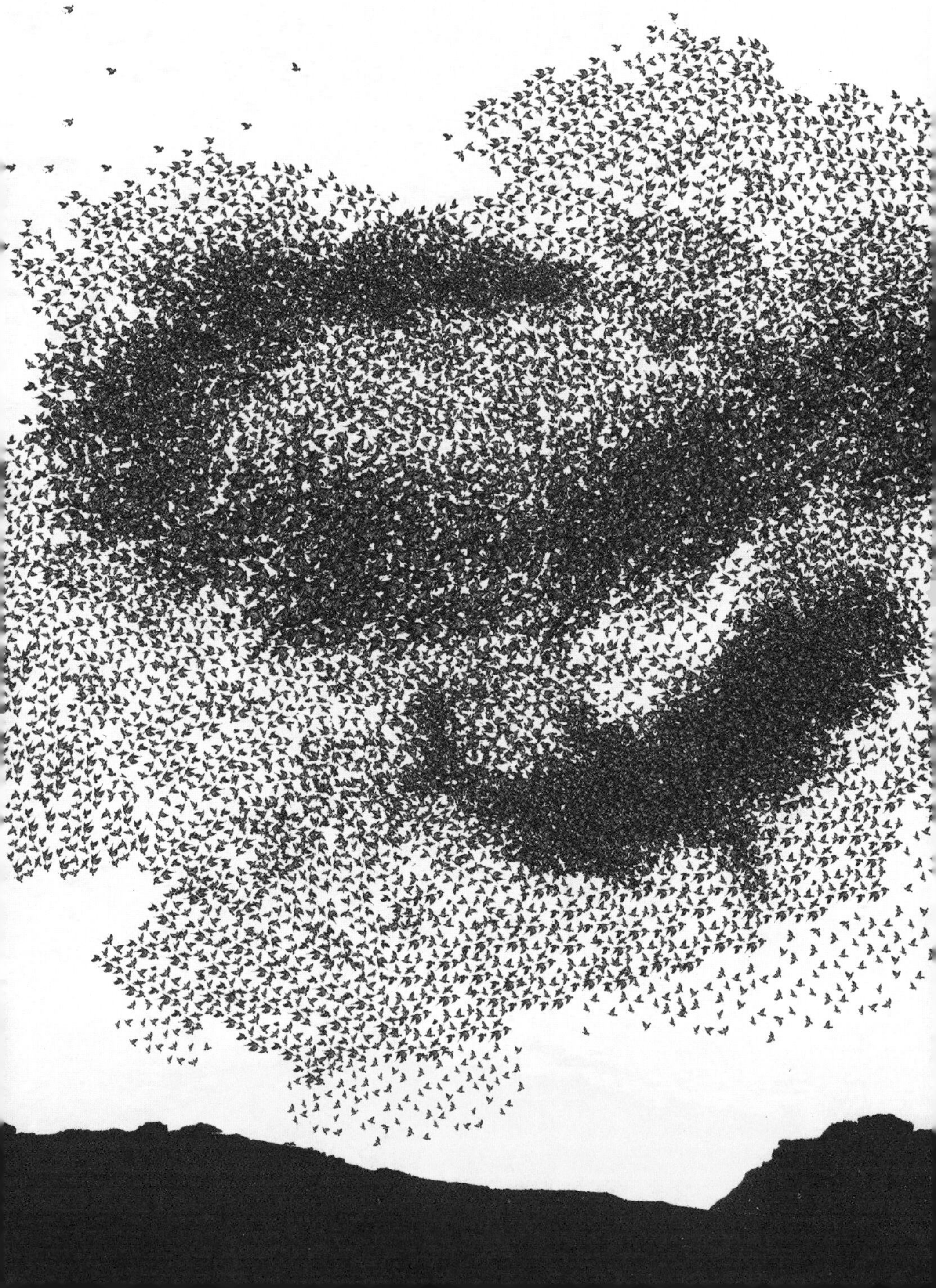

Mum takes my hand as the birds shimmer like a scarf,

lifting and lowering, like waves.

Until, finally, they find a safe place to land.

ACKNOWLEDGEMENTS

Of all the stories we've told, this has the most of our hearts – and so it also has plenty of what others have given us. The love, the support, the belief and the encouragement.

Our families are our pole stars, and this book is because of them: parents, siblings, grandparents, niblings, aunts and uncles. Our especial thanks to Tilly, for modelling Julia, and to Andrea, for reading multiple drafts. Thank you to Tilly, Fred, Emily, Pippa, Isla, Ted, Leo, baby Regan and Sabine, for inspiring us daily with your sheer existence.

We have been lucky to work with three extraordinary editors. Helen Thomas, who believed in and shaped Julia's story from the start, and ensured we remembered that 'there's a crack in everything, that's how the light gets in'. Sarah Lambert, who looked after us so beautifully and always showed such care and kindness. And to Rachel Wade, launching this book into the world. We're so excited for future adventures with you.

There are really three makers of this story. Alison Padley, our designer, has worked a deep and special enchantment on our words and images. You're a stone-cold genius.

Our team at Hachette Children's Group – it's a true delight to work with you. We feel part of a family and more than that, part of the magic you're weaving in the world of books. Especial thanks to wonderful editor Nazima Abdillahi, our phenomenal publicist Emily Thomas, brilliant marketing director Naomi Berwin, amazing production controller Helen Hughes, and all the numerous people at HCG, Orion, and beyond, who willed and worked this book into existence.

Hellie Ogden – there are never the right words. Thank you for helping us through this next chapter, and finding us a safe place to land. Thank you Rebecca Carter for looking after us, and all at Janklow & Nesbit UK. Thanks to Harriet Moore and all at David Higham Associates.

Thank you to Peter Mallet, photographer extraordinaire, who ensured nothing was lost in translation from paper artwork to digital files. Thank you to the broader network built around Tom's artwork: Paul Smith, Matt Price, Mandy Fowler, Freya Pocklington, Simon Palfrey, Pablo de Orellana, Mark Jones and Ali Souleman.

Julia has had amazing cheerleaders from the very first moment. Thank you to some of our favourite authors and people: Katie Webber and Kevin Tsang, Kate Rundell, Cressida Cowell, Sophie Anderson, Ross Montgomery, Cat Doyle, Anna James, Florentyna Martin, Hilary McKay, Emma Carroll and Tom Fletcher for their early, early support of this book.

The children's, YA, and adult book community have been glorious champions of us and our work, as well as huge inspirations. Thank you especially to Lizzie Huxley-Jones, Anna James, Maz Evans, MG Leonard, Lucy Strange, Cat Doyle, Jasbinder Bilan, Sita Bramachari, James Nicols, Lauren James, Melinda Salisbury, Robin Stevens, Frances Hardinge, Mariam Khan, Aisha Bushby, Liz Hyder, Jessie Burton, Nikesh Shukla, Patrice Lawrence, Cat Johnson and Samantha Shannon. Thank you to the Skunk Pirates for a safe space to speak all things writing.

Thank you to the booksellers from independent bookshops, including but not limited to Liznojan Books, the Kenilworth Bookshop, The Book House, Mostly Books, Lighthouse Books, Portobello Books, Mainstreet Trading, Toppings St Andrews, and the bound. Thank you to the incredible teams at Waterstones, Blackwell's and Foyles – especially our local Waterstones Oxford, and Oxford's two wonderful Blackwell's branches. We'd be lost without your support.

Librarians and teachers are the beating heart of the children's book community, and we are so thankful for how you champion stories as the truly life-changing things they are. We know there are so many of you in classrooms and libraries all over the country working to create a love of reading – you are the too-often unsung heroes of our industry. Special mention to Steph Elliot, who has been there since the beginning.

Thank you to all the bloggers and reviewers who spread the word about stories, so often for the sheer love of them. Especial thanks to Fiona Noble, Simon Savidge, Gavin Hetherington, Jo Clarke, and Daniel Bassett.

Our beloved Daisy Johnson and Sarvat Hasin – stupid words. They are never enough. But we love you, we love your work, we love that we get to have you in our lives. Thank you for being there through the good, the bad, and the downright ugly.

To our wider community of friends. Each of you is so precious to us. Especial thanks to those who were there while we wrestled with this story: Matt Bradshaw, Lucy Ayrton, Paul Fitchett, Laura Theis, Jess Oliver, and Elizabeth Macneal.

To four very loved children, who we adore very much: Evie, baby Tsang, Rowan and Thom.

To the various cats who have graced our laptops during the creation of this story – Luna, Oscar, and of course Noodle.

Thank you to you, the reader. Julia was ours, and now she's yours too.

To our twins, Rosemary and Lavender, who we hoped would one day hear this story.

To each other, for it all.

Kiran Millwood Hargrave and her husband Tom de Freston met in 2009, when Kiran was a student and Tom was artist-in-residence at Cambridge University. They have been a couple and collaborators ever since, but *Julia and the Shark* is their first novel. Kiran is the award-winning, bestselling author of stories including *The Girl of Ink & Stars*, *The Way Past Winter*, and *The Deathless Girls*, and Tom is making his illustrative debut having worked as an acclaimed artist for many years. They live in Oxford with their rescue cats Luna and Marly, in a house between a river and a forest.

FURTHER READING

See booktrust.org.uk/booklists/ for brilliant recommendations by theme. Here are some of our favourite books on these topics.

NATURE

The Lost Words – Robert Macfarlane and Jackie Morris (5+)
Beetle Boy trilogy – MG Leonard (8+)
A Wolf Called Wander – Rosanne Parry (8+)
Here We Are – Oliver Jeffers (3+)
Diary of a Young Naturalist – Dara McAnulty (12+)

MENTAL HEALTH

Paper Avalanche – Lisa Williamson (12+)
Tiny Infinities – JH Diehl (9+)
Am I Normal Yet? – Holly Bourne (14+)
Aubrey and the Terrible Yoot – Horatio Clare and Jane Matthews (8+)
The Red Tree – Shaun Tan (9+)

RESOURCES

The Greenland Shark is an extreme example of how amazing and bizarre nature can be. We believe protecting and conserving the natural world, both on land and in the sea, is of vital importance to all of us, because it impacts processes like climate change. But you don't have to live by the sea or be a marine biologist to help protect animals. Here are some resources where you can learn more about the natural world, and how to look after it.

rspb.org.uk/fun-and-learning/ – ideas from the RSPB on how to get closer to the nature in your local surroundings, from bird counting to creating bug hotels

treetoolsforschools.org.uk – activities and information with a focus on trees

nature-shetland.co.uk – amazing pictures and stories about wildlife in Shetland

mcsuk.org – Marine Conservation Society is an activist-focused organisation full of facts and ideas

wwf.org.uk/get-involved/schools/resources – the World Wide Fund for Nature is the world's largest conservation charity

Julia's mum has a mental illness called bipolar disorder. As you have read, it can be easily managed with the right support. There's a whole range of mental health issues, and not all of them are as severe as what Julia's mum experiences. But sometimes we all feel a bit sad or overwhelmed, and might not know how to deal with it. We believe it's so important to talk about these feelings without shame or embarrassment, because that's the only way to process them. Both of us, Kiran and Tom, have experienced this ourselves.

The most important thing is getting the right support, and the only way to do that is to talk to a trusted adult – a parent, a teacher, a school counsellor, or use one of the resources below to speak to a trained professional. The more we talk, the less we bottle up, and the better we feel. Here are some places you can learn more about the issues we talk about in *Julia and the Shark*.

bbc.co.uk/newsround – Newsround has a wealth of resources about mental health and how to look after yours – just scroll down to the 'Mental Health' tab

youngminds.org.uk – a treasure trove of resources about children and young people's mental health

mind.org.uk/information-support/for-children-and-young-people/ – a leading mental health charity's dedicated page for children and young people

nipinthebud.org – informative and approachable videos to get kids talking about mental health

giveusashout.org – a text service where you can talk about how you're feeling with a trained professional